Over-paid, Over-sexed and
Over Here

To Brenda Brooks, who inspired this book and without whose encouragement, expertise and sheer hard work we could not have coped.

Jim and Norman

Over-paid, Over-sexed and Over Here

From RAF Eagles to 4th Fighter Group Hawks

Lt. Col. James A Goodson and Norman Franks

WINGHAM PRESS – CANTERBURY

First published in 1991 by
Wingham Press Limited, Seymour Place,
28 High Street, Wingham, Kent CT3 1AB

ISBN 1 873454 09 0

Typeset by DP Press, Sevenoaks, Kent
Printed in Great Britain by
Biddles Ltd., Guildford and Kings Lynn

List of Contents

List of illustrations

Photographs (between pages134 and 135)

Hal Marting.
John Godfrey and Don Gentile.
Mike Sobanski – 4th Fighter Group.
Pierce McKennon – 4th Fighter Group.
Bob Mannix.
Mike Miluck.
Don Blakeslee.
Duane Beeson – 4th Fighter Group.
Jim Clark – 4th Fighter Group.
John and Don pose in front of a red nosed Mustang.
Don Gentile's pranged Mustang "Shangri-La".
Kid Hofer with his "Salem Representative".
The boys letting their hair down in the Debden Mess.
Visit by Mr Lovett, US Secretary for Air.
Blakeslee and General Bill Kepner.
Swede Carlson – 4th Fighter Group.
Red-Dog Norley – 4th Fighter Group.
56th Fighter Group – Hub Zemke.
Lieutenant William G Spencer, 334th Squadron, 4th GP.
Kid Hofer and Jim Goodson.
Colonel Don Blakeslee, CO of the 4th FG.
Wee Michael McPharlin, 71 Eagle Squadron.
Bill Spencer with his P.51 Mustang, 1945.
Eagle Squadron's Memorial Plaque – RAF Debden.
4th FG Insignia and Eagle Squadron patch

Prologue

We were the happy warriors! Oh yes, we were against Hitler and his band of Nazi thugs and of course we were very much in support of the embattled British, standing alone against the power of Hitler and Nazi Germany; but we didn't even pretend to be impassioned defenders of democracy against the threat of Fascism.

What we really wanted was to fly! We wanted adventure!

To our amazement, not only was the RAF prepared to give this to us, but we didn't even have to pay – they paid US! It may not have been much by modern standards – I think it was 7/6d per day – but we would happily have done it for nothing.

I suppose if we'd thought seriously about it, we would have realised that there was a very real danger of losing our lives, either during the hazardous accelerated training or at the hands of the well-trained, experienced and dedicated German Air Force; but Death was something that happened to the other guy. This theory was never mentioned, but it was the basic conviction of every pilot.

We certainly never thought of ourselves as heroes and even now, fifty years later, as I look back on those carefree characters, I'm not sure I think of them as heroes. They were, however, great and wonderful friends, and it is to them that this book is dedicated, with respect and deep affection.

Chapter 1
The Trail Blazers

I AM sometimes asked, "What was it like for you Americans when you came over here during the War?"

The answer is simple; we were treated extremely well, the English were very nice to us. They did, of course, say we were "Over-paid, over-sexed and over here!" and after 50 years I still have two out of the three going for me, so perhaps that's not too bad! As usual with the British sense of humour, it was a phrase which summed up some feelings with a basis of half-truth or wishful thinking.

Compared to their own way of life, and certainly when comparing British wages with the Americans' pay, the US boys were well (over) paid. That by 1942 the majority of eligible bachelors and married men were in the British forces, either serving overseas or, when in Britain, away from their homes and loved-ones, was a fact. This gave rise to the feeling that the newly arrived Americans were looked upon as glamorous by the women of Britain. Thus it was that the Americans – by now being collectively called GIs (which stood, like all military "equipment", for Government Issue) – were seen to have a free run of the homeland ladies. Being always thought to be after the "main chance", they were soon dubbed "over-sexed".

And collectively, if they were deemed over-paid and over-sexed, that might have been acceptable but for one thing – they were over here! Not that many British women in the 18 to 40 (but not exclusively so!) age range minded, but their men, whatever age, certainly did, and so did the more straight-laced gentry, who would always see the Americans, or any other Allied soldiery, as either colonials or foreigners.

One has to remember that in the early 1940s, war or not, Britain was a very different place to what it is today. To the British, the Americans in particular were fascinating, even dazzling, individuals. Few people then were the world travellers they are now and the only Americans the average British man or woman had seen were those portrayed in the cinema. The Hollywood legends were very real to many, whether they be matinee cowboys like Roy Rogers or Gene Autrey, great adventurers such as Gary Cooper, swash-buckling dare-devils like Douglas Fairbanks, or screen idols – male or female – Jean Harlow, Mary Pickford, Tyrone Power, Clark Gable, and the like. Americans too were different, had different lifestyles. Few people in Britain, for instance, had refrigerators or telephones, or motor-cars; many did not even have a bathroom. In America, these were almost basic items of everyday life. Many Americans lived in areas of good climate and housing, whereas in Britain climate was always, or seemed to be, the main talking point, one day rarely being like the next. As for homes, Britain seemed to live in terraced, two-up, two-down, houses, behind a factory or gasworks. American GIs looked bronzed, healthy and athletic, so no wonder the women of Britain fell easily for their charms. And the American serviceman was a long way from his home town, his high-school sweetheart, in a strange land and maybe with death waiting for him round the next corner. It easily developed in the British minds that these Yanks certainly were, over-paid, over-sexed and what is more, they were over here – in Great Britain!

Vic France probably epitomised what the English thought of as the average American airman. We called him "The Playboy".

He was tall, good-looking and well-dressed. Of course he wore the uniform which we all did, but in his case it was tailored to accentuate the broad shoulders, trim hips and long frame to the point where it was hard to recognise it as the same uniform. Occasionally, when he reached into his pocket, there was a flash of crimson silk lining. There were also other subtle differences.

On the shoulder, above the Eagle Squadron badge, where the rest of us had a discreet "USA", Vic had a discreet "Texas". The first thing most of us did was discard the standard-issue RAF footwear, but Vic replaced it with Texas boots.

The girls fell for him in droves. I remember when we were based at Southend, I went one evening into the bar of the Queens Hotel. It was full of British Army officers, several of them accompanied by attractive girls. It was approaching closing time when Vic ambled in, pausing to say "Hi" to the girls and their escorts and finally moving out of the bar. Almost immediately, three of the girls excused themselves and left the bar. They were last seen climbing into Vic's taxi-cab.

On April 18th, 1944, we had at last established the position of being able to escort the bombers all over Germany. On this particular raid, I heard Blakeslee call, "Everybody out!" Then I heard a familiar Texas drawl:

"There's a bunch of 109s on the rear Fort. Reckon we'll go back and help."

"I'll cover you, Vic, but we're low on ammo and damn low on gas, so break off as soon as you can, or you won't make it back."

"Well, if I don't, tell my girl so long for me."

"Which one, Vic?" I asked.

"All of them!" he said.

Then all I heard were the disjointed snatches which come over the radio during a dogfight ... "You got him, Vic," "Break right, there's one on your tail!" ... "OK, I got him off" ... "He's going in on the bomber again" ...

I was closer to the straggler now and could see the fighters around him. Then I saw him peel off slowly and go into his death-dive. Vic hadn't been able to get to that one German fighter soon enough. He'd got one of them, and saved his wingman, but when I heard him, I knew he was mad.

"The rest of you guys go home – I'm gonna get that bastard!"

"For God's sake, Vic, break off!" I said. "Let him go!"

"Not this baby!" he said.

By now I could see the 109 diving for the deck and behind him the lone Mustang carrying the curves and 10-gallon hat of "Miss Dallas". I watched as the two planes hurtled down in a screaming vertical dive, winding up to terminal velocity.

My own plane was shuddering as I followed them down. The controls were rigid and I had to ease it out by slowly winding the trim handle back a fraction.

"Pull out, Vic!" I yelled. "Pull out, goddam it!"

But there was no stopping him now. "I'm hitting him, I'm gonna get him!"

He got him alright. A great ball of flame flared on the ground where the German went in. Almost immediately, a second seering flash burst close to the first, as Miss Dallas followed her victim in.

I'd made a few phone calls before I walked into the Salted Almond Bar and ordered drinks for the girls who were there.

Audrey said, "Vic?"

"Yep."

Someone asked, "When?"

"Today."

Jackie said, "Cheers!" and we all raised our glasses.

After a while, the girls started to drift off and I was thinking of getting back to Debden when Jackie stopped me. "There's another one," she said, "the special one."

I went over. She declined a drink and didn't even sit down.

"It's Vic," I said. "He'd have wanted you to know. He went out in a blaze of glory!"

It was a mistake. Women know there's no glory in death. It takes men years to learn that.

The girl got up to go. Jean said, "She shouldn't be so cut-up – he wasn't exactly faithful to her."

Rita turned on her and flashed her dark Spanish eyes. "He was faithful," she said defiantly, "to ALL of us!"

We stepped out into the evening bustle of Piccadilly, with its stream of soldiers, sailors and airmen of all nationalities. It was a starry night and we looked up at the sky.

"Do you think Vic's gone to Heaven?" asked Rita.

"If he has," said Audrey, "the angels won't know what's hit them!"

Vic was one of the over-paid, over-sexed and over here.

* * *

At the beginning of the Second World War, the Royal Air Force had any number of "colonials" within its ranks. Men had come from Australia, New Zealand, Canada, South Africa, Rhodesia, and so on, so it is not surprising that there were a handful of Americans who had joined its ranks. There was no great problem about Americans being in the RAF, so long as they swore allegiance to the King of England and his country.

Most of those Americans serving or training in the RAF in 1939 to early 1940 were guided not by any warlike or high moral thinking, but merely wanting to share in the delight of flying and flying within a professional service which would train them well. When war did come, they, like their fellow pilots, felt equal to the task ahead, seeing the war as an adventure; a dangerous adventure but nevertheless, a challenge.

And those who saw the chance to be a part of good challenging evil, well, they were in the right place to help.

These Americans would go largely un-noticed by the general public. By the time the "shooting war" finally came in May 1940, that same public saw just a collective whole, a command of fighter pilots fighting against the German aggressor. It made no difference what nationality a fighter pilot was, so long as he was fighting for Britain in her hour of need. The media and history was to make more of nationalities later but not then. However, we can look in some detail at the "first Americans" to fly and fight with RAF Fighter Command in World War II.

In 1940 there were just nine Americans (or Anglo-Americans) who would serve in Fighter Command, in what has now become described as that fateful spring and summer. They were:

Flight Lieutenant J W E Davies–	79	Squadron (Hurricane)
Flying Officer C D Palmer	–	1 Squadron (Hurricane)
Pilot Officer W M L Fiske	–	601 Squadron (Hurricane)
Pilot Officer A G Donahue	–	64 Squadron (Spitfire)
Pilot Officer E Q Tobin	–	609 Squadron (Spitfire)
Pilot Officer V C Keough	–	609 Squadron (Spitfire)
Pilot Officer A Mamedoff	–	609 Squadron (Spitfire)
Pilot Officer P H Leckrone	–	616 Squadron (Spitfire)
Pilot Officer J K Haviland	–	151 Squadron (Hurricane)
Pilot Officer H W Reilly	–	66 Squadron (Spitfire)
Pilot Officer C R Davis	–	601 Squadron (Hurricane)
Pilot Officer O J Peterson	–	1 RCAF Sqdn (Hurricane)
Pilot Officer deP Brown	–	1 RCAF Sqdn (Hurricane)

Of these, James William Elias Davies, was the first to see action against the enemy. From New Jersey, Jimmy had joined the RAF pre-war, went to 79 Squadron in March 1937 when it was formed at RAF Biggin Hill and by the time May 1940 and action came around, he was a flight commander. Back in 1937, 79 Squadron had been flying Gloster Gauntlet biplane fighters but these had been exchanged for Hawker Hurricanes in November, 1938.

Sqdn. Ldr. Donald (Dimsie) Stones, DFC, flew with him and had the highest regard for him. He first met Jimmy in the Mess at Biggin Hill in February 1940, when posted to 32 Squadron. Jimmy was serving with 79 Squadron and they shared the Mess, since both 32 and 79 had been resident pre-war squadrons there.

Dimsie told me, "Jimmy Davies and Flight Sergeant F S Brown were scrambled at 10am on 21 November to patrol over Hawkinge when an X-raid (X–14) – an assumed hostile radar plot – came to the attention of the Operations Room duty fighter controller. They were vectored out over the Channel towards Calais and saw a Dornier 127 bomber. Seeing the two Hurricanes, the Dornier pilot dived, but they caught up with him and attacked, sending the luckless Dornier down into the clouds. When the two RAF pilots saw it next, it was diving upside-down below the cloud, then went into the sea eight miles north of the French port.

"Not only was it Jimmy Davies' first victory, it was 79's and also the first destroyed by Fighter Command's No. 11 Group, which covered the South East of England.

"When I was posted to 79 Squadron in late March 1940, Jimmy was supernumerary Flight Lieutenant and commanded "A" Flight after F/ Lt. Bob Edwards was shot down and wounded in early May. Jimmy made a splendid flight commander and I was glad to serve under him in "A" Flight until he was so tragically killed on 27 June. He had great charm, and was always cheerful and full of energy. His exuberance on the ground was described by all of us in one phrase: "Jimmy's whizzing again!"

"We shared many combats. I remember two in particular. On 27 May, our section of "A" Flight patrolled Gravelines to Veurne during the Dunkirk evacuation and ran into a formation of Me–110s. One attacked Jimmy, but overshot him and turned in front of me. I was lucky with my first burst and hit one of his engines and maybe the cockpit. He dived steeply to the sea past Jimmy, who also got in a burst, and later confirmed that it hit the sea whilst I was engaging another Me–110. We filled in our combat reports at base and I suggested we should share the Me–110 which went into the sea. Jimmy would have none of it, insisting that it was on its way in before he fired, and gave me the credit for it. That is what a generous fighter pilot Jimmy was.

"Our second joint success was on 8 June, when Jimmy, P/O J E R Wood and I put down an He–111 near Le Treport.

"When the German Blitzkrieg erupted on the Western Front on 10 May, 1940, 79 Squadron was sent to France to support the British and French land forces. Initially, it was based at Vitry and, four days later,

Davies and Sergeant Harry Cartwright each shot down a Junkers 88 bomber while operating out of Merville. The next day he was leading a protection patrol off the Belgian port of Ostende, but within a few more days, 79, along with other RAF squadrons in France, were forced to withdraw back to England."

From Biggin Hill, Jimmy and 79 continued to operate over France almost daily, as the Allied forces retreated south west. He shot down a Messerschmitt 110 fighter on 27 May, with another probably destroyed. Then on 7 June, the Squadron escorted Blenheim light bombers on a raid over France, then afterwards flew a patrol to Abbeville. They engaged single-engined Me–109 fighters and shot down four, possibly six. Davies claimed one of the certainties.

The next day came the news of the award of the Distinguished Flying Cross – the first for an American in World War II, and among the first for the Squadron. Another pilot similarly honoured was Flying Officer Don "Dimsie" Stones. Then on June 27, news came that His Majesty the King would be coming to Biggin to present awards to some of the pilots, Jimmy and Dimsie among them. However, before that event, 79 and 32 Squadrons left to escort Blenheims from Manston to St Valery on a photographic sortie. Upon leaving the French coast, three Me–109 fighters were seen by one of the pilots but his warning cry was not heard. He was shot up and forced to bale out but worse still, another of the 109s bounced 79 and shot down the Hurricane flown by Jimmy Davies.

Not long after the rest of the Squadron landed the King arrived, pinned the various DFCs and DFMs onto the breasts of the recipients until just one lone DFC medal remained on the table. The King asked whose it was and was visibly moved when told that the man who should have received it had not returned from the morning's operation. With so many "firsts" to his name, it was sad that he had to be the first American to die with Fighter Command in the war.

Cyril Dampier Palmer, known affectionately as "Pussy", came from Cleveland, Ohio and regarded himself as Anglo-American. He too had joined the RAF before the war and was an operational pilot when it began. Flying with the famous No. 1 Squadron, he went to France in September 1939, and like Jimmy Davies, had an early success when he shared in the destruction of a Dornier 217 flying a reconnaissance sortie on 23 November. Where the similarity ended was when the

German rear gunner hit his Hurricane, forcing Pussy to make a forced landing in a field.

When the German "Blitzkrieg" began on 10 May, 1940, he was in the thick of the fighting, and was supposed to have shot down four more German aircraft before the Squadron was forced to withdraw to England. Two of his known victories came on 14 and 17 May, an Me–109 and Me–110. He received the DFC and then became an instructor. He returned to operational flying in 1942 but was killed in action over Brest while an acting squadron leader. Jimmy Davies did not live long enough to see the coming Battle of Britain, but the others did.

William Mead Lindsley Fiske III, known to everyone as Billy, was probably known more outside the RAF by this time. Although an American (born in Chicago in 1911) he was the son of an international New York millionaire stockbroker living in Paris. Despite his American citizenship, Billy Fiske was very much an Anglophile, for he had been educated at Trinity College, Cambridge, and later joined the London office of his father's company. In his spare time he had become a well known racing car driver and bob-sleigh champion, a first-rate shot, played golf and sailed a yacht. In fact he held a record for the Cresta Run at St Moritz and captained the US Olympic team that won the bob-sleigh event in 1932. At the age of 19 he drove in the 24-hour Le Mans race in a Stutz car. At one stage he held the record – very "unofficial" – for driving his 41/2 litre Bentley from Cambridge to London, a record other students failed to take from him. He could also drive the 19 miles from Cambridge to Mildenhall (to play golf) in 17 minutes . . .! He married Rose, the former Countess of Warwick in 1939.

He was the Golden Boy; good looks, wealth, charm, intelligence, he had it all. He excelled in most sports and was good in business. He was very American, but completely international at the same time. The English loved him, and he loved them.

It was not surprising that someone like Billy should also want to fly, and in September, 1939, he joined the RAF. In August he had been at the New York office, but returned to England on the Aquitania on the 30th. With his background it was natural that he "got fighters" and that he managed to get himself posted to 601 (Auxiliary) Squadron – known as the Millionaire's Squadron because of all the well-to-do pilots on its strength.

He joined 601 on 12 July, 1940, just as the Battle of Britain was starting to warm up. Eventually he became operational and on the morning of 11 August, flying as number three to Blue Section, he and 601 engaged some Me–110s, twenty miles south of Swanage. His section leader developed engine trouble and had to return, so Billy led the attack. In the fight which followed, Billy Fiske hit a 110 which dived with one engine on fire but he could not see its end as he was then attacked by another 110. He was credited with a probable in this scrap with ZG.2 – Zerstorergeschwader No. 2.

Two days later, on the 13th, Billy's B Flight had a morning engagement with a formation of Ju88s from Kampfgeschwader No. 54. He attacked and shot down one, both its engines streaming smoke, then attacked and damaged two more. One was credited as a probable when it was last seen, streaming smoke as it headed south over the Solent, surrounded by AA fire.

Later that same morning, 601 were scrambled again and shortly after mid-day, they engaged Me–110s over Portland, escorting more Ju88s. Fiske attacked and claimed two probables and two damaged from Lehrgeschwader No. 1. His own Hurricane was damaged but he got it home.

Friday 16 August saw 601 in action yet again, this time against Stuka dive-bombers over Bognor Regis, close to their home base at Tangmere, which the Luftwaffe aircraft also bombed. Billy's Hurricane was damaged in the air, a shell or bullet hitting the fuel tank behind the engine, which exploded. The controller advised him to head the plane out to sea and bale out. Billy's reaction was typical; "No, I think I can save the kite. I'm coming in."

At first, it looked as though he might make it; the fire went out and the approach and landing were perfect. It wasn't until the plane was halfway down the runway that it blew up as he crashed into a bomb crater.

Billy Fiske was terribly burned about the face, hands and one leg, but they pulled him clear of his damaged fighter and got him to hospital. It was a wonder that, with the injuries he had sustained, he had managed to get back at all. He seemed more concerned about the damage to his fighter than his own injuries, asking how badly it was damaged and saying that he'd soon be back. He died the next day.

He could have been buried with other heroes in the Arlington National Cemetery in Washington DC but he was laid to rest where he would have wanted to be and where England wanted him to be, at Boxgrove Priory near Tangmere.

A year later a plaque was placed in St Paul's Cathedral, in a ceremony attended by Sir Archibald Sinclair, the Secretary of State for Air. On it were his name and the words – "An American Citizen who died that England might live."

Pilot Officer Arthur Gerald Donahue, known to his friends as "Art", was born in St Charles, Minnesota, in 1913. He had learned to fly privately and before his 19th birthday had his private and commercial flying licences. Between work on the family farm he sold pleasure flights and did some barnstorming, before starting an aerial taxi and air-training company in 1938, with a pal in Laredo, Texas.

With a war in Europe, Art joined the RAF in Canada, sailed to England where he eventually went to No. 7 OTU, prior to joining 64 Squadron at RAF Kenley on 3 August, 1940. He was in action almost at once, being shot up by some Me–109s off the French coast on the 5th. More flights came on the 8th, 9th and 11th, then he was again shot up by 109s on the 12th off the south coast of England, baling out with wounds to his right leg and some slight burns.

He rejoined the Squadron in mid-September but on the 29th he was posted to 71 Squadron – the first American Eagle Squadron – but as it was a non-operational unit at the time, soon got himself back to 64 and was again on Ops. by October.

In late 1940 he went to 91 Squadron, then back to the US for some leave in March and April 1941, before returning to 91. He shot down a Messerschmitt 109F on 17 August and claimed another German in September, then went to 258 Squadron which was about to go overseas. Then the Japanese bombed Pearl Harbour and Art Donohue found himself and his Squadron at Palembang, Sumatra, flying sorties over Singapore, being attached to 232 Squadron. He was wounded in the leg while ground strafing Jap troops on 16 February, and evacuated to Ceylon. He later received the DFC.

Back in England he rejoined his old 91 "Jim Crow" Squadron as an acting Flight Lieutenant. Meantime, he wrote two books, "Tally Ho! Yankee in a Spitfire" and "Last Flight from Singapore." During a combat with a Ju88 on 11 September 1942, he shot down the enemy but his own Spitfire was hit and he called to say he was going to ditch. Bad weather prevented a rescue and he was not seen again.

* * *

Phillip Howard Leckrone, known as both Phil and "Zeke", was from Salam, Illinois. After joining the RAF, he completed his training at 7 OTU, before being posted to 616 Squadron on 2 September, 1940. Operating from RAF Coltishall, in Fighter Command's 12 Group (part of the Group's Wing led by the famous legless pilot Douglas Bader), he saw action on 16 September. His Section was scrambled at 0922 am when a hostile aircraft was plotted approaching a convoy code-named "Pilot".

At 10,000 feet they sighted a Ju88 and Phil and his leader, Flight Lieutenant C M MacFie, attacked but saw no definite results from their fire. It was a long patrol and chase, the number three of the section having to come down in the sea when his fuel ran out, but he was rescued. MacFie and Leckrone landed at Bircham Newton to refuel, returning to "Colts" at 1223. They claimed the Ju88 as damaged and it is understood now that this was a machine from 4(F)/122 which failed to return from a reconnaissance mission over the North Sea.

Phil Leckrone was posted, as he was an American, to the first Eagle Squadron on 12 October but was killed whilst engaged on a formation flying practice on 5 January, 1941. He was the embryo unit's first casualty. He is buried in Kirton-in-Lindsey cemetery.

John Kenneth Haviland was born in January, 1921, at Mount Kisco, New York, the son of a US Navy officer and an English mother. He had spent most of his early life in Engand, completing his education at Nottingham University. He obtained his private pilot's licence, then decided to join the RAFVR.

At the beginning of the war he was called-up and on completion of his training went into Army Co-Operation Command, but then volunteered for fighters. After a period with 6 OTU, he was sent to 151 Squadron on 23 September, to join B Flight under Flight Lieutenant R L Smith.

On his first day with the Squadron he collided with Sergeant J McPhee whilst on formation practice. McPhee baled out of his now tail-less Hurricane, while Haviland force-landed his Hurricane in a paddock.

He began flying operational sorties on 30 September and flew several before the Squadron began converting from Hurricanes to Defiant two-seater night fighters in December. After leaving 151, he became an instructor, then flew two tours of night intruder and bomber support operations. As a flight lieutenant with 141 Squadron, he received the DFC in early 1945.

Leaving the RAF in December of that year, he completed a degree course and went to Canada where he served with the RCAF Reserve, flying Vampires. Later he became a Professor at the School of Engineering at the University of Virginia, involved with aerospace projects.

Much has been written about Eugene Quimby Tobin, Vernon Charles Keough and Andrew Mamedoff, the trio of Americans who joined 609 Squadron prior to the formation of the first Eagle Squadron. Already the wheels had been set in motion to secure American pilots to join the RAF and form some kind of volunteer squadron, and these three had been among the first to be recruited.

Tobin, known as "Red", was recruited at Mines Field, near Inglewood, California. He was working as a guide at the Metro-Goldwyn-Mayer film studios, spending his free-time flying rented aircraft from Mines Field. He wanted to fly more and found the offer of cash and free flying too much to resist!

Tobin quickly contacted his friend Andy Mamedoff, who came from Thompson, Connecticut, another flyer, who had spent some time on air taxi work and barnstorming. The offer initially was to go to Finland and help the Finns fight the Russians as sort of mercenaries, which was alright by them. No sooner had they said they'd go, packed, left their jobs and said their goodbyes to family and friends, than the Russo-Finnish war came to an end. Not wishing to look foolish, having already "burnt their boats", Tobin and Mamedoff agreed to go to France, so headed for Montreal in Canada.

In Canada the two flyers met up with Vernon Keough, known as "Shorty" which was not surprising – he was just four feet, ten inches tall! Coming from Brooklyn, he had been a professional parachutist at fairs and carnivals up and down the American East Coast. Sometimes his purse money was good, sometimes not so good. Often he would help boost the influx of funds (he always took the money before he jumped!!) by turning up with a very tatty, threadbare looking parachute, which he would make sure everyone would see him stuffing into the back-pack harness. He never used this 'chute, of course, but it gingered up the public and helped them part with their money!

Finally the three American volunteers were heading for France by boat, just like some Americans had done back in 1915–16. By the time they arrived in Paris, the German Blitzkrieg had begun and everyone was much too busy to see to them. With France in turmoil and fast being over-run, the Americans had to make their own way out of their predicament. Luckily they managed to get a ship to England, just hours before the Germans arrived to capture their port of exit.

Once in England, and still determined to fly against the Germans, they tried to join the RAF, only to be advised to return to Canada and try from there! Britain was mindful of America's neutrality and any US citizens wishing to volunteer needed first to join the ranks of the Royal Canadian Air Force – in Canada. However, they contacted a Member of Parliament, whose name had been given to them, and finally, on 5 July, 1940, Tobin, Mamedoff and Keough, together with Virgil Olsen and Michael Luczhow, joined the ranks of the Royal Air Force.

Once past their Operational Training Unit courses, the three were posted together to No. 609 Squadron, on 5 August, based at RAF Middle Wallop. Despite their flying experience, the trio were hardly combat ready and wisely, the CO, Horace Darley, did not allow them to fly in action at once. But with the desperate fighting over England, every fighter pilot was needed and so by mid-August, the "Yanks" were operational.

The 24th was Andy Mamedoff's 28th birthday. He scrambled with the Squadron and got into combat with enemy fighters, which were escorting scores of bombers over Southampton that afternoon. Mamedoff was flying Spitfire No. L1082 which was a veteran. In fact it had been 609's very first Spitfire, taken in charge a year earlier. Unhappily, Mamedoff let a fighter get behind him and put a cannon shell into it. This shell appeared to have smashed through the tail, zipped straight along the fuselage, through the radio, exploded and spent itself on the armour plate behind Mamedoff's back! Andy brought the damaged fighter back, although the tail wheel collapsed on landing, but its fighting days were over. There were a few holes in the fuselage, two bullets through the propeller and a hole through the starboard elevator which Andy could stand in!

The Luftwaffe mounted a raid the next day which RAF fighters intercepted near the south coast town of Weymouth, as they headed for Portland. Squadron Leader Darley led his pilots into escorting Me–110s of V/LG1 and II/ZG2 as well as Me–109s from III/JG2, although the Spitfire pilots were then themselves engaged by Me–109 fighters from JG53. At least two 110s were shot down by 609 Squadron and five others damaged, while two ME–109s of JG2 were also shot down off the Isle of Wight. Red Tobin put in a claim for one Me–110 damaged and possibly destroyed but before he could see more he became unconscious as he had not switched on his oxygen! He came to when just 1,000 feet above the sea.

The air battles continued but it was not until 15 September that Tobin was able to make another claim. The Luftwaffe had now started to attack London and 609 engaged bombers south of the city shortly after mid-day. Tobin singled out a Dornier bomber, attacked it and in company with another pilot, shot it down, Tobin already having been engaged himself by three yellow-nosed Me–109 fighters.

It is understood that the Dornier (a Do217, coded F1 + FS) was from the 8th Staffel of KG76, and in fact it crash landed at Castle Farm, Shoreham, a little after noon. The other pilot who shared this kill was Flying Officer John Dundas DFC, also of 609. Dundas was to gain a dozen victories during 1940 before his own death in action in November. Dundas' brother Hugh, was a pilot with 616 Squadron in the Battle and went on to become Group Captain Dundas, DSO DFC (later Sir Hugh).

Tobin recorded in his diary:

"I caught a Dornier, chased him, shot his aileron off, hit his glycol tank. He went into a cloud. I went down after him, saw a 215 make a crash landing. Crew of three got out, sat on the wing. Geoffrey Gaunt, one of my best friends missing. I saw a Spit during the fight going down on fire. Sure hope it wasn't Geoff. If it was, well, from now on he'll be flying in clearer skies."

Shorty Keough was also in the fighting on the 15th, flying as No. 2 to Pilot Officer Mike Appleby in Green Section. The section shot down a Dornier 217 from 5/KG2 which force landed in a field at Eighteen Pounder Farm, Westfield, near Hastings at 12.10 pm.

Carl Raymond Davis was born of American parents in South Africa and is more generally referred to as a South African. He came to England when he was 13 and ended his education at Trinity College, Cambridge, to become a mining engineer. Joining the Auxiliary Air

Force in 1936 he went to 601 Squadron and in the Battle of Britain won the DFC before being killed in action on 6 September, aged 29. He had shot down about ten Germans.

DePeyster Brown and Otto John Peterson were both members of the RCAF and came to England with No. 1 Canadian Squadron. Brown transferred to the USAAF in May 1942. Otto Peterson was born in Eckville, Atlanta in 1915, joining the RCAF in 1938. Aged 24 he was killed in action on 27 September, 1940.

There has been some suggestion that there may have been other Americans who fought with the RAF in 1940, mostly under the guise of being Canadians. Pilot Officer H W Reilley is one, who it is understood was born in Detroit. He spent part of his life in London, Ontario, and when he served with the RAF gave his nationality as Canadian but swore friends to secrecy about his true place of birth. Hugh Reilley died in action on 17 October, 1940, flying Spitfires with 66 Squadron. He was shot down not far from Biggin Hill by the German ace Werner Molders, of JG.51.

These then were the first American fighter pilots to see action with the RAF. But already there were other Americans in Britain starting on their great adventures. Most would serve in the Eagle Squadrons and their exploits were to become legendary.

AMERICAN PILOTS WHO FLEW IN THE BATTLE OF BRITAIN

NAME	SERVICE No.	SQDN.
DePeyster Brown	C1094	1 (RCAF)
Carl Raymond Davis	90131	601
Arthur Gerald Donahue	81624	64
William Mead Lindsley Fiske	78092	601
John Kenneth Haviland*	82690	151
Vernon Charles Keough	81630	609
Phillip Howard Leckrone	84655	616
Andrew Mamedoff	81621	609
Otto John Peterson	C900	1 (RCAF)
Hugh William Reilley	43043	64 & 66
Eugene Quimby Tobin	81622	609

*Note: John Haviland is the only American to have fought in the Battle of Britain and survived the War.

Chapter 2

Fledgling Eagles

EVEN before the Battle of Britain began, there was movement behind the scenes to organise a possible American fighter squadron which could be made available to RAF Fighter Command. Something similar had occurred in the Great War of 1914–18. In that conflict, American volunteers had been formed into a fighting squadron within the French Air Service. Known officially as Escadrille N.124, and unofficially as the Lafayette Squadron, this unit had served France well between 1916 and the beginning of 1918.

So popular had the concept been that there were more Americans than could be assigned to a single squadron. Others, therefore, served in other French units and collectively they became part of the Lafayette Flying Corps. When the United States finally entered the war and her forces arrived in France, N.124 became the 103rd Aero (Pursuit) Squadron USAS. It gave the embryo USAS a fully experienced squadron in the battle zone and the Squadron and the Corps helped to provide experienced flight, squadron and later group commanders for the American Air Service.

Now, 22 years after the end of the First World War, the same general idea was being formulated. Too late to help France – France had fallen in June 1940 – American volunteer pilots could at least help Britain, in a war that would last a long time, provided she survived the immediate crisis and could ward off invasion from the Continent.

The new organisation was the brain-child of Charles Sweeny – described as a "well-heeled American sportsman, businessman and socialite" – who lived in London. Charles Sweeny was 30 years old and he engaged two other Sweenys to help in the preliminaries. One was his brother Robert – Bobby, the well-known golfer, who had become the British Amateur Golf Champion in 1937 – the other was their uncle, Colonel Charles Sweeny, who hailed from Salt Lake City, Utah. Uncle Charles was equally well-known as a traveller and soldier of fortune. He had twice entered the American military academy at

West Point and was twice expelled, in 1900 and again in 1901. Despite this, he was determined to become a soldier.

Uncle Charles' story then began to read like a chapter out of a "Boy's Own" magazine. He had been the hero of freedom uprisings in Mexico, Venezuela and Nicaragua. He had become a Colonel in the French Foreign Legion in the First World War and then became a colonel in the American Expeditionary Force. He was an aide to the French General Weygand, supporting the Poles against the Russian Bolsheviks in 1920; an adviser to Kemal Ataturk in the Greco-Turkish war of 1922; a French Foreign Legionnaire fighting a Berber revolt in 1925; a military adviser to the Republican forces in the Spanish Civil War in the late 30s.

Initially, Charles Sweeny formed an army unit of Americans, known as the "First American Reconnaissance (Motorised) Squadron", made up of Americans living or working in London, to help defend the country if an invasion came. Fortunately perhaps, it was never to be tested in battle!

Then came the idea of the fighter squadron. This became the start of the first Eagle Squadron – the name actually being suggested by Charles' father, Robert, a prominent American businessman in London.

Charles Sweeny, knowing the right people in London, who equally knew the right people at Air Ministry, had his idea accepted (although the "powers" needed to tread carefully through the minefield of the US Neutrality Act) and this in due course turned into a well organised programme in America and Canada, which soon began to recruit would-be pilots to fly with the RAF.

This was put under the command of a famous First War fighter "ace" – Billy Bishop VC, now an Air Vice Marshal. Billy Bishop asked an American, Clayton Knight, who had been in the Royal Flying Corps in World War I and became a well-known aviation artist, to exercise some control over the influx of Americans who began to pour over the border into Canada. Together with his friend Homer Smith (who was Charles Sweeny's cousin), Knight formed a small committee which, first clandestinely and then openly, set up interviewing and screening offices in the USA. Those with 30 flying hours were eligible to join the Eagle Squadrons directly.

Charles Sweeny was pleased at the way it had all gone, for he knew only too well that America must eventually come into the war and that his American volunteers, with operational experience with the RAF, would help form a nucleus of pilots with "know-how" to assist the untried USAAF.

The Air Ministry, with the Secretary of State for Air, Sir Archibald Sinclair, having negotiated the US Neutrality problem set about forming an RAF fighter squadron to take the American volunteers. They selected RAF squadron number 71, which had not been used since World War I, activating it in September 1940 specifically to house the Americans. The new unit was to be based at RAF Church Fenton, to the east of Leeds, Yorkshire, and equipped with Miles Master trainers until its new pilots were ready for an operational aeroplane.

Its emblem became the American eagle, the design for which Charles Sweeny took from the eagle design of his US passport, with the letters "E.S." above it. Uncle Charles became the squadron's honorary commander, while the unit's first leader was Squadron Leader W M Churchill DSO DFC RAF.

* * *

Walter Myers Churchill, was posted to command No. 71 Squadron on 29 September 1940. An experienced RAF officer, he had been in the service since 1931 and had seen considerable front line action in France. He had a handful of victories in air combat, been decorated twice and had a famous name, though not related at all to the British Prime Minister.

The task then was to find pilots to join the new Squadron. Those men being recruited across the Atlantic would take time to get to Britain to train, so the net was cast for other candidates. Three obvious men were Tobin, Mamedoff and Keough, who were fighting with 609 Squadron down south. These three were posted in shortly before Churchill, on the 19th. On the same day that Churchill arrived, so too did Art Donahue from 64 Squadron. A senior flight commander came next, another RAF officer, Flight Lieutenant G A Brown, posted in from 253 Squadron.

George Alfred Brown was 28, and had joined the RAF in 1937. In the Battle of Britain he had been shot down over Maidstone by Me–109s and wounded in the shoulder and legs, but returned to his unit two weeks later. Now he took on the job of A Flight Commander, in 71.

In Charles Sweeny's plan of things, the American Volunteer Squadron's first CO would have been Billy Fiske. It was an obvious choice but one that might well not have been approved by Air Ministry. For one thing he was still only a Pilot Officer, but his death in action had put an end to that thought. It was still essential in the eyes of the RAF that the initial leaders be RAF officers, although accepting that a future American CO would be desirable. To this end, they found an American officer with both operational and command experience within the ranks of the British Fleet Air Arm, one W E G "Bill" Taylor, aged 35, who had been a former US Navy pilot, had been attached to the FAA and had flown some carrier operations. He was posted in on 4 October as CO designate but then had to go off and learn how to fly single-seat RAF fighters.

A couple of days later Phil Leckrone was prized away from 616 Squadron and before the month was out, Luke Allen had arrived from No. 5 AFTS and the B Flight Commander, R C Wilkinson DFM and bar, had joined. Royce Clifford Wilkinson, was nearing 27 and had been a former Halton RAF apprentice. Later becoming a pilot he had flown in France with Walter Churchill in May 1940, so no doubt Churchill had some influence over his posting. His double Distinguished Flying Medal, earned in France, was yet another influence on the young Americans.

Not that any of it influenced Art Donahue much. Cheesed off that he had left a perfectly good operational Spitfire squadron to come to a non-operational, hardly equipped and almost pilotless new squadron, he quickly got himself posted back to 64 and never saw the Eagles again.

Meantime, No. 5 AFTS churned out 11 more pilots during November and December, all of whom arrived at Church Fenton. Some would make names for themselves with the Squadron. The eleven, which then brought the squadron up to strength, were: Bryon Kennerly, Arthur "Indian Jim" Moore, Chesley Peterson, Gus Daymond, Jim McGinnis, Bud Orbison, Dean Satterlee, Mike Kolendorski, Ken Taylor, John Ayer and Charlie Bateman. Of these, Peterson and Daymond would end up as the top scoring Eagle pilots.

Despite the seemingly keen enthusiasm the RAF showed towards the formation of the Eagle Squadron, the first Eagles themselves were less than enthusiastic once they had arrived at Church Fenton. They still did not have an operational aeroplane, having to be content with their Master training machines. Newly formed RAF squadrons usually got a few Hurricanes or Spitfires, even if they were "clapped out" and "war weary" types. Then, as if to add insult to injury, the RAF tried to "snow" them, by giving them an American fighter – the tubby Brewster Buffalo.

One can imagine some Air Ministry bureaucrat smiling to himself when coming up with the idea that this bunch of American "heroes" could help sort out the embarrassing situation of having been lumbered with these all but useless American Buffaloes. Aptly named, some would say. Many who flew it in the RAF complimented the designers in having produced a lovely "club" machine; very nice for swanning about on a Sunday afternoon, but absolutely no use in modern-day combat. The Americans themselves quickly discovered in the Pacific war that they were no match for the Jap Zero fighters.

Walter Churchill, when he found his squadron had got them, was appalled. Viewing the three stubby fighters, Churchill's main concern was how to get rid of them. Fortunately Phil Leckrone overshot in one on landing four days after they arrived and put it on its back – the Buffalo had a tendency to "float" on final landing approach. Churchill himself had an emergency landing when he flew one and condemned them as a death-trap. So he "suggested" to a couple of pilots that if they ground-looped the remaining Buffalos, he would not be too angry. Thus 71 were quickly out of Buffalo fighters and began to receive real aeroplanes – Hurricanes. The units also moved to Kirton-in-Lindsey, south of Scunthorpe

* * *

I write about the Hurricane with admiration and affection, tinged with a little sorrow. In a way, it was sad that this great old war-horse was put in the shade by its successor. The beautiful Spitfire imme-diately took the limelight and even took the credit for winning the Battle of Britain, in which there were far more Hurricanes involved than Spitfires.

Of course, the Spitfire was a lovely plane, combining speed, manoeuvrability and beauty. But let's not forget the old Hurricane, as those of us who flew it never will. She forgave many mistakes that the Spitfire wouldn't, both in the air and on the ground, and in the early days, when we took to the air with so little experience, we needed a lot of forgiveness.

The Spit was a little bitch on the ground. The long nose blocking your forward vision completely meant that you had to constantly weave right and left, and if you took too long before taking off, you could lose your brakes entirely through lack of air, or even overheat the engine. The narrow landing-gear also made it prone to ground-looping on landing or take-off if the field was uneven.

In the Hurricane, you could trundle around on the ground as you liked, and you had to be really ham-fisted to ground loop it. In the air, too, the Hurricane was much steadier than the Spitfire. Johnnie Johnson's first comment after being in combat in a Spitfire was "The Hurricane was a much better gun-platform."

I knew exactly what he meant. The first time I got onto the tail of an enemy plane in a Spitfire, I missed him. It wasn't because I opened fire before I was in range, or anything like that; I should have blown him to bits, and would have if I'd been flying a Hurricane. But the firing button on the Spitfire was on the top of the control column and the Spitfire was so sensitive that, when I pressed the trigger, the nose pitched down and I missed the target.

The same applied on landing. The Hurricane just came in, plunked itself down and rolled to a stop. One always knew a pilot who had just transferred to Spitfires – he bounced three times down the runway!

The Hurricane could also take a lot of punishment. On one of my first missions escorting bombers to Le Havre and St. Omer, we ran into a real hornet's nest of Me–109s and FW–190s. I don't know whether it was fighters or flak that got me, but I was damned lucky that either Fate or the amount of plating behind me protected me. There were nasty jagged holes in the wings, too.

Halfway across the Channel, I saw another Hurricane beside me. My Flight Commander was giving my plane the once-over. His Canadian drawl over the radio was completely unemotional:

"You'll never make it. Get out before it blows up!"

I must have hesitated too long.

"Hit the silk, goddam it!"

My canopy was already open. I started getting off my helmet and its appendages of oxygen mask and radio wires, and slipped out of the seat harness. With great difficulty, I heaved myself out of the seat, fighting the rush of air outside, and crawled out onto the wing. There was no smoke out there.

I looked at the Channel far below. It looked a long way down and promised to be cold. The smoke had cleared as the plane side-slipped and the cockpit looked warmer than the alternative. I clambered back in.

The engine was running rough; the plane was hard to handle; the controls were obviously badly hit. Somehow I nursed her across the Channel, past the golf courses at Sandwich Bay and down to the longest runway in England at Manston.

There wasn't much left of the fabric or the tailplane. Before they took me off to the hospital, I hobbled over and patted what was left of the fuselage.

"Thanks, old girl! You were a real lady!"

* * *

The new year of 1941 did not start well for the Squadron. On the 5th, Phil Leckrone was killed in a flying accident. He was flying in a three-man formation with Shorty Keough and Bud Orbison at 20,000 feet when Phil collided with Orbison and went into a gradual dive. Shorty followed him down, shouting to him over the R/T but Phil made no reply or any attempt at baling out, so must have been unconscious, either by the collision or by lack of oxygen prior to it. The doomed Hurricane went straight into the ground just outside Scunthorpe. Orbison did very well to land back at base with a badly damaged left wing.

Just over a month later Orbison himself was killed whilst flying in thick cloud. He must have lost his bearings and spun in from about 4,000 feet. Then, in one of those strange quirks of fate, the third man of that trio, Shorty Keough himself, was lost six days later, on 15 February.

The boys had gone to RAF Finningley on an overnight evacuation practice. A section of Hurricanes was scrambled to fly a protection patrol over a convoy just off the east coast the next morning. Pilot Officer Nat Maranz (who had arrived on 8 January) and Shorty went

Flying Officer Jimmy Davies, was the first American fighter pilot to receive the British DFC. Flying with 79 Squadron RAF, he saw action during the Battle of France but was killed in action in July 1940. Seen here, 5th from the left, in France, May 1940. 3rd from the left is his friend Don "Dimsie" Stones DFC.

Pilot Officer Phil Leckrone flew with 616 Squadron in the Battle of Britain, but died in a flying accident with 71 Squadron in early 1941.

Billy Fiske, died of injuries sustained in the Battle of Britain, flying with 601 Squadron RAF, after bringing back his badly damaged fighter.

Flying Officer C D "Pussy" Palmer DFC, saw action in the Battle of France and later commanded a British fighter squadron. Killed in action over Brest in 1942.

Pilot Officer Art Donahue flew with 64 Squadron in the Battle of Britain and after a very brief stay with 71 Squadron, saw action in the Far East. Killed in action in September 1942 with 91 Squadron RAF.

Andy Mamedoff with his 609 Squadron Spitfire, after being badly shot up on his birthday – 24 August, 1940. Note his leg is through the hole in the rear elevator.

Andy Mamedoff inspects bullet holes through his propeller – 24 August, 1940.

609 Squadron in the Battle of Britain with Andy Mamedoff and Red Tobin amongst them. Seated: Frankie Howell DFC, Keith Ogilvie DFC, Red Tobin and Staples. Standing: Andy Mamedoff, John Dundas DFC and John Bisdee DFC.

609 Squadron. Shorty Keough standing, left, with Red Tobin seated left.

Canadian Keith Ogilvie left, and Red Tobin, 609 Squadron, 1940.

Hurricane I of 71 Eagle Squadron, coded XR-Z.

The Orde drawing of Squadron Leader Walter Churchill DSO DFC, CO of 71 Eagle Squadron in 1940–41.

Oscar Coen DFC.

Ground crews of 71 Squadron, with Hurricane I.

Hurricane XR-J of 71 Squadron, late 1940.

Hurricane IIb of 121 Squadron AV-R (Z3427). Sel Edner shared the probable destruction of a Ju88 in this machine on 8 August, 1941, the Squadron's first combat claim.

Prince Bernhard of the Netherlands visits 71 Squadron, l to r: Ed Bateman, Andy Mamedoff, Bob Sweeny, the Prince, Bill Taylor (CO), Robbie Robinson (Adj), Prince's Aide.

into cloud, Maranz breaking away when at 7,000 feet and still diving. For some reason Shorty stayed in the dive and must have come out of the cloud too low to recover and went into the sea. Coastguards heard the sound of a crash and a couple of days later the tops of a pair of flying boots, size 5, were found with some wreckage. Only little Shorty Keough could wear such small boots.

The Squadron had become operational back in December, (Bill Taylor had taken over from Churchill in February) but convoy patrols were the only war-like activities assigned to them. After all, they were still working up, and during the recent winter months, there hadn't been too much happening in the south of England, although the fighter offensive over the Channel and northern France was now beginning to get underway. 71's first engagement came on 17 April, again over a convoy. Gus Daymond saw a Dornier 217 bomber fleetingly and fired but could not determine any result. The Squadron also moved its base again in this month, going to Martlesham Heath, near Ipswich.

Among some new arrivals on 19 April was Oscar Coen, who was to make a name for himself with the Eagles, and Virgil Olsen. Olsen had been in France with Tobin and Mamedoff but failed to get away in time. In fact it was not until September that he managed to get out of France. Another new arrival in May was Pilot Officer Bill Dunn.

William Robert Dunn, like so many of the Eagle pilots, had come to the Squadron by a very circuitous route. He was from Minneapolis, and was nearing his 23rd birthday when the war began. He had had his first ride in an aeroplane when he was about 12, in a barnstormer OX–5 Powers Travel Air biplane and he also had an uncle who had flown in World War I, who owned a Waco 9 biplane. His mother remarried, and Bill's stepfather too had been a World War I pilot, so by the time he was 15, he had logged some 100 odd hours of flight time as a student pilot, but was not yet old enough to apply for a licence.

Keen to join the US Air Corps, he applied when he was 17 but despite his flying hours was conned into joining the infantry as a private and try as he might, he got nowhere when he tried to transfer to the Air Corps. He finished his time in the army in 1937, managed a few more flying lessons but then the war in Europe began and Bill immediately set off for the Canadian border. His plan was to join the RCAF but he was told they were not able to accept American volunteers! Without any money he felt obliged to join something so went into the Canadian army.

He ended up in the Seaforth Highlanders of Canada and by December he was in England. His outfit was, by the summer of 1940, in the south of England, so Sergeant Bill Dunn found himself in the Battle of Britain – but on the ground. Even so he was in the action during an attack on Southampton and RAF Tangmere, and on 16 August, (the day Billy Fiske was mortally wounded), Bill manned a Lewis gun at his camp at nearby Borden.When Ju87 dive-bombers screamed down, he helped shoot down two in quick succession!

His chance to fly finally came in October, when the Air Ministry sought volunteers from the army to become pilots to replace the losses Fighter Command had suffered during the summer. With a slight exaggeration about the number of flying hours he had, he was accepted, trained, commissioned and by May 1941 was an obvious candidate for the Eagles.

A couple of days after Bill arrived, Chesley Peterson – or just plain "Pete" – was granted the acting rank of Flight Lieutenant in the RAF. He was, therefore, the first American in the Eagle Squadron on General Duties to be raised above the rank of Pilot Officer. In view of his later service and actions, it is obvious that his superiors had seen something special in Pete. And they were right.

As if the Eagle Squadron were now "on the map" – or perhaps it was just plain curiosity, – the "Father of the RAF", Lord Trenchard, paid the Squadron a visit on 15 May, making certain he spoke to all the pilots.

If this had been an auspicious event, that same evening provided more excitement. A Section was scrambled and set off across the Channel, which comprised Pilot Officer J K Alexander and J F Flynn. The Squadron was later able to record its "first blood" and its first aircraft shot-up in action. However, the truth was more salutary.

Near Calais 109s had come down, Flynn chasing one as another got on his tail. Keith Alexander had fired at the second Messerschmitt 109 that was attacking John's Hurricane. In the excitement of the occasion, Alexander's fire not only damaged the German fighter but blasted into Flynn's machine as well. The 109 broke away as Flynn began the struggle to get his machine back to the English coast, having also caught a bit of shrapnel in his arm. He was able to make Manston where he managed a landing. In June, Keith Alexander was posted to No. 1 Squadron RAF and later became an instructor in Rhodesia.

Two days later came the first real loss in action. Mike Kolendorski, a man of Polish extraction from California, and mad keen to get at the enemy, failed to extricate himself from an action over the North Sea. He spotted a German and went right down after it and was lost in the clouds. It is thought that he got suckered into a trap and that another German shot him down. His body was later washed up south of the Hook of Holland.

* * *

In June the Squadron was deemed ready for the big league, moving down to North Weald, in Essex. From here they could still fly convoy patrols over the North Sea, but would also be within range of more interesting operations across the Channel. On other Ops they would also be able to fly to a more southerly airfield to refuel before heading out to France.

It was now time for the Eagles to prove themselves. They had had a good deal of publicity due to the very nature of who and what they were, but despite some eight months of life, the squadron had achieved very little, and this had not been helped by the Alexander/Flynn scrap.

General H H "Hap" Arnold, head of the USAAF in the States, had even visited London and apparently been told by Air Marshal Sholto Douglas that 71's performance was far from satisfactory, which seems a little harsh given the period of general inactivity they had just come through. News of this had stung the Eagles and Peterson had gone over everyone's head, straight to the AOC of 12 Group, Hugh Saunders, to request a more active duty, hence the initial move to Martlesham. Fortunately he had not been penalised for this bit of temerity. Now, having moved to North Weald, things must improve. They also had a new CO, another RAF officer, Squadron Leader H deC A Woodhouse – "Paddy".

Henry deClifford Anthony Woodhouse AFC, had been with Training Command for some time, winning the Air Force Cross, but he had lived in New York three years earlier. However, although keen to get into action, he had seen little real action himself. Undoubtedly the Eagles would have liked someone a little more combat-hardened at this particular moment. He came to 71 from 610 Squadron where he had been a flight commander. He had a half share in one Ju88 destroyed to his name. Then came 2 July, 1941.

The Squadron were put on stand-by – there was a show on. The North Weald Wing and its Squadrons would be taking part in two escort shows, first to Hurricane-bombers and then as part of a Circus operation – Circus 29. Circus was part of Fighter Command's new operational plan to take the air war to the enemy. In order to bring the Luftwaffe to battle, a small formation of bombers – usually light twin-engined Blenheims – would go for a target in northern France, escorted by several squadrons of RAF fighters. The plan then would be for the fighters to engage and shoot down their German counterparts when they came up. It didn't always work that way, but it was the way things were organised in 1941.

The twelve pilots of 71 Squadron were called early, breakfasted, briefed and in their Hurricanes soon afterwards. They escorted the bomb-carrying Hurricanes to the French coast and back, being home at North Weald by 10. Here word was received that they were down for the second show – Circus 29 – take off was 1150.

The target was a power station at Lille, and there were six bombers each from 21 and 226 Squadrons. Somehow they missed the target and bombed Merville, losing two of their aircraft. Paddy Woodhouse led his Eagles, with Bill Dunn flying as his No. 2. The Germans did react to this raid and soon Me–109s were darting about, trying to pick off the bombers as they headed in or give a brief burst at a Spitfire or Hurricane as they slashed down and away.

Woodhouse fired a burst at one diving 109 from 150 yards and it poured smoke, rolled over and plunged earthwards. Some of the Eagles saw it crash. It was now just after mid-day and the attacks eased as the Circus continued inland. Twenty minutes later the 109s – or their friends – were back. Again came the sleek fighters, curving down trying to get at the bombers. A 109E came through the bombers and was spotted by Bill Dunn, but it broke to port and headed right in front of Bill's Hurricane. He jabbed the gun-button with the German no more than 75–100 yards ahead of him. His bullets smashed into the enemy fighter as he closed to 50 yards, then it was on fire and going over, diving headlong for the ground where he and others saw it explode.

Gus Daymond was after another 109 at almost the same moment. He fired but the 109 turned and put some bullets into Gus's fighter. Gus also turned, caught the German, opened fire and raked the Messerschmitt which streamed black smoke, rolled and went down to the west of Lille, its pilot taking to his parachute. Kill number three for the Eagles. Bob Mannix sliced in behind another, fired and saw it stagger away belching smoke but that was all so he could only claim a probable.

In just thirty minutes the Eagle Squadron had proved themselves in action. The CO had gained the Squadron's first confirmed victory, while Bill and Gus had clobbered two more at almost the same time. Bill timed his combat report as being 12.35, Gus at 12.40, so credit for the first American Eagle pilot to get a Hun went to Bill Dunn.

Eleven gleeful pilots touched down at North Weald, excited and exalted. Only then did they realise that someone was missing. The pilots looked at each other, then realised it was Bill Hall who was not back. Bill Hall was an experienced pilot – a bush pilot in Alaska and Quebec – could it really be him? Someone remembered seeing a Hurricane heading down, streaming smoke. It must have been him. Happily news later came that he was a prisoner – wounded, but alive. He would return to more leisurely flying in Canada after the war.

The important thing, however, was that the Squadron had seen their first major action and had come out on top. They might still have things to prove to themselves as well as to others, but they were on their way.

Chapter 3

The Second & Third
Eagle Squadrons

By the time 71 Squadron were in the full swing of operations, there
was a second Eagle Squadron in being – No. 121 Squadron RAF. This
was formed at 71's former stamping ground at Kirton on 14 May, 1941,
command being given to Squadron Leader R P R Powell DFC.

Robin Peter Reginald Powell, known to everyone as Peter, was yet
another pre-war pilot. Aged 24, he was ex-Cranwell and had flown
with the first RAF Hurricane Squadron – No. 111, back in 1936. He
had been awarded the DFC for actions over France and Dunkirk the
previous year, then continued to fly throughout the Battle of Britain.
121 was his first command. Arriving with him was Hugh Kennard, as
senior Flight Commander. He too was a pre-war RAF officer who had
flown in the Battle of Britain and then become a Flight Commander
with one of the first Polish squadrons. Two days later, Royce Wilkinson
joined 121 from 71 as Flight Commander, bringing with him the
experience gained while working up 71 Squadron.

The first crop of squadron pilots also arrived on the 16th, Indian Jim
Moore and Nat Maranz brought their experience from 71, then came
Collier Mize, Bob Reed, Fred Scuddy, Brad Smith, Reade Tilley and
Bert Stewart. Before the month was out three more had arrived, Earl
"Tootie" Mason, Loran "Gunner" Laughlin and Carrol "Red" McColpin.
Reade Tilley and Red McColpin would do pretty well.

Unlike most of 71 Squadron, who had come in from training units,
a lot of the guys who were assigned to 121 had been with RAF
squadrons, albeit briefly. Obviously, with more American volunteers
coming through from the Clayton Knight Organisation than could be
assigned to just one squadron, others had to find homes prior to a
second Eagle squadron being activated. Thus it was that Reed, Mize
and Scuddy came in via 43 Squadron RAF. The pilots who joined in
May, Laughlin and McColpin, had been with 607 Squadron.

Laughlin was the first Eagle to die in 121, in a flying accident on
June 21. Training accidents, whilst tragic and seemingly a waste of

life,were a part of the risks in all forces. It is sadly a fact that more young men were killed learning to fly than were to to die in actual combat situations throughout both world wars.

The Squadron had Hurricanes from the start, firstly some old Mark I models, then in July the Mark IIb. With these they began an intensive working-up period until they were deemed ready to fly convoy patrols at the beginning of August. On the 5th came the first scramble, which involved Viv Watkins and Reade Tilley but they found nothing. Three days later came the first bit of excitement when sections were out over another North Sea convoy. Sel Edner and Jack Mooney were 50 miles out from Hull when they spotted a Ju88 bomber and gave chase. Both opened fire, keeping it up until their ammo ran out. They saw the 88 losing height, dropping down gradually from 2,500 to just 300 feet with dense smoke coming from it, but they did not see whether it actually crashed. Both men gained a healthy respect for German rear gunners, as both fighters were found to have bullet holes in them when they landed.

Then on 18 August, twelve pilots of 121, led by Peter Powell took off for West Malling in Kent, refuelled and then became part of a Fighter Sweep to the French coast. A Sweep was an operation without bombers to protect. They were either flown with the hope of meeting enemy fighters, or, more usually, in indirect support of a Circus Operation being flown to a nearby area. In this case the Sweep might be lucky enough to run into German fighters going to or returning from the bomber operation. There was a brief skirmish, Peter Powell latching onto a lone 109F near Gravelines, but he could only claim it as probably destroyed. However, it was almost a "first" for the Squadron.

Some more shows occurred. Hugh Kennard led the Squadron on another Sweep from West Malling on the 21st, but this time all they found was German flak from Dunkirk, and on the 27th, on another show in company with 65 and 257 Squadrons, they didn't even get flak!

During September some more patrols were flown and on the 15th Earl Mason was killed in yet another flying accident. The Squadron began to be a little despondent in September because Red McColpin an Don Geffene were posted to 71 on the 9th, to be followed by Ed Miluck and Bert Stewart on the 15th and then by Sergeant Griffin on the 28th. The Squadron began to think they were little more than a holding unit to replenish losses by 71! Griffin was returned on 6 October, so perhaps someone said something.

* * *

The third American Eagle Squadron – No. 133 – was formed at the end of July, 1941, this time at RAF Coltishall, near Norwich. George Brown was posted over from 71 Squadron as its first commanding officer, then during August a whole bunch of pilots arrived, including one flight commander, Flight Lieutenant Scott RAF, who was almost immediately posted out again to 601 Squadron. He was replaced by Andy Mamedoff, from 71, on 2 September, a fitting reward for one of the original Eagles. He had just recently been married, to an English girl, Penny Craven, of the Craven cigarette family. Towards the end of September, the A Flight Commander arrived, H A S Johnston.

Hugh Anthony Stephen Johnston, known inevitably as "Johnny", although also known as Tim, was 27 years old. He'd been to Oxford and then went into the Colonial Service but joined the RAFVR in 1940. He had served with 257 Squadron at Coltishall, flying Hurricanes, so was in the right place at the right time when this flight commander vacancy arose. He remained with 133 for seven months before being posted out to Malta, where he was to win the DFC. He wrote a famous wartime book on his experiences – "Tattered Battlements" – published anonymously in 1943. He returned to England to command fighter squadrons at the time of the invasion of Europe, and won a bar to his DFC.

The Squadron had Hurricanes – Mark IIb – and it became operational within two months. It moved to Duxford in August 1941 but despite being at this more "operational" station, it did not see any action, and then went to Collyweston, west of Peterborough. It was not there too long before going to Fowlmere, near Cambridge, but then disaster struck.

The new Squadron had already suffered its first casualties – yes, in training – on 27 September. Walt Soares and his number two, Charles Barrell, collided in a turn into final approach and were killed, being too low to recover. Then in October it was decided, for reasons which never did seem to be discovered, that the Squadron's training should be completed in Northern Ireland of all places. On 8 October, 15

Hurricanes took off from Fowlmere at 1.30 pm and landed without incident at Seeland at 2.20. From here the final part of the journey would be flown, to Eglington, near Londonderry, in Northern Ireland. The weather wasn't too good with storms forecast, so George Brown and Tim Johnston took off with four other pilots at 3.30, leaving Andy Mamedoff to bring in the other nine. They took off at 4.40, by which time the weather was really bad.

The next refuelling stop was Andreas on the Isle of Man, half way across the Irish Sea. Of the first six, Johnston and two others got to the island and landed at Jurby at 4.15, the other three at Andreas five minutes later. Of the second party, four got through to Andreas, two returned to Seeland, while four others crashed. All four pilots were lost, amongst them Andy Mamedoff.

The new B Flight commander was Ed Bateman, from 71 Squadron, who just a few weeks earlier had been part of the fly-past over Andy's wedding celebrations. The Squadron was to remain at Eglington, in a sea of mud and knee deep in water, till December. It was a real low point in 133's history.

* * *

Meanwhile, 121 Squadron were continuing their operations but had yet to record their first confirmed success. Day convoy patrols and the occasional show over France filled their days and a dusk patrol ended disastrously for Reade Tilley on 2 October. Flying in the dark is perilous at the best of times, especially over a blacked-out Britain. When Reade's radio failed he suddenly had no contact, help or advice from the ground. As his fuel ran out he was forced to depart from his Hurricane near Burton-on-Trent, suffering a broken leg when he hit the ground.

In October 1941, both 121 and 133 Squadrons began to re-equip with Britain's well-known fighter – the Spitfire.

The Spitfire was a lady, and everyone who flew her had a love affair with her – she was that kind of lady!

When you got used to the Spit, you became part of it. You didn't aim your guns, you aimed yourself. The controls were so sensitive you didn't have the impression of forcing the plane to follow your will; it was as if your will was automatically converted into action. So little effort was needed to handle her that one was inclined to move the plane rather than move one's body.

Strictly against the rules, I sometimes used to smoke a cigar when flying. If I dropped my lighter, it never occurred to me to grope around the floor for it. I simply moved the stick about an inch and caught the lighter as the plane rolled over.

The basic design of the Spitfire was so intrinsically sound that it could, and did, accept more and more powerful engines. The Germans tried to do the same thing with the Me–109 but gave up after the 'G' model when, fortunately for them, they were able to switch to jet planes.

It is difficult to compare the different models of FW–190 and Me–109 with the different models of Spitfires, but throughout the development of both sides, the Spit retained its superiority over the German aircraft in rate of climb and rate of turn. Since it was conceived and used as a defensive fighter, that was what it was meant to do.

Although the Germans used the dive as an evasive tactic, the Spitfire could stay with them and stood a fair chance of catching them when they finally levelled out, even if it was at ground level. Johnnie Johnson confirms that many of the over 30 victories he had over 109s and 190s were as a result of catching them after a dive.

But it wasn't just the performance of the Spitfire which endeared it to its pilots. The plane had a mystique which led one to become one with the machine and which extended even beyond the pilots.

It even extended to the Luftwaffe. Peter Townsend visited in hospital a German pilot he had shot down, who said how pleased he was to meet the Spitfire pilot who had shot him down.

"No, no," said Peter, "I was flying a Hurricane!"

"No, it was a Spitfire!"

They argued back and forth for some time before the Luftwaffe pilot said, "Alright, but do me a favour – if you meet any other German pilots, tell them that I was shot down by a Spitfire!"

* * *

No. 71 Squadron began to re-equip with Spitfires in August. During July they had continued to fly operations over France in their Hurricanes, despite the majority of Fighter Command units operating with

Spitfires. Bill Dunn and Gus Daymond both claimed Me–109s destroyed on 6 July, on Circus 35, Peterson getting a probable. Bill
shared his with a Polish pilot in 306 Squadron – Leon Jaugsch, who
after the war emigrated to California, both men corresponding with
each other regularly. Bill got another 109 over France on the 21st.

On August 3, Gus bagged a Dornier over the North Sea on a convoy
patrol which made it three each, but then on the 9th, Bill destroyed
a 109 west of Mardyck. Not that there was any race on, but the media
were keen to make something of it and perhaps get excited about the
first Eagle "Ace". Bill ended all speculation on 27 August by downing
two Messerschmits on Circus 86. However, some of their pals ganged
up on the American and put some bits of metal into his Spitfire and
he felt a blow to his right foot and right leg. He was creased across
the back of his head by another bullet.

In pain but with his Spitfire still flying he headed for home and
landed safely. The medics inspected the damage, finding two bullet
holes in his right calf, but a 20 mm shell had taken off the front of
his foot, including three toes. He was out of the fight as far as 71 was
concerned but Bill was far from out of the war. He'd get back to it
in due time.

Gus Daymond got his fourth victory – a 109F – on Circus 93, 4
September, his first in a Spitfire. Tom Wallace also bagged one while
Bob Mannix got another probable. Rhubarbs could be exciting, if
costly – to both sides. The idea was to fly over to France in poor
weather, in sections of two or perhaps four, and shoot up anything that
looked German. If they got into trouble, the RAF pilots could nip into
cloud and head for home. That was the theory anyway. The main
problem however, was that one generally had to fly low and if caught
by ground fire, one was often too low to do much but hit the deck.
If lucky one could end up as a prisoner, if not so lucky . . . ! The boys
in 71 seemed to have been doing OK on Sweeps and Circus operations,
but that all changed on 7 September.

Twelve Spitfires flew a sweep over enemy territory, led by Squadron
Leader Stan Meares DFC, who had taken over command of 71 a couple
of weeks previously. Meares had somehow missed out on the Battle
of Britain, being with Command HQ but had been a flight commander
with 611 Squadron in 1941 and then commanded 74 Squadron that
June.

Mechanical defect forced three pilots to abort, so just nine of 71's Spitfires headed across into France with the rest of the Wing. They were engaged by scores of 109s which reacted violently to the RAF intrusion. Pete Peterson bagged his first 109 and Jack Fessler knocked pieces off another, but three Spitfires failed to return. Forrest Dowling got shot-up and slightly injured, crash landing near New Romney, but Red Tobin, Hillard Fenlaw and Bill Nichols were missing. Only Nichols survived – as a prisoner of war. Fenlaw had only been married recently – to an English girl. Red Tobin's loss was a blow. Now the second of the original Eagles was dead. And Andy Mamedoff, posted to 133 just five days earlier, would, as already related, die when flying to the Isle of Man on 8 October.

Ten days after the Sweep, 71 escorted bombers over France and were hit again. This time Bill Geiger and Tommy McGerty failed to get home. Bill, not yet 22 years old, had flown nearly 30 Sweeps and Circus Ops, but ended up a prisoner. Eighteen year old McGerty, from Los Angeles, who had told his parents he was only a Link Trainer instructor, so they wouldn't worry, was killed. His folks would receive a devastating telegram now. And all the Eagles got was a damaged 109 by Pete.

A slight redress to the balance sheet came the next day, Pete getting a 109 over France. Then Gus Daymond and Johnnie Flynn flew on a late afternoon Rhubarb mission to the French coast on the 19th. They got into a huddle with some 109s and each shot down one, Gus damaging another. Red McColpin shot down his first 109 on Circus 102, between Lille and the French coast on the 21st, Wallace Tribkin possibly getting a second.

Carroll Warren McColpin, was born in Buffalo, New York. By the time the war in Europe started, he had nearly 50 flying hours on 28 different aeroplane types, mostly biplanes but he had some monoplane time. Before the war he managed his own electrical testing equipment company, helping to support his mother, a brother and four sisters. Feeling disgusted with the American Government policy to the war and the draft, he decided to join the RAF and fight.

"We were at war, why not admit it! I joined via the Clayton Knight test in Los Angeles but refused to sign-up until I was in London and assured I'd be assigned to a fighter base. I was worried that, with my experience, if I signed earlier I'd be kept in Canada as an instructor.

I had been self-taught on aeronautical engineering and navigation studies."

He went to Montreal and was soon on a ship out of Halifax to Liverpool, then by train to London. He then had three weeks at No. 56 OTU, flying Hurricanes.

"My first ride, I had to have the mechanic show me where the switches were and how to start the engine. Gunnery and night training were almost nil. It was a period where we taught ourselves all the basics and hoped for the best."

However, Red, or Mac as he was also called, wasn't over-keen to join the Eagle Squadron at first. He knew many of the pilots and didn't want to trust his life in combat to them. So, after training, he went to 607 Squadron, which had quite a mix of nationalities, English, Norwegian, Belgian, Czech, New Zealand and Australian as well as two Americans. He finally went to 121 Squadron in May 1941, then to 71 in September.

Circus 103B, flown on 27 September, produced some more kills. Sam Mauriello got a 109F, Ross Scarborough another, Pete and Jim Crawley, a probable each and Oscar Coen a damaged. Then came 2 October, and McColpin scored the Squadron's first double kills.

McColpin was flying as wingman to Stan Meares when he saw some 109Fs climbing up towards them. Calling a warning to the CO, they both dived and attacked. Both fired into 109s, both falling in flames. McColpin then turned after another which went down and the pilot baled out. Two quick kills and the latest Eagle was on his way!

Chapter 4

Gongs and a new year

PETE Peterson and Gus Daymond were both awarded the British Distinguished Flying Cross on 5 October, 1941. At this time, Pete had shot down two Me–109s, with two probables and a damaged . Gus had claimed four 109s and a Dornier, making him 71's second "ace" on 19 September. Chesley Gordon Peterson, was from Salt Lake City, Utah, and he had actually joined the US Air Corps before the war. Then he was "washed out" for " lack of inherent flying ability", from which we must assume he was judged no damn good. Boy, were they wrong! Not wishing to take that from anyone, the tall, sandy-haired, soft-spoken Peterson volunteered for the RAF in 1940, still only aged 19 (although he still carried the altered birth certificate, changed to show the Air Corps that he was 21), and by November of that year was with the first Eagle Squadron in England.

But before that, being a "flunked out" aviation cadet, he had gone to work for the Douglas Aircraft Company, out in California, where he teamed up with "Indian Joe" Moore – another failure! When they, and a few other hopefuls, heard that Colonel Sweeny was at a Santa Monica hotel trying to organise pilots to fight for France, he was quickly sought out. Sweeny took their names and by February 1940 they were on their way, initially to Canada, then to England, although by then, France had been invaded and plans changed. In England he made the grade at last with no more question of lack of ability.

Like most of the early Eagles, Pete was certain that America would eventually have to come into the war, and he wasn't going to wait around. Perhaps over the years a sense has grown up that these early Americans were little more than adventurous mercenaries, with more bull-shit than brains. This is very far from the truth. Pete and the others were almost all professional, or would-be professional airmen, with a real sense of duty and a sense of pride in their country. So much so that they decided to get into "this man's war" and do something about Hitler and his gangsters before they took over the world. Of course, there had to be something of the adventurer in them. Who else would journey halfway round the world, to fly, fight and perhaps to die, just for the hell of it? But they had their priorities right.

And being trained and indoctrinated by the British Royal Air Force gave them a solid base from which to work and, for a number who would gain high rank in the USAAF later on, a true sense of how to do things properly.

Gregory Augustus Daymond, was from Great Falls, Montana, but had seen something of the world, flying not only in the States, but also in South America and South Africa. Also aged just 19, he nevertheless had six years flying experience behind him!

When the war in Europe began, Daymond was a make-up artist in a Hollywood film studio. Now, less than two years later, he was the Eagle Squadron's second "ace", with five victories and the DFC, and would soon be promoted to flight lieutenant.

Success of a slightly different kind came in October. Oscar Coen, from North Dakota, didn't get back from a Rhubarb mission on the 20th. This might well have been the quick end to a promising airforce career, but not only did he survive the action but returned to tell the tale.

Coen, a former schoolteacher, was still dining out on the story of a similar mission when he and "Lulu" Hollander had attacked a target in France to good effect. But this was much to the consternation of Wing Commander Myles Duke Woolley when he checked over the combat film. The Wingco recognised the target as the only Benedictine factory left in France – and they'd blown it in two!

Coen was flying on Pete's wing on the 20th, and had been itching to fly another sortie over France. Pete agreed and they found a goods train near Lille. Pete said he'd take the engine, and Oscar should go for the freight cars. They both proceeded to work the train over but then one of the cars exploded – it must have been full of ammo. Pete saw Oscar's Spitfire stagger away, streaming glycol. He yelled to Pete that he'd been hit, then that he was baling out, Pete seeing the parachute open. He was low but obviously got away with it. Obviously, because he was back with the Squadron just after Christmas.

As was usual, the boys at North Weald, knowing he'd baled out, said casually that Oscar would be back in a month, knowing full well that the chances of being anything else but a POW were slim. But Oscar did get back, although it took him more than a month. Fortunately, he had some help from the French Underground Movement, who got him out of France via the Pyrenees and Gibraltar, where he was put on a plane and flown to England.

By prior arrangement, Oscar had agreed that Mike McPharlin could have his boots if at any time he "failed to return". Mike had soon "lifted" them, but the first thing the new owner heard when Oscar returned, was: "Mac, take off those damn boots!"

A week after Oscar went missing, a Rhubarb claimed another victim, this time Jack Fessler. He had flown out with Wally Tribkin and they too had paid attention to a freight train in the marshalling yards at Boulogne. Fessler also had the misfortune of bringing himself down, for as the loco engine blew up, some debris lodged in his radiator and oil cooler. The Spitfire didn't go too far with that sort of problem and soon Jack was putting the crippled fighter down into a ploughed field. He ended up a prisoner of the Germans.

No. 71 Squadron got its third "ace" in October. Red McColpin shot down a Henschel 126 light observation plane he surprised on a Rhubarb sortie on the 16th, then proceeded to shoot up a train. Then on the 27th he bagged another brace of Me–109s and strafed yet another loco on yet another Rhubarb. As already stated, Rhubarbs could be dangerous but what also made them attractive was that if one got really lucky they could be not only exciting but rewarding. On some of these trips you could see absolutely nothing, just as if France had been emptied of not only Germans but French people as well. Other days, like the 27th, Germans were all over the place. Red was the third Eagle to be awarded the British DFC.

Then in November, tragedy. Stan Meares and Ross Scarborough were killed in a stupid training accident. They collided in mid-air and both crashed to their deaths. Meares had just received the DFC and only just been married. The new CO was Pete – the first Eagle to have command of the Squadron. In the same month – November – the British King pinned DFC medals onto the proud breasts of Pete, Gus and Red McColpin.

* * *

The other two Eagle Squadrons were still at Kirton Lindsey and

Eglington respectively. 133 were still smarting from their loss of four pilots when flying across to Northern Ireland, then at the beginning of November, 121 nearly had a similar tragedy.

On the 2nd, seven pilots took off in Hurricanes which had belonged to 136 Squadron, they having just left for the Far East. The Hurricanes were being ferried down to Cardiff. Bad weather greeted them as they headed south west. Gene Watkins, (who was leading the flight in a Spitfire), Bob Sprague and Martin landed at RAF Chivenor, later proceeding from there. However, Pilot Officer Cox crashed at Okehampton, breaking three fingers, Johnnie Lynch baled out over Cleve, North Cornwall, while three others made forced landings, Pilot Officers Amos and Ken Holder near Bideford, Don McLeod on the Cornish Moors.

Then, on the 15th, Malta Stepp and John Brown, while on patrol near York, attacked and fired at what they identified as a Ju88, but it turned out to be an RAF Blenheim. The two Eagles swore that the rear gunner fired at them – and he may have done – but as he was killed when the Blenheim was shot down, we shall never know. The first the poor Blenheim pilot knew was when his port engine burst into flames and cut out. He baled out but the rear gunner went down with the bomber.

Misidentification of aircraft was nothing new. Friendly aircraft had been shooting each other down since the war started. Excitement, inexperience, pumping adrenaline, the eyes seeing what they wanted to see – all contributed to these tragedies. The two men were later cleared of blame but it was an action the Eagles could well have done without.

The next day, Harold Marting and Almos were on patrol over the convoy "Plumb" and they did see a real Ju88. Marting gave chase, opened fire, hitting the 88's fuselage and shooting off an aileron. He could only claim a damaged, but it was the first success – of a kind – since August! Hal Marting recorded in his diary;

"November 16: Was scrambled to a convoy patrol at 11 am and was stooging around it with my No. 2, Griffin, when I saw a Ju88 come out of a cloud and drop two bombs. Went after it right away and made five attacks of which three were at very good range and I could see my fire going into him. The rear gunner gave me a short squirt and as my shots were going into the fuselage all around him, I think he was hit as I saw him let go of his gun and drop out of sight. Also saw his port aileron fall off on the next attack. Finally lost him in cloud and landed at Catfoss, out of gas. Had to stay there overnight."

Hal Marting got back to Kirton the next day to find that he, Bob Sprague and Johnnie Lynch were posted to 71 Squadron. What might have been good news was obviously tinged with caution, as Hal then wrote in his diary:

"November 17: Found out tonight that I am going to 71 Squadron in the morning.

"November 18: Left Kirton at 0830 and arrived here at 1600. Reported to the CO of the Squadron, S/L Peterson. He and the others are USA, including the doctor and excepting the adjutant and intelligence officer. Seems to be a nice bunch of fellows here now. All but two or three of the original Eagles are prisoner or dead."

With the coming of winter, most of the day Ops were curtailed, the first two Eagle Squadrons flying Rhubarbs instead. Richard Patterson was lost on one of these on 7 December – an inauspicious day for the Americans – the day the Japanese bombed Pearl Harbor.

Before the news actually arrived, 121 Squadron flew a Ramrod Operation on the 8th, as Hal Marting recorded:

"December 8: We were on a big show today over France. Three Wings of us (about 96 aircraft) escorted a group of eight Hurricane bombers to their target. Our Wing was close escort and our squadron was the anti-flak fighters. We took off at 1136 and climbed to 17,000 ft and joined 222 Squadron who was the other half of our Wing. One Wing was just above us and another at 24,000. The 'Hurries' were just below and slightly ahead of us.

"About half way across the Channel we started letting down and we crossed the coast of France at about 5,000, the other two Wings staying up as top cover to take care of the 109s. About ten miles SE of Le Touquet, the Hurries peeled off to their target which was a sugar and alcohol factory, and blew hell out of it. We went right down with them to shoot at gun posts and protect the Hurries; 222 stayed at about 2,000 ft to protect us from 109s. We continued on south to an airdrome we had spotted and shot that up. I picked out a gun post which was firing at us and put that out of action. F/L Daymond and F/O Mauriello got a 109 each which were on the ground. McColpin set fire to a barracks. 222 had one fellow shot down and one of the top cover was lost – all by 109s. Very little flak anywhere. I was flying No. 2 to our CO, S/L Peterson. Came back at 'O' feet."

It was not until the following day that the news of Pearl Harbor came to Hal's ears and he confided to his diary:

"December 9: Heard the news about Japan's declaration of war and it was quite a shock to all of us to learn of the unpreparedness of the US. That is a shameful thing and will take some explaining.

"All sorts of rumours are running around about us here in the Eagles but I imagine we will continue on as before. Some want to go home and some want the whole squadron sent to Singapore but I don't imagine either will be done. Nor can I see us becoming a part of the Army Air Corps as to do so we would have to take orders from officers with none of our experience and there would be trouble for sure."

A few days later, Ken Holder flew out on a patrol over the Channel and failed to get home. He was the first Eagle lost following America's entry into the war. He was also the last one lost in the momentous year of 1941.

* * *

Peter Powell left 121 Squadron early in the New Year of 1942, his place being taken by Squadron Leader Hugh Kennard, the senior flight commander. With the weather still decidedly wintry, Rhubarbs continued to be flown during these early weeks of 1942, and even the Germans began to take advantage of the weather to come in over the east coast of Britain.

However, 133 Squadron finally got to see some action at the start of February. They were now back in England, at Kirton Lindsey, back from the wilderness of Northern Ireland. The Squadron diary (RAF Form 540, for the "officially minded") recorded: "Average winter day, as expected in Lincolnshire; cloud base 2,000 feet, 10/10ths cloud, visibility three to four miles. 133 had its first series of combats and chases with enemy aircraft . . ."

The first was a Ju88 which Flight Lieutenant Tim Johnston spotted at around 9.30 am, flying north up the east coast, ten miles north of Spurn Head. On being chased, the Junkers pilot disappeared into cloud and was not seen again. The real fun started in the afternoon, between

3 and 3.30 pm. Johnston was again airborne, with Jackie Jackson on his wing. Red McColpin and Sergeant Wally Wicker were also out over a convoy. The first two had scraps with several Dorniers and although they didn't see any go down, the escort vessel astern of the convoy reported one Dornier falling into the sea. 253 Squadron's aircraft were also in contact with enemy aircraft so they got a share in the kill too.

McColpin had even more fun over the ships. No sooner did he arrive than he began a more or less uninterrupted series of actions with one or more Dorniers, lasting 15 minutes. He knocked out the gunner on one bomber, then shot some pieces off one engine of the same or another Dornier.

"February 17: We flew again today for the first time since Jan. 22. We were Scrambled just before lunch and were up an hour. Finally saw the Hun I was after but didn't get a shot at him. Ceiling was about 1,500 and the clouds were 2,000 feet thick. The Hun was a Do.217E, one of their newest types. He was on my starboard and a little behind me about 300 yards away but pulled up into cloud when I turned.

"Coen and Stewart emptied their guns at one over convoy this afternoon but didn't knock it down. I was over the same convoy but was at the other end and never got to see it. Tribkin also saw one but like mine it pulled into cloud and got away."

This was how Hal Marting of 71, recorded this day's activities, although he didn't mention that Coen and Stewart's Dornier went into cloud trailing smoke.

Back with 121 Squadron, Don McLeod and Jimmie Peck flew a Rhubarb Op. the next day, hoping to shoot-up the seaplane base at LeCrotoy. They missed the target, flew over the top of Boulogne but saw nothing of interest. They then headed for Le Touquet but still found nothing worth strafing so flew home. Some days it was like that.

The chaps in 121 Squadron had still to record their first confirmed kill. "Jim" Daley claimed a damaged 109 on a Wing Sweep over France on 8 March but they lost William "Casey" Jones – last seen heading down losing glycol – and the Wing Leader!

Yet before March was out, 121 had their first victory. In a Wing Sweep on the afternoon of the 23rd, in company with 222 and the Canadian 403 Squadrons, they headed out over Manston, flying round

Dunkirk, St Omer and back to Dungeness. Just outside Calais they were engaged by the first Focke Wulf 190 fighters they had seen in the air. Jack Mooney had a go at four of them, one of which went in about a mile out to sea, with Daley and Flight Lieutenant Tom Allen firing at others without seeing results.

The next day Reade Tilley fired at another 190 but all he could claim was a probable, even though it dived upside down into cloud with thick black smoke pouring out of it.

Not to be out-done, 133 Squadron, which had now started operating within the 12 Group Wing set-up, flew their second Sweep on 26 April. Making rendezvous with other squadrons over Eastchurch, they crossed out over North Foreland and set course for Mardyck. Making landfall at this point they then headed down the coast to cross in at Boulogne. Blue Section, led by McColpin, attacked a bunch of FW190s, Mac sending one down to crash into the sea. McColpin had been flying as No. 2 to the Wing Leader, Wing Commander P R Walker DFC.

There were two more probable 190s on the 27th, by Bob Pewitt and William Baker, but they lost Flight Sergeant Wicker of 133 Squadron. It was another Wing Show, 133 flying as top cover squadron. Some 30 Focke Wulfs were engaged over Ostend and as the Wing finally disengaged and turned for home, Wicker's voice came over the radio – very faintly – saying that he'd been hit. He failed to get home and his body was washed ashore at Dover two days later. The Squadron were certainly having a variety of operations for on the 29th, Eric Doorly, on a night sortie over York during a "blitz", damaged a Dornier but seems to have had his glycol tank hit which forced him to bale out. He landed safely in a field.

* * *

Seventy-One Squadron also got into the action in April. On the 17th, Johnny Lynch and Leo Nomis – "Chief" Nomis, as he had Sioux Indian ancestry – were out on a convoy patrol. Lynch saw a Ju88 and both men gave chase. Down to 50 feet, Lynch's first burst kicked up sea water ahead of the Junkers, but his second took chunks out of the fuselage and the rear gunner stopped firing; but not before the gunner scored hits on Lynch's Spitfire! Nomis saw his leader pull up and turn, with smoke streaming from his engine, to head for home, crash landing at Bentley, three miles from Orfordness. Nomis continued the attack until his ammo ran out and as he pulled up to one side, had the satisfaction of seeing the 88 dive into the sea.

Ten days later the Squadron escorted Hurri-bombers to St. Omer (Circus 142) and lost Johnnie Flynn, but the boys destroyed five enemy aircraft, with one more probable and three damaged. It was their best score yet. Pete Peterson got a brace of 190s, with one damaged, while Oscar Coen and Willie McPharlin shared three 190s. Art Roscoe got the probable.

April was also hotting up for 121 Squadron. They flew a Sweep on the 12th, with Kennard, Skinner and Barry Mahon claiming FW190s damaged, with Tom Allen getting a probable and a damaged. Skinner claimed two and as Tom Allen had seen a fighter crash, Skinner had one raised to a confirmed destroyed. He got another on the 14th, an escort mission – shooting down two FW190s and one damaged. On another sweep on the 17th, they lost one pilot while another had most of his tail blown off, then on the 24th, two pilots claimed an unusual victory.

After successfully escorting Bostons to Flushing, Daley and Leroy Skinner spotted what they thought was a Ju52 transport aircraft. They peeled off and attacked it several times, as it trailed white smoke and shed pieces. From above, the Wing Leader, David Scott-Malden, and Tom Allen, watched as the enemy plane caught fire and went into the sea with a mighty splash. Later, when they compared notes and checked with photos and their own cine-gun film, they discovered that rather than a Ju52, what they had shot down was a Junkers W–34 training/communication aircraft. But no matter what the type, Daley had his first confirmed success and Skinner his third for the month.

But for LeRoy (Roy) Skinner, time was running out. On 28 April, 121 flew out with Treble Two Squadron on a Sweep, making rendezvous with six Bostons over Bradwell Bay. The target was St. Omer. Ten miles inland from Dunkirk the enemy fighters appeared and began to mix it. Sel Edner sent one down out of control, pouring out smoke, and Sergeant Kay may have hit another. Carl Bodding's Spitfire was hit and went down. Someone saw him go down and thought he saw a parachute, but it was low, and a couple of miles inland from the coast. In the event, Bodding left it too late and he hit the ground before his 'chute deployed. Skinner also failed to get home. He was not seen after the engagement began and after he peeled off to chase a German fighter. Later he was reported a "guest" of the Germans.

As May began, the Eagles lost more pilots. On the 4th, 121 Squadron flew an escort mission in company with the Biggin Hill Wing to Le Havre, with Bostons. Several running fights started, Tom Allen possibly damaging one but Ralph Freiberg and Bob Brossmer didn't make it back.

With May came the fighting weather, the summer season; operations would be on the increase. 71 Squadron, still at Martlesham Heath, were about to move to RAF Debden, Essex. 121 at North Weald, would be off to Rochford in June, while 133, got the premier posting in May – to RAF Station Biggin Hill. The squadron commanders now were Peterson, Kennard and E H "Tommy" Thomas – and they were all now flying the Spitfire Vb with two 20 mm cannons and four .303 machine-guns.

Chapter 5

The Summer of '42

THE arrival at Biggin Hill of one of the Eagle Squadrons was quite a milestone for the Americans. Biggin Hill was RAF Fighter Command's foremost fighter station, having claimed the destruction of more German aircraft than any other base.

Its various squadrons had seen action over France and Dunkirk and were, of course, in the forefront of the action during the Battle of Britain. Its famous Wing Leader in the summer of 1941 had been Wing Commander A G "Sailor" Malan DSO DFC, currently the Command's top scoring pilot with 35 victories. The Wing Leader now was Jamie Rankin DSO DFC with a score of around 20 victories. Station Commander was Group Captain Dickie Barwell DFC. One of the other squadrons in the Wing was No. 124, commanded by Myles Duke Woolley DFC. "Duke" (or "Dook", as the Americans called him) would gain much respect for the Americans and later would lead some of them from RAF Debden.

The Americans made quite an impact going to Biggin. Even though America was officially in the war, there was still no major sign of their mighty presence in England, the three Eagle Squadrons being the only visible evidence of any Americans, despite the fact that they were still officially "volunteers" fighting with the RAF.

Stories abounded about the Eagles' exploits, from McColpin being voted the most dangerous poker player on the base, to Ches Robertson's shout over the radio on his first sortie over France – "Hey, they're shootin' at me!"

One of the most famous remarks over the radio came when one of the Eagles ran into a dozen Me–109s over the Channel when flying alone. He exhorted his friends, whom he knew to be flying nearby, "I'm up here at 18,000 ft and I've got about fifty 109s up here – cornered!" He only just made it back. When he asked one of his colleagues why he had not come to help, the friend said that he thought that as the other guy had them cornered he could take care of them himself!

The Biggin Hill Eagles made their first real sortie from their new base on 7 May but it was not until 17 May on a fighter Sweep over Abbeville, that they really stirred up a hornet's nest. Red McColpin blasted a 109F out of the sky, and possibly a second, whle Moran Morris also claimed a probable. The euphoria was short lived. Two days later, on another Sweep, Bob Pewitt was seen going down with two fighters on his tail over the Channel, and Davis Florence was lost. Pewitt was later rescued from the sea but died of head injuries soon afterwards. The fact that two 190s and a 109F were shot down didn't help much.

One of the other Biggin Hill squadrons was the Canadian 401 – or to be exact, it was at Gravesend, Biggin's satellite airfield. One of its pilots was an American in the RCAF – Flying Officer D J M Blakeslee. Some say that immediately he heard that an American manned squadron was at Biggin he requested a transfer. Others say that when he arrived he wasn't too impressed with what he found. Whatever the truth, it was a red letter day for the squadron and the Eagles, not to mention the American Air force.

Donald James Matthew Blakeslee was from Fairport Harbor, Ohio, aged 24. He had joined the RCAF and after pilot training had been assigned to 401 Squadron in 1941. He already had at least one kill to his name and was about to receive the British DFC. When he received it the citation read:

"This officer has completed a large number of sorties over enemy territory. He has destroyed one, probably destroyed two and damaged several more hostile aircraft. He is a fine leader whose keenness has proved most inspiring."

That the compiler of this citation should record his leadership and keenness is not surprising, for Don Blakeslee was to prove one of the US Air Force's most brilliant fighter leaders and Group Commanders of all time.

I remember very clearly the first time I met Blakeslee. It was a day or so after I had been sent to Great Sampford and 133 Squadron, following the disastrous Morlaix raid. After dinner, we found our way by bicycle to Saffron Walden and The Rose and Crown, the old pub on the Market Square. We weaved our way back to Great Sampford, parked the bikes and approached the barracks.

Suddenly, the wooden door of the hut was shattered as if by an explosion. A body came hurtling through, closely followed by another. They were followed by two kit bags. A six-foot figure appeared in the doorway. His open-necked shirt and buttoned blue tunic made his shoulders seem even broader than they were. His head was lowered like a bull about to charge, showing his close-cropped hair and broad forehead over blue eyes. His powerful chin added to the impression of forcefulness and drive.

The two sprawled figures began to pick themselves up slowly and painfully. They were RAF administration officers. Ray, Whitey and I moved towards the door, but it was still blocked by the glowering figure.

"You pilots?" he asked.

We nodded and he let us in.

"I'm Don Blakeslee." He said it as if no other explanation was necessary. He was right.

* * *

May proved an exciting month for 121 Squadron as well. Sel Edner had attacked an FW190 during a North Weald Sweep on the 17th. He was dead on target for he only fired a one-second burst of cannon and machine-guns and the Focke Wulf exploded. Daley flamed another, while Jack Mooney and Barry Mahon each claimed 190s damaged.

Jack Mooney and Barry Mahon were two more up-and-coming Eagle pilots. Mooney already had his first kill and Barry a couple of damaged so far. Mooney was an aggressive Irish-American and seemed to show no fear. Despite the fact that he was due to be married early in July, he continued to seek out the enemy and fly on the hottest missions. He even went down and shot up enemy ground targets after a sortie if he had any ammo left. In this he was the forerunner of what many American fighter pilots would do later in the war.

Barry Mahon had gained his private flying licence back in 1938, in California. When he was posted to 121, he knew he had arrived at the right place as soon as he entered the Officer's Mess. As he put his case down he heard yells and calls from upstairs and then a bunch of pilots came racing down the stairs – in formation, on bicycles – only to end μp in a heap of metal and bodies at the bottom. Perfectly normal behaviour for officers and gentlemen – even American officers and gentlemen!

Enemy aircraft were not the only targets for fighter pilots. On 27 May, 121 flew a shipping recce (reconnaissance) off Flushing Harbour. Squadron Leader Kennard saw two mine-sweepers and a destroyer and took his No. 2 – Sergeant Kelly – down into a screaming attack on one of the 'sweepers, ordering Daley and Sergeant Vance onto the other. Barry Mahon and Gene Fetrow followed Kennard's example and also went for the first vessel. Both ships were badly shot about, Daley and Vance's target sending up a column of smoke after an explosion.As they pulled up, Daley saw eight Me–109s above and immediately attacked one which Vance saw dive into the sea. Vance put some lead into another which staggered away smoking. Mahon also scored a damaged on a third 109.

Hugh Kennard flew a similar mission on the 31st, this time to the northeast of Walcheren, and again they found two mine-sweepers. Kennard ordered an attack on one of them, Flight Lieutenant Tom Allen and Sergeant Vance going in. Whether Tom Allen was hit or merely misjudged his second strafing run is uncertain, (Mahon thought he saw a trail of glycol) but Vance saw his leader's Spitfire hit the water on the far side of the target and bounce up into the air. Allen's voice came over the radio saying that his machine was "coming apart" and that he proposed to ditch. As he was going at something like 100 mph, he failed to get a good angle onto the sea and nosed in and down. The fighter sank almost immediately. The others saw no sign of Allen, who came from South Carolina. Having survived, they flew off, leaving the two ships damaged, one sinking. Allen's place was taken by John DuFour, posted in from 71 Squadron.

On the first day of June, Daley was notified of the award of the DFC, the citation for which read:

"Pilot Officer Daley is an extremely keen officer who shows out-standing devotion to duty. Since February 1942 he has completed 51 operational sorties over Northern France, Holland and Belgium and has destroyed at least two enemy aircraft."

Now the handsome Jim Daley, from Amarillo, Texas, had three victories.

The next day, a new pilot came to 121 Squadron, Pilot Officer Don

Willis, posted in from completing his training at No. 61 OTU. Not that he needed a lot of training! Don had joined the Finnish Airforce during the Russian/Finnish war back in 1939/40. Later he went into the Norwegian Airforce when the Germans invaded their country. Escaping to England after Norway's defeat, he joined the RAF and with an excellent report from the CO of his OTU, was welcomed to 121.

Scoring multiple kills was pretty rare and never easy, but Jack Mooney and Barry Mahon made it look easy on 8 June. Twelve Spitfires of the Squadron flew a Rodeo mission (now the more general name for a Fighter Sweep) to St. Omer. Luftwaffe fighters didn't always react to a pure fighter sweep – why should they, in itself it posed no threat – but today they came up and made contact.

Jack Mooney, as aggressive as ever, went down on one FW190 and sent it crashing to the ground. Immediately afterwards he attacked another and saw it fall in flames and crash. Meanwhile, Mahon was attacked by a 190 but he out-fought it and shot it, and then a second 190 went down.

On 16 June, Jack Mooney was just under three weeks away from his wedding day. But he chose this day to fly a Rhubarb with Sel Edner. The two fighter pilots made landfall to the east of Ostend, flew southwest for half a mile to where the main Bruges to Ostend railway was located and took a look. Sure enough, they spotted a freight train heading towards Ostend. Both attacked from astern of the train, Edner giving it a four-second burst which brought the loco to a standstill. As he pulled up and round he was suddenly aware that Mooney was nowhere to be seen. He gave a call over the radio and circled round but there was no sight or sound of Jack. Hoping that his partner had merely had his radio hit or it had failed, Edner flew to the Bruges–Ostend Canal and shot-up three barges, each heavily laden with packing cases, leaving all three burning. Then he headed for home.

Landing, he quickly asked about Mooney, but he had not got back. He never did. John Joseph Mooney was already dead. Sel Edner could have wished for a different way for promotion, but with Mooney gone, he was made B Flight Commander.

The day Mooney was lost was the same day that Hugh Kennard's DFC citation appeared in the London Gazette. It was a popular award for the Squadron:

"Squadron Leader Kennard has completed 58 offensive operations since he was appointed to command the Squadron in January 1942. In May 1942 he had led the squadron in a successful combat against eight enemy aircraft, two of which were destroyed, one probably destroyed and another damaged. A few days later he led a flight in a successful attack against a mine-sweeper. Later in May, Squadron Leader Kennard led his squadron to attack an armed trawler off the Dutch coast. The trawler was observed to sink. Squadron Leader Kennard has commanded his squadron skilfully and has set an excellent example at all times."

* * *

Recent weeks had seen a lull in 71 Squadron's activities, but with the move to Debden, they were back in the mainstream of things. The morning of June 1st was fine and clear, the pilots being called to briefing at noon. Forty-five minutes later they were airborne, together with 350 Belgian Squadron, followed by 111 Squadron, meeting up with 65 Squadron over Debden, thereby completing the Wing formation, for Circus 176.

They crossed out over the English coast at about 1.12 pm at Deal, crossing into France 25 minutes later, having picked up eight Hurri-bombers. The Debden Wing's job was that of Target Support, with 65 Squadron flying at 20,000 feet, 111 at 22,000, 71 at 23,000 and the Belgians at 25,000.

A number of enemy fighters were encountered, Pete Peterson firing at two, claiming one destroyed and the other damaged. Then one got him, blowing a large hole in Pete's Spitfire. There were an estimated 50 enemy fighters engaging the Wing by this time.

Gus Daymond and his section were pounced on by three FW190s and a dog-fight started. George Teicheira, Gus's wingman, was hit badly and Gus saw him go down towards the sea. Gus was now being hotly engaged by five 190s, and without a wingman to help out, he was fighting for his life. The fight took them out to sea off Ostend, until one FW made a mistake, allowing the American to get in a quick burst of cannon fire. It was enough. He saw two or three strikes on the German and it fell away. He then managed to shake off the others and streak for home, landing at Manston with just 2 1/2 gallons of petrol left, and feeling totally worn out. He put in a claim for a damaged, but two other pilots had seen the 190 go into the sea, so he had his 6th official victory. Bob Sprague scored a damaged, while Gene Potter claimed a probable. Oscar Coen fired at three but was too busy to see if anything happened to them. Pilot Officer George Teicheira didn't get home, but everyone else landed back at base at around 2.30 pm. 71 were back in action.

Don Blakeslee got his first crack at the enemy as an Eagle pilot on 27 June. He and Flight Sergeant C W "George" Harp were one of three two-man sections sent off early to patrol the Tenterden area of Kent as hostile plots were on radar. When at 27,000 feet, Blakeslee and Harp both spotted a Ju88 below which they then proceeded to chase, but the 88 pilot stuffed his nose down and was going away at a hell of a speed. They both opened fire, but without seeing much in the way of definite results. Not being able to close the range beyond 400 yards, all they could hope for was a "damaged".

July saw a continuation of various actions. Gil Halsey and Sergeant Stanhope of 121 chased another "early-bird" Ju88 back to the French coast on the 8th, leaving it with smoke trailing from one engine. More Rodeo Ops were flown in mid-July without major opposition, then poor weather on the 14th persuaded Barry Mahon to fly a Rhubarb along with Sergeant Carpenter.

They crossed into France near St. Inglevert and the nearby airfield. This seemed a good enough target. So they proceeded to strafe the place. They then headed south, finding a train which they also shot-up, as well as a gun emplacement which had the temerity to open fire at them!

A massed Rhubarb operation was flown on the 15th, in company with units from Hornchurch and that evening, 121 flew on a Roadstead Operation (an attack on enemy ships), flying with the two Norwegian Squadrons – 331 and 332. Off the enemy coast, 121's pilots found a mine-sweeper and attacked, leaving it burning from stem to stern.

Rhubarbs and shipping recce sorties continued towards the end of July, with varying degrees of success. On the 26th the pilots caught a German E-boat off Calais and left it burning and sinking. Then on the 31st, Hugh Kennard was hit.

It was yet another Circus (No. 201), in company with the North Weald, Debden and Tangmere Wings. Boston light bombers were going for the fighter airfield of Abbeville-Drucat. Part of the show was

133 Squadron from Debden, who flew with 65 and 72 Squadrons. Shows were like this – a small formation of bombers with massive fighter support.

121 were assigned to patrol near the French coast, to the north of the operation and in indirect support of it. They engaged FW190s and Me–109s. In a tremendous scrap over Berck and the north of the Somme, Kennard shot down a 109F, Edner got two more, with Sergeant Kelly getting another and Barry Mahon two FW190s (his second double); Frank Boyle got a probable.

Unfortunately, this success was offset by the losses in 133 Squadron, who went in with the bombers as they were part of the close escort Wing. Just as they crossed the French coast on the way back after bombing, several FW190s made an appearance. Combat began, William Baker shooting down one over Le Crotoy, whilst Jessie Taylor, although wounded in the foot and forehead, got a 190 and damaged a 109F. Jessie, in fact, fought his way out of trouble. He knew the ropes for he had been in combat for ten months, but it was anger that spurred him on this day.

The bullet that creased his forehead made him temporarily blind and it was while being unable to see that he got both alarmed and angry. This brought his sight back to one eye. With a bullet in the foot too, most pilots would have headed for home but Taylor was angry. Seeing at least three enemy fighters circling him, waiting for him to crash, he turned on them, claiming two 190s and damaging a 109, although he only got credit for one 190 and the 109. Jack Jackson finally escorted him home, with his Spitfire riddled with holes, which totalled 107 when they came to count them. However, Taylor had been lucky; when the dust settled, three other pilots were not around.

Flight Lieutenant C C "Pop" King, 35 years old and from Oregon, "Woody" Harp, from Georgia and "Ike" Eichar, from Illionois were all killed. Sadly all were experienced pilots, far from novices likely to be picked off in their early sorties. Pop King had been flying since he was 18, had been an instructor in the RCAF and even ferried bombers across to England before coming to 133. If he had a lot of flying hours, so did Woody Harp – probably more than most, for he had been a barnstormer in the States, a "wing-walker" and stunt flyer. He had warned Jessie Taylor that he had a 190 behind him, and that was the last anyone heard of Woody, probably clobbered as he warned his friend of the danger. Eichar had been flying combat for five months, so had the experience.

Six confirmed kills for the Squadron was a record but Kennard's Spitfire was hit and the squadron leader wounded in one knee and the buttocks, and Norm Young was missing. Kennard managed to get his crippled aircraft back over the Channel to make a successful crash landing at RAF Lympne but he was lost to the Squadron. His place as CO went to yet another British officer, Squadron Leader W D Williams.

William Dudley Williams DFC, joined the RAFVR in 1938 and in May 1940 was with 152 Squadron. He won his DFC for actions during the Battle of Britain. He became a flight instructor in late 1941, command of the second Eagle Squadron being his first job away from Training Command.

* * *

Rhubarbs were never confined to winter months. In Britain, even the summer could produce good Rhubarb weather. On 19 July, Johnnie Lynch and Joe Helgason took off from Debden to do some local flying and latched onto Spitfires of the North Weald Wing on a Group Rhubarb, attaching themselves to 222 Squadron. Near Dunkirk, and heading towards Nieuport, the two Eagles were flying in wide echelon, with Joe to the left of Johnnie, as the main Wing formation turned to the right and headed back along the enemy coast.

In that turn, Lynch and Helgason were between 222 and the coast when up ahead, two FW190s broke cloud in a shallow dive, approaching the Spitfires head-on. When in range, Lynch fired a short burst at the 190 furthest out from the coast. The German fighter was already firing at someone, but the sudden appearance of Lynch's Spitfire caused him to stop. Helgason also opened fire at an oncoming 190, but the other one seemed to have disappeared.

In a second the three fighters flashed by each other and as Lynch looked back, he saw the 190 half roll onto its back. Checking forward again before contemplating a turn after the 190s, Lynch saw four more 190s above, just below the cloud layer, also approaching head-on. Lynch opened fire at them, splitting them up, then he pulled up into the cloud to avoid a section of Spitfires.

Helgason by this time had called that his engine was causing trouble

Bill Dunn in his 71 Squadron Spitfire, 1941.

Spitfire Vb of 71 Squadron, summer 1941, with battle damage after Bill Dunn shot down his fifth enemy plane but was wounded at the same time.

P/O T C Worral and P/O Howard Coffin, 126 Squadron Malta. Coffin was one of the first Americans to see action over the island.

Claude Weaver, high scoring American with 185 Squadron.

Jim Goodson (right) first saw service with 416 Canadian Squadron. With him is Jackie Rae, who later become a TV personality in Britain in the 1960's.

Gus Daymond DFC (2nd from left), top scoring Eagle pilot, after a combat.

Don Willis, 71 Squadron.

121 Squadron pilots raise the US flag, now that America has entered the war. With the pole, Ken Holder, Don McLeod and Dick McHan; Rear: Vincent, Shenk, "Shine" Parker, Casey Jones.

The memorial tablet to Billy Fiske in St Paul's Cathedral.

PILOT OFFICER
WILLIAM MEADE LINDSLEY
FISKE III
ROYAL AIR FORCE
AN AMERICAN CITIZEN
WHO DIED
THAT ENGLAND MIGHT LIVE
AUGUST 18TH 1940.

Jack Mooney of 121 Squadron chats to the Station Commander of North Weald in December 1941 after a show. Gerald Maxwell shot down 26 German aircraft in the First World War.

Jim Peck, Eagle pilot and 126 Squadron.   Richard "Sunday" McHan, 126 Squadron, Malta.

Pilots of 121 Squadron, November, 1941 – front: Don McLeod, Fred Gamble, Peter Powell (BR CO), Fred Almos, Casey Jones and Sgt Shenk. Rear: Jim Peck, Mike Duff, Malta Stepp and Dick McHan. McLeod, Peck and McHan later saw action over Malta.

Leo "Chief" Nomis; after a brief stay on Malta, went to 92 Squadron in North Africa.

Spitfire Vb of 133 Squadron at Kirton in Lindsey, early 1942. Note the pint jug by the cockpit and the slogan, "Mild & Bitter".

Spitfire Vb XR-C (AA855) crash landed in France, 27 October, 1941. PO M W Fessler was taken prisoner.

Probably the oldest Eagle – Harold Strickland, 71 Squadron.

Stan Anderson, saw action with the Eagle Squadron and later with the 4th FG but was then killed in action.

Dixie Alexander, saw action with the Eagles from England, shooting down enemy planes over Dieppe. Later saw combat in Italy.

Reade Tilley, 71 Squadron and 126 Squadron on Malta.

and when Lynch broke cloud again, the sky was clear. He could only claim the 190 as being last seen on its back at 500 feet, but then a call came from Wing Commander Scott-Malden that he and his pilots had seen the Focke Wulf go into the sea. Lynch and Helgason shared the victory.

Gus Daymond led a four-man Rhubarb Op towards the end of July, the two sections splitting up as they crossed into France. Daymond and his No. 2 "Jessie" Taylor, shot up a water tower and, on their way out, Daymond blasted a gun emplacement. The other section got caught by some flak which damaged Bob Sprague's aircraft.

Meanwhile, 133 Squadron had been busy. On 20 July, they flew with 72 Squadron on a massed Rhubarb to Le Treport. Here the squadrons split up into pairs and headed to various inland locations, about five miles from the coast. The 72 Squadron boys flew at 5,000 feet to cover the American pilots. Several targets were shot-up, including a Navigational Beam Station, which had been specially mentioned at the pilot briefings. Next day, 133 took their turn to fly cover for another squadron on a similar Rhubarb Op.

* * *

On the first day of August, sections of 71 Squadron flew on some Air Sea Rescue sorties from Debden, refuelling at Martlesham Heath, from where one of the Walrus Rescue Flights operated. Some enemy fighters tried to interfere with these operations and Jim "Jerko" Gray, from Hollister, California, blew up a 190 in mid-air with a well-aimed burst, Bob Sprague chased another which he finally left belching smoke. Another 190 came in behind him, but he shook it off.

Joe Helgason was killed on the 6th. He beat-up a gun-emplacement near the airfield, misjudged it and crashed. He died instantly. Another waste of a good life.

In mid-August there were more American voices at Biggin Hill. At last the vanguard of the mighty American 8th Air Force was beginning to arrive in Britain. Some personnel had started to arrive in the early part of the year but it was not until July 1 that the first American aircraft landed at Prestwick – a Boeing B.17E four-engined bomber of the 97th Bomb Group. More bombers and P.38 "Lightning" twin-boomed, twin-engined fighters came in during the month, then some

C.47 transport aircraft. The build-up had started.

The previous month, pilots and men of the 31st Fighter Group had arrived in England by sea. They had received a telegram from General H "Hap" Arnold, Commanding Officer of the US Army Air Forces, which read: "You have been chosen to be the spearhead of the United States combat forces in the European Theatre of Operations. Congratulations and good luck". They would be quickly followed by the 1st, 14th and 52nd Fighter Groups.

The 31st Group were assigned to the 8th Air Force, then under the command of Major General Carl "Tooey" Spaatz, a veteran airforce flyer who had seen action in World War I. (He shot down two German planes while flying with the 13th Pursuit Squadron in France in 1918.) The Group would initially fly the British Spitfire, a change from their P.39 Airocobras – a machine that would have been totally out-classed by the 190 and 109s of the Luftwaffe.

The 31st Group had three squadrons, the 307th, 308th and 309th Fighter Squadrons. Once they had some experience on Spits, the unit was activated, with the 307th going to Biggin Hill, the 308th to Kenley, and the 309th to Westhampnett, a satellite of RAF Tangmere. From here they began their first tentative operations against enemy occupied France, in company with their RAF brothers-in-arms.

On the 18th August, 133 flew a Rodeo mission in company with the 307th and 65 Squadron RAF. They made a wide detour inland from Dunkirk and were just inland from Sangatte when they were attacked by about ten Focke Wulfs. Led by Don Blakeslee, the Squadron made a 360 degree orbit, and turned inside a couple of the 190s, which allowed Blakeslee to give one a good burst. As the Squadron Diarist recorded: "Plenty of cannon shots hit the enemy aircraft and the pilot evidently thought it best to bale out – he did! The remaining enemy aircraft disappeared."

When 133 landed back from this afternoon mission, there was obviously something in the wind. The pilots were not allowed off base and the unit commanders were summoned to a special briefing. The fighter aircraft too were having thin black and white stripes painted on them. Something big was about to happen.

Chapter 6

Dieppe

For some time the Russians had been urging the British Prime Minister, Winston Churchill, to open up a second front to help relieve the pressure on the Eastern Front. Germany's invasion of Russia in June 1941, had been a huge success and had pushed back the battle line to the very gates of Moscow. However, Churchill knew only too well that with a vital war going on in the Middle East, now a war raging in the Far East, with British forces having retreated through Burma to the Indian borders, and with his own forces in southern England no match for Hitler's might in France, he could not even contemplate an invasion of France at this stage of the war.

Nevertheless, he thought it would be a good idea to make a strike in force against the French coast somewhere. It would be good training, would test both his own forces and the German defences, and if nothing else, ensure that the Germans kept forces in France and away from Russia, in case the British – and now their new American allies – did come.

Much has been written about "Operation Jubilee" – the massive raid by British commandos and Canadian troops on the harbour town of Dieppe. It was not an invasion, merely a "reconnaissance in strength", the object being to get men and tanks ashore, hold the town for most of the day, blow up installations and a nearby airfield, then retire.

Lessons were learned, experience gained and the Luftwaffe were engaged in large numbers by the RAF. However, although at the time – and with the claims made – it seemed as though RAF Fighter Command had scored a great victory, the cold factual truth was that it had not. It did shoot down a number of German aircraft, of course, although not as many as either hoped or claimed at the time, but it lost a lot more.

What Don Blakeslee and the others soon discovered upon their return from the Rodeo on the 18th August, was that the next day would see this big raid on Dieppe and they, the other Eagle Squadrons and the 31st Fighter Group, would be part of it.

Detailed briefings were made that evening and the first aircraft were off at dawn, helping to cover the assault force of ships that had sailed the night before, so as to be off Dieppe at sun-up.

The Eagle pilots of 71 Squadron were first off at 0450 hours, Pete Peterson leading, to cover the Dieppe anchorage. It was still dark, which caused Harold Strickland problems when his section leader turned off his navigation lights, and "Strick" lost him. Carrying on alone, Strickland – who had recently celebrated his 39th birthday – spotted a Focke Wulf 190 having a sniff-round. He attacked it and before losing it in the gloom, knocked some pieces off it. Pilot Officer Brewster Morgan saw a 190 too and later recorded:

"It was a mishmash from the start, and soon I became separated and lost. I guessed that I was about 35 miles south of Dieppe and was heading north to rejoin when a Focke Wulfe 190 made a firing pass at me. I lost him but as I rendezvoused with the Squadron, I noticed that my engine was heating up. I guessed that I had been hit by the German. I was ordered to return to England. I barely cleared the cliffs at Beachy Head when I saw the emergency airfield near Friston. I knew that my engine might seize at any moment and that I had to come straight in and land. The problem was that there was a Boston bomber burning in the middle of the runway. I came in low over the bomber, and made a gear-up landing."

Don Blakeslee led 133 out at 0720, again to orbit over Dieppe and keep enemy aircraft away. Enemy fighters were now reacting to the attack force and several FW190s appeared. A fight started with Blakeslee and Bill Baker claiming 190s destroyed while Dixie Alexander got a probable.

By the time 133 were landing back, 121 were heading south for Dieppe, led by Seldon Edner. They too were engaged by enemy fighters. In a whirling dog-fight, Edner got a 190, and Gil "Gunner" Halsey and Leon Blanding claimed probables. "Snuffy" Smith scored a damaged. However, three pilots were lost, Gene Fetrow, Jim Taylor and Barry Mahon. Fetrow was later fished out of the water and returned home, Taylor was killed and Barry Mahon became a prisoner.

In the fight, Mahon had got a 190 burning, then pulled up as his guns fell silent – out of ammo. As he curved away, he got a feeling and looked back and down. Sure enough a yellow-nosed 190 was climbing after him, and well in range. The German couldn't get the right deflection with Barry in his climbing turn but then the American stalled and fell right through the 190's line of fire. That did it. The 190's fire raked his Spitfire, blew off the gun panels and smashed the engine, which put oil all over the cockpit hood. As more shells blasted his right wing, and oil got into his eyes, Mahon rolled over onto his back, jettisoned the canopy and went out.

Floating down, still smarting from the oil in his eyes, he decided it would be better to leave his 'chute before he hit the water, but misjudged his height. Instead of being just a few feet above the sea, he was more like 50, and as he splashed down, seemed to go right to the bottom of the Channel. However, his Mae West shot him to the surface and moments later he was in his dinghy. He remained in his rubber boat for the rest of the day until, having failed to be picked up by either returning ships or rescue craft, he drifted ashore on the French coast.

As he was put into a truck with other prisoners, mostly Canadian troops, he found a German who spoke English and asked where they were being taken. The German showed him a road on a map, whereupon Mahon said that the road indicated was going to be strafed by his squadron that afternoon. The German took no notice, until Spitfires did indeed come over and shoot up the road. The downed Eagle was too busy crouching in a ditch to see if it was indeed 121 who were doing the strafing.

Blakeslee led 133 out for their second show at 1015. By this time the Germans knew something big was on and had sent bombers to attack the shipping off Dieppe. 133 were in the midst of masses of air fights as they reached the harbour, the sky seemingly full of Ju88s, Do217s and FW190s. When they disengaged for the flight home, they had destroyed one Ju88, two 190s and damaged four, with three Dorniers also damaged. Blakeslee had damaged one of each, Don Gentile had got a 190 and an 88, Gil Wright, although shot-up himself, had scored a damaged. Gordon Brettell, a new flight commander, got the other 190. Others who damaged aircraft were Richard Beatty, Baker, Eric Doorly and Dick Gudmundsen – the latter being a US Army Air Corps pilot.

Peterson flew out at the head of 71 again shortly before 11 am, damaging a Ju88. Then, as noon ticked round, 121 under Squadron Leader Williams were over the harbour, in deteriorating weather. Flak was heavy and Jim Daley's machine was hit. A large hole was blasted through the tailplane and the engine cut out. Daley was preparing to jump when the motor restarted.

Blakeslee and 133 were out on their third sorties by 12.30, and again they saw action. Jim Nelson and Dixie Alexander both shot down Dornier bombers, while Blakeslee damaged a 190. They were overlapped by 71 Squadron who caught the tail-end of this battle. Pete Peterson again leading, went down on a Ju88 and opened fire, the WingCo – Myles Duke Woolley, leading the Debden Wing, seeing it go into the sea. However, the German rear-gunner got in a telling burst on Pete's Spit and smoke started to fill the cockpit. With his engine on fire Pete went over the side and pulled the rip-cord.

As he floated towards the water, the sound of aero engines above him and gunfire from the coast, he remembered his service revolver which he carried in his flying boot. Not only would his boots soon have to come off but he must also throw away the gun. As it would be lost anyway, he pulled it out and shot off the six rounds in a show of bravado, then, fully satisfied, threw it into the sea, which was fast approaching. Moments later he splashed down and within minutes was picked up by a Naval MTB.

This was not the end of his adventures for the torpedo boat was later strafed by enemy fighters, and an RAF pilot who had also been rescued and was sitting next to Peterson, was hit and killed.

Two other pilots scored hits on 88s, Stan Anderson and Willie McPharlin shared a probable with Oscar Coen. But Wee Willie was also hit and also had to bale out. Later, as he sat in his dinghy, he decided that he ought to try to row to England rather than wait around, just in case the rescue boys didn't spot him. In order to boost his strength, he decided to break into his escape kit and scoffed everything, which included Oxo and Horlicks tablets – as well as the supply of Benzedrine! Charged up with this lot, and especially the Benzedrine, he felt super-charged and paddled away like a windmill, but was then spotted and rescued.

However, he was so wide awake, and with nobody really knowing what the after effects might be, someone was assigned to be with him for however long it took to wear off. Willie was as bright as a button for the next 48 hours or so – then in a moment, was out like a light. He woke up some hours later with no apparent ill-effects and the pilots' faith in Benzedrine reached a new high.

By this time the survivors of the Raid were on their way home. Few of them had got off the beaches and made the town and those who had were now either dead or prisoners. Cross-fire from the headlands and the town itself had proved murderous to the Canadian troops. When finally the boats got the living off, they left hundreds of dead or dying where they had fallen. Of those who were taken off, several hundred had been wounded. In the end, nearly two thousand were unable to get away and were captured.

The final sorties by the RAF and thus by the Eagles were in covering the return of the ships, which were harried by enemy aircraft right back to the English coast.

Bill Williams led 121 out over the convoy shortly after 4 pm. They tried in vain to intercept fighters making hit-and-run attacks by diving in and out of the clouds at the boats. "Doc" Osborne's engine caught fire over the sea but he got over the coast, baled out and landed safely. Duke Woolley led the Debden Wing out in the late afternoon, Gus Daymond leading 71 on the final mission of the day. They saw plenty of German aircraft but were unable to make any interceptions. On Blakeslee's fourth and last sortie for 133, they saw no enemy planes at all.

Overall it had been a testing but disastrous day for the Combined Forces who had gone to Dieppe. The Eagles had had mixed fortunes. They had seen a lot of action, and claimed eight destroyed, five probables and twelve damaged. They had lost one pilot killed, one taken prisoner and seven Spitfires with another five damaged.

Any loss is grievous to a Squadron, but Barry Mahon's was particularly sad. Jim Daley was devastated by it, feeling certain that Barry had been killed. Luckily news soon reached the Squadron that Barry was safe even if a prisoner. On the 20th, the day after Operation Jubilee, came the news of Barry's award of the DFC.

Pete Peterson received the Distinguished Service Order from the British after the Dieppe Show. Gus Daymond too was soon to receive a bar to his DFC – the first American Eagle to have a bar. (A second DFC, akin to the American's Oak Leaf Clusters to their medals.)

Peterson's citation read:

"This officer has completed a large number of sorties over enemy occupied territory. He has at all times displayed high qualities of leadership and courage which have contributed materially to the fine fighting of his Squadron. During the operations over Dieppe, Squadron Leader Peterson destroyed a Ju88, bringing his victories to six. His devotion to duty has been outstanding."

Gus Daymond's citation read:

"Since being awarded the DFC, this officer has completed many sorties over enemy territory. He has always led his flight with great skill and courage and has destroyed seven enemy aircraft. In the recent Dieppe operations, Flight Lieutenant Daymond flew with distinction."

* * *

Mention should also be made of the 31st Fighter Group's activities over Dieppe. The 307th Squadron flew four sorties that day, but lost two pilots, claiming one victory and a couple of probables. The 308th also flew four sorties, lost two pilots, and claimed one probable; the 309th completed four missions, lost one pilot and three Spitfires, but claimed one destroyed, one probable and a damaged. The 309th had the honour of scoring the first victory by a USAAF pilot in Europe. Lieutenant Sam Junkin Jr, of Natchez, Mississippi, got an FW190 on the first sortie although he was also shot down, wounded and rescued.

Twenty-four American 8th Air Force B.17 bombers from the 97th Bombardment Group – which comprised the 340th, 341st, 342nd and 444th Bomb Squadrons, based at Polebrook and Grafton Underwood – bombed Abbeville during the raid, the German's main fighter base in the area. They had no losses.

The Group CO was Lieutenant Colonel Frank A Armstrong Jr who had, just two days earlier – the 17th August – flown on the 8th Air Force's first heavy bomber mission of the war. Rouen had been the target for the 12 B.17s, and aboard one B.17 had been General Ira Eaker, CO of the 8th Air Force. Frank Armstrong's pilot that historic day was Major Paul Tibbets. Three years later, Paul Tibbets, by then a full Colonel, would fly the B.29 Superfortress "Enola Gay", to drop the first atomic bomb over Hiroshima, Japan. (6 August, 1945. 509th Composite Bomb Group, 20th US Air Force.)

* * *

Despite Don Blakeslee's actions over recent weeks as well as over Dieppe, not to mention the award of his British DFC, he got himself into trouble shortly afterwards. That "trouble" cost him a demotion. This was surprising in itself, especially as Don had just been given command of 133 Squadron. It also came at a particularly bad time, for 133 were about to re-equip with Spitfire Mark IX – the fighter every fighter pilot would give his eye-teeth for. The Spitfire V had long been outclassed by the FW190 in most respects, but the new Mark IX could beat the 190 and what is more, it looked for all the world like a Mark V, so it could give the poor Luftwaffe pilots a nasty shock.

News that Blakeslee had been "busted" in rank and looked as if he was about to be banished to some training backwater, caught everybody by surprise. Poor Don had been caught "in the act"!

As I recall it, General "Tooey" Spaatz was on an inspection visit, and when walking round the airfield buildings with a full entourage of RAF and American "brass", out from a bedroom window clambered two WAAFs. Everyone was lost for words, but when later the Station Commander discovered the owner of the room, it was found to be that of Don Blakeslee. At first, when Don was carpeted and his sentence announced, one senior officer was apparently heard to comment – "For one WAAF yes, but for two, have you considered promotion?"

Gordon Brettell took over acting command of 133, but then Carroll McColpin, who had been back to the States following his tour of duty with all three Eagle Squadrons, returned and was given command of 133. He was the third American to command an RAF fighter squadron, after Pete and Newt Anderson.

* * *

Operations continued quickly after Dieppe. 71 Squadron flew a Circus Op to St. Omer on the 27th, Myles Duke Woolley and Gus Daymond both shooting down FW190s, with Tony Seaman getting a damaged. Sergeant Jack Evans failed to return. Gus's German baled out almost as soon as the 20mm shells began to hit his Focke Wulf. It was Daymond's last victory, making a total of seven air and one ground kills, plus one damaged. He would ever remain as the top scoring Eagle pilot in the RAF.

Four days later, W D "Bill" Taylor and Stan Anderson set out on an evening Rhubarb. Over the Belgian coast, Taylor was hit by machine-gun fire from the ground and forced to bale out between Ostend and

Blankenburg, about 20 miles out. Anderson circled round, seeing Bill
in his dinghy, waving his tiny signal flag happily. Anderson gave a
"Mayday" for a fix, but could only get to 500 feet due to low cloud.
Two rescue Walrus aircraft were sent out but they failed to locate him.
To die in action was one thing but to die whilst sitting in a rubber
dinghy in the North Sea was another. Bill Taylor just didn't make it.

Pilot Officer Don Young of 121 Squadron got lucky on 5 September.
Gene Fetrow and Sergeant F M Fink were scrambled that afternoon,
and Young, who was doing some local flying near Biggin, heard the
call over his radio. He headed towards the reported hostile aircraft,
finding a Ju88 at 20,000 feet over base being harried by his two
squadron pals. By the time he had closed in the 88 was trailing smoke
and flame and starting a dive for the coast. Young followed, giving the
bomber two bursts of cannon fire after which the Junkers dropped into
the sea with a huge splash, some miles east of the Naze. By being in
the right place at the right time he got a third share in the kill. It was
also the last victory scored by the Squadron.

In September, 133 returned to Biggin Hill, now fully operational
with the Spitfire IX and began operating with the new Mark. The day
after 121 got the Ju88, 133 escorted 36 Fortresses, together with the
Canadians of 401 Squadron. The target was an aircraft factory at
Meaulte. The Forts were seven minutes early at the rendezvous point
but 133 being "wise guys" were seven minutes early too!

Ten FW190s jumped the formation while they were crossing into
France. They didn't seem too keen to mix it, but 133 became slightly
split-up. The American air-gunners must have started to panic. They
began firing at the Spitfires. This didn't please the Eagle boys one bit,
so they left them to it and dived to sea level and came home, leaving
the bombers to look after themselves! That Eric Doorly and Dick
Gudmundson failed to get home, didn't help matters either.

In the event, the two lost pilots had been shot down by 190s, as
confirmed by Eric Doorley when he eventually turned up. He had
managed to bale out, evaded capture and helped by French people got
across into Spain and then home. But it was a lesson of sorts, for as
both Americans and British escort pilots were to discover over the next
couple of years, B.17 and B.24 gunners usually shot first and asked
questions later!

There is a wonderful line in a wartime 8th Air Force booklet, concerning a B.17 ball gunner, whose philosophy was ". . . anything with less than four engines oughta get it!"

Next day, the 7th, 133 escorted Forts to Rotterdam's shipyards. The Squadron headed out for the city where their orders were to orbit for three minutes when the bombers would head on in and bomb. The B.17s did arrive – after orbiting for 20 minutes! As the experienced Americans watched their newly arrived brothers bomb, it did little for their confidence. The bombers appeared to split into pairs, drop their bombs all over the place and then scoot for home. Some 190s did take a look on the way back, Billy Baker riddling one with gunfire. It was only allowed as a probable but it seemed unlikely the 190 got home.

"Spike" Miley claimed 133's last victory. He was on a dawn show, fifty miles out from Deal on the morning of 16 September, when he spotted two FW190s flying west. He turned into the attack and fired a long burst at the leading FW as it turned towards him. The two fighters met head-on, then another head-on pass followed. He then battled with both 190s, scoring hits on one which began to trail smoke but then they flew off and Miley didn't feel inclined to follow.

Preparations were now in hand to transfer the three Squadrons over to the US Air Force, but before that, there was Morlaix.

Chapter 7

Morlaix – and goodbye

OPERATIONS in support of the 8th Air Force Bomber Command were becoming part of the routine. Although the build-up of the 8th's fighter force was underway, the RAF had naturally to continue as the main means of escort for some months to come. It was natural too that the Eagle Squadrons would take their share in these escorts.

The Operation scheduled for 26 September, 1942, was in itself no different from previous shows. The 8th's Fortresses were still only probing Hitler's defended Europe, still learning, still gaining experience. There would be time for deep penetration raids later. For now, and for the 26th, the target was to be German airfields around Cherbourg – Maupertus and Morlaix/Poujean.

Twenty-six B.17s from the 301st Bomb Group would be the main force, with two diversion raids planned, one of 17 bombers from the 92nd Group, and 32 from the 92nd and 97th Groups. Thirty-six P.38 Lightnings of the 1st Fighter Group were also down as escort but they were recalled shortly after they took off.

The operation was planned in two parts, preceded by a diversion to the Le Havre area, designed to get enemy fighters into the air and be back at their aerodromes refuelling when the main force went in. No fewer than 16 squadrons of fighters would take part in the escort, with 11 Group as diversion support. This comprised 61 aircraft; all three American squadrons of the 31st Group, plus 24 Spitfires from 616 and 124 Squadrons from Tangmere. Even this diversion sortie did not go according to plan, as only eight Fortresses were seen by the fighter pilots and one of those soon turned for home. Then four of 124 Squadron's aircraft turned back due to severe icing and two of the 307th US Squadron aborted for similar reasons. What was left of the formation flew to within 15 miles of Le Havre then swept round towards St. Omer and home. Some enemy fighters were picked up by British radar but they did not make an appearance.

For part of the main raid, against Maupertus, RAF 10 Group had

24 Spitfire IXs from 611 and 402 Squadrons, who were to act as high cover and close escort to the Forts. They took off at 4.54 pm, making rendezvous over Portland Bill at 5.30, but the formation was five minutes late because of the weather. The P.38s took off from Ibsley at the same time as the Spits were off but they did not see anything of the bombers and, as already stated, they were recalled. Rear cover was to be provided by Spitfire Vs from 308 and 315 Polish Squadrons from Middle Wallop, but again all aircraft were recalled.

For the raid on Morlaix, close escort would be provided by Spitfire IXs from 401 and 133 Squadrons from Bolt Head and 64 Squadron from Harrowbeer. Fourteen Spits of 133 had flown from Great Sampford to Bolt Head at 12.30 that afternoon and at 1.50, after a very sketchy briefing, the 12 selected pilots took off with 401 with orders to make rendezvous with the B.17s in mid-Channel, approximately half-way from Bolt Head to Morlaix.

The twelve pilots and their aircraft were:

FL E G Brettell	BS313	FL M E Jackson	BS279
PO L T Ryerson	BS275	PO R E Smith	BS447
PO W H Baker	BS446	PO C A Cook	BS640
PO D D Smith	BS137	PO R N Beaty	BS418
PO G B Sperry	BS638	PO G H Middleton	BS301
PO G G Wright	BS138	PO G P Neville	BS140

Spare pilot had been Pilot Officer Don Gentile (BS445), who was disgusted at being left behind. Some way out over the Channel, Beaty's Spitfire had engine trouble and, after flying along for some time, he decided that he really ought to return. He staggered back against the wind, ran out of petrol and force landed in a small field near Kingsbridge. The eleven others flew on.

Squadron Leader P B "Laddie" Lucas DFC, had recently returned from Malta, and was now at Fighter Command Headquarters, under Air Chief Marshal Sholto-Douglas. He remembers:

"It was a Saturday and Sholto had gone down to Chequers with Churchill and the Chiefs of Staff and I was Squadron Leader Ops 1.B under Theodore McEvoy and Barrie Heath, who was Wing Commander Ops. I was therefore on duty with everyone away for the weekend.

"I got on well with Sholto, knew him quite well and I can recall him saying that he didn't want to be disturbed while at Chequers unless it was something absolutely vital. I thought nothing of it but as it happened we did have a problem arise.

"The Americans were going to bomb Morlaix with their B.17s; it was one of their first raids and they were terribly inexperienced. The fighter escort boys were under Exeter Control – 10 Group, and the operational order was that the new Spitfire IXs should rendezvous with the Forts in mid-Channel at around 17,000 feet and would then climb to 22,000, go over and bomb, then return. It was a simple, straightforward operation, and the weather was given as about 6/10ths cloud, varying up to 15,000 feet over the Channel and therefore, at 17,000, it would be clearer.

"The wind was given as blowing to the southwest if the Forts were going, say, due south. The remit was that the Spit IXs would do the forward target cover and after bombing they would come back.

"No.133 Squadron was led that day by their English flight commander Gordon Brettell, as Red McColpin was busy making arrangements for the change over to the 8th Air Force. Off they went and the weather, in fact, was found to be almost unbroken cloud up to 14–15,000 feet and the rendezvous failed to take place. Brettell led the Squadron over the top of the cloud, couldn't see a sign of the bombers, assumed they were further on, so thought he'd better go on and try to catch them up.

"He therefore flew on towards the target on his given ETA and when he reached his ETA, with still no sign of the bombers, decided to turn and return home."

However, what Brettell and his pilots did not realise, and being above cloud with no sight of the ground, had no way of checking, was that the wind, given at briefing as an estimated 40 mph, was in fact in excess of 100 mph!

Laddie Lucas was in the Ops Room at Fighter Command and told us:

"You could see the radar plots being placed down and I can remember seeing them going miles down south and eventually they disappeared off our board. I rang up the Sector Controller at Exeter and asked what was happening to these fellows, we can't see them, can you? But he said, no, they'd gone off their board too! I said, "They'll never get back from there," but the Controller said that they were now out of radio touch and had been for the last 20 minutes!

"Brettell, eventually heading back, still over cloud, flew on an ETA heading, then began to let down through the cloud, not having seen any land at all since mid-Channel. At around 4,000 feet they broke cloud and Brettell called, "Close up you fellows and make it tight." So they all closed up, Brettell thinking as he looked down that he was seeing the Cornish countryside. In fact it was the Brittany peninsular. They went pretty well over the top of Brest, a hornet's nest at the best of times, whereupon all the flak opened up on them. What the Exeter Controller then heard was Brettell calling, "For Christ's sake tell those bastards to stop shooting at us, can't they see we're friendly!" – but one after another these guys were shot down or began to run out of juice and those still in the air began to let down and force land.

"One chap, Bob Smith, realising finally he wasn't going to get home, flew inland until he ran out of fuel, put the Spitfire down in a field, destroyed it and walked off. He was later picked up by the Resistance who got him across the Pyrenees and he turned up again in England.

"However, 133 – all with brand new Spitfire IXs – had been lost, so I was put in a hell of a fix to decide whether to inform   Sholto or leave it until he came back from Chequers. Finally it was decided he should be told, so I rang him up. I said, "Sir, I'm afraid there's bad news", and he asked, "What is it, Laddie?" He sounded quite sharp and obviously annoyed at being disturbed. So I told him, and then there was a pause. Now I'd always admired Sholto, for whoever he was with, you always felt he was batting on the same level. He was very bright. He made no comment but then simply said, "Will you please get me the following people in my office, tomorrow morning, 9 am; AOC 10 Group, Sector Controller Exeter, Controller, Exeter, Wing Leaders and so on. And let's have a full report on the operation when I get there." That was all he said, then put the 'phone down.

"They duly had their meeting, although I didn't attend. What had of course happened was that the Met people had got it all wrong. Poor Brettell shouldn't have gone on when he failed to make rendezvous n that sort of weather. No doubt for the best of reasons, but with the wrong judgement, he chose to go on. With the unreported wind strength they had been blown almost down to the Spanish border, certainly down beyond Bordeaux. Thus when they did head back, into this same wind, instead of letting down over Cornwall they were just about over Brest. It is, or course, very easy to say what he should have done but it is very difficult leading those shows thinking that someone might think you're LMF or something, if you turn for home too readily. But if you are above cloud, with the sun shining, blue sky above etc. you would have no idea of the wind strength.

"Perhaps the B.17 boys should have given Control a warning for they should have known there was a wind problem but the real point was they were inexperienced and obviously keeping radio silence as they had been told to do. Yet it's very easy to say so afterwards."

One of the Wing Leaders on that mission was Wing Commander W G G Duncan-Smith DSO, DFC, who recalls:

"I was leading the North Weald Wing. We were above cloud so I was flying on my watch – 30,000 feet, as we had Spitfire IXs. I quickly realised we had a terrific following wind so told my chaps we'd be turning soon and we'd have to forget the bombers. The Forts headed out past Cherbourg before turning but by then, 133 Squadron were in trouble and soon began letting down over the peninsular. Some crash landed or landed on German airfields, presenting the enemy with some samples of our new Mark IXs."

The rest of the 11 Group Wing, 64 and 401 Squadrons also very nearly ran into trouble. The Canadians were flying top cover, 133 had been in the middle, 64 below. According to 401 Squadron, the briefing at Exeter was without Wing Commander Brian Kingcome and so Squadron Leader Tony Gaze led the Wing, although Kingcome arrived at the last minute from London, and flew at the head of 401 Squadron. As the squadrons then became split due to the cloud, 133 were suddenly on their own.

Tony Gaze also realised that the winds were stronger than forecast, but then some of them could see the ground at this point, so had some point of reference. Some time later, they could hear the Americans calling for a positional fix and they had run into German AA fire from the Cherbourg area. By then they could do nothing for them – they would not have enough petrol to recross the Channel. Some FW190s also made an appearance, and the Eagles, already in deep trouble, had to fend them off. Marion Jackson shot down one, but then flak caught him and he baled out. By this time others were also going down – out of gas.

At Sholto-Douglas' subsequent meeting at Fighter Command HQ, Generals Tooey Spaatz, Ira Eaker and Monk Hunter were in attendance. Here it was confirmed that the winds had caused the problem and with the thick cloud obscuring the ground the American pilots had no way of knowing that they were being blown so far south. Once they turned this same wind held them back

Of the 11 pilots who were left over Cherbourg, Ryerson, Baker, Smith and Neville were killed, Brettell, Sperry, Wright, Jackson, Cook and Middleton were prisoners and Bob Smith evading. Gordon Brettell was later in Stalag Luft III, and took part in the mass escape in March 1944 (The Great Escape) being one of the 50 officers murdered by the Gestapo when recaptured. Suggestions that he was too inexperienced to have led 133 on this September day must be refuted by his recent award of the DFC, the citation for which read:

"This officer has taken part in 111 sorties over enemy territory. He has always displayed great keenness to engage the enemy. On one occasion he was wounded in combat and on recovery, he resumed operational flying with renewed zest. He is an excellent Flight Commander."

Some heads did "roll" – someone had to take responsibility. The Exeter Controllers took some of the "flak", the weather men too. What was obvious was that in future, there must be far more co-operation between the British and American efforts.

Myles Duke Woolley, the Debden Wing Leader, knew Gordon Brettell and remembers:

"I knew Gordon very well for we'd both done some motor racing together before the war. He wrote to me from prison camp and said that when they'd got down below the cloud he realised something was awfully wrong, for the ground below certainly wasn't Devon or Cornwall. Furthermore, all sorts of shit and corruption was flying up at them.

"Brian Kingcome then heard a very faint cry from the Controller. Some of the "jabber" going on was to the effect that the Americans had encountered all this flak and Exeter was telling them to "Head north, head north!"

"Brian was already heading north but he also called the Americans, but there was such a lot of talk on the radio it was hard to get through. The Americans did tend to gabble a bit on the radio; I used to slaughter the Eagle boys I had in my Wing for it and eventually they became very good at R/T discipline.

"When eventually Gordon's fuel ran out he took to his parachute but broke several toes when he landed. He was quickly captured and ended up in Stalag Luft III.

"The Wing Leader was always totally calm and unruffled, and I asked him later what had happened. He said "There was nothing I could do, 'Duke', I just headed north, with the leanest mixture that kept the engines running and as the chaps baled out, I called up Control, giving one Mayday after another!"

"They had got stuck in a jet stream, of course. We didn't know much about jet streams in those days and we were completely mystified by it at the time. I was horrified. I'd sent down one squadron and was only getting back one pilot and no aircraft.

"However, one good thing to come from this tragedy helped the Eagle Squadrons very much. There had been some feeling between the three squadrons. My difficulty in building the Wing was that 71 Squadron, being the first squadron, tended to look down on the second (121), while the second looked down on the third (133); the third looked down on everyone because of being looked down on! It was a ridiculous situation.

"What we were now able to do was to sort the three squadrons out between us so as to end this situation. So we very carefully sorted out the pilots who had the potential to be good CO's, good flight commanders, section leaders, and so on, irrespective of to which squadron they had belonged. I said to Pete Peterson that it was no good just promoting all 71's chaps, we must fill vacancies from all three squadrons. Thus we scrambled everyone up and by switching them about, we suddenly had an American Wing! It was probably easier for me to do, than one of the American commanders, but it worked and solved the problem."

* * *

All three Eagle Squadrons were now in Duke Woolley's Wing, 121 and 133 having moved to Debden on 23 September, (133 being actually located at the nearby satellite of Great Sampford) just three days before

Morlaix; 71 were already on base. The loss of 133 came right in the middle of the plans to hand-over the three squadrons to the US 8th Air Force, so it was a particular embarrassment to all concerned.

Initially, Duke Woolley had had only 71 in his fighter Wing, but as the date of the transfer approached, he lost his RAF squadrons, the Wing then being solely American.

I had been flying with No. 416 RCAF. I was quite happy flying with the Canadians but all that changed when 133 were lost over Brest. Sergeant Fuchs and I had been sent up to London for interviews just before the Morlaix mission. We passed the interview I guess. In any event I was hurriedly posted to 133 in order to make the numbers up!

I well remember turning up at Great Sampford, the satellite airfield of Debden. I walked into the silent Nissen hut which had been the officer's quarters. I knocked on the first door, waited, then pushed upon the door. The two beds were neatly made, obviously by the batman. There were uniforms hung up; by the wash basin, the shaving kits and tooth brushes; on the small table a half-finished letter: "Dear Mum, thanks for your letter of August 5 . . . We're kept pretty busy flying missions almost every day . . . Don't worry about me . . . " I felt I was intruding so left the room and went into the next, and then the next . . .

"There were ten of them in all, and all empty – except the last one. There, sitting on his bed, looking dazed, sat a dark, unusually handsome pilot officer.

"Where is everybody?" I asked. He shook his head.

"I'm Jim Goodson," I continued.

"Don Gentile," he said, and then, "No one came back."

"Back from where?" I asked.

"The mission. I was down as spare pilot so I didn't go."

"No one came back?" I persisted. Gentile shook his head. He looked so forlorn I thought he might burst into tears. If someone had told me then, that this good-looking, frightened, insecure youngster, would, within a few months, be famous as America's leading fighter ace, I would have thought he was crazy.

The squadron commanders from the date of the transfer were Squadron Leader Gus Daymond (71), Squadron Leader Jim Daley (121), and Squadron Leader Mac McColpin (133). From that Tuesday, 29 September, 1942, the three men became Majors in the USAAF, the three squadrons becoming the 334th, 335th and 336th of the American 4th Fighter Group, US 8th Air Force.

Duke Woolley: "I got on with the Americans very well, but tactically speaking they were a little impetuous, wanting the war won the day after tomorrow, which was a most dangerous thing to do, and in any case, totally unnecessary. We were in for a five or six year war and so to go blazing round trying to win it by Wednesday week was not on.

"At first I had thought 71 just another squadron. I was rather demanding in those days, so I'm sure if they'd been inefficient, I would have told them so, but, of course, they weren't. The pilots, on average, were older than those on RAF squadrons. They were dead keen and they had all done a vast amount of flying – something virtually unheard of in a normal RAF squadron. When finally the squadrons were handed over to the Americans, we had to have a parade, attended by various high ranking dignitaries from both the RAF and USAAF. The march-past, of course, would be led by 71 Squadron, commanded now by Gus Daymond. The trouble was, poor old Gus couldn't march!

"I didn't find this out until about a day before the parade. On the order – "By the left, quick march," Gus would strike out with not only his left foot but also his left arm! Therefore, he would go along for about six or seven paces with both feet and both the same arms together. Then, keeping his arms going, he'd change step, producing a sort of ripple effect back along the columns.

"I got absolutely furious about this and tried desperately to get Gus to move off with opposite leg and arm but he merely said, "Never could do it, Duke. Sorry!"

"Well, he tried but it was no good. Pete, of course, was giggling away and not helping a bit. Finally I said to Gus, "Look, if you could change your feet after six or seven paces, do you think you could change your arms instead?" But that didn't work either. Finally we tried to march him off with both arms perfectly still and by his sides, until after about six paces he could begin to swing his arms opposite to each leg. "I'll try, Duke!"

"After about twenty dry runs he finally had it off pat. I don't know if there is any movie film of that parade but if there is, you'll find that there's Gus with no arms working at all for about six or eight steps as he led 71 off the mark and past the VIPs.

"At that parade, they dished out a number of American DFCs, to Pete, Gus and me. I didn't realise that this was the first American DFC ever given to a non-American."

There had also been some recent British DFC awards to the Eagles. Selden Edner and Bill Baker of 133 and Sam Mauriello of 71, although Baker had been lost over Morlaix.

It was a wet Tuesday when the Eagles became the 4th Fighter Group. Among the brass was Sholto Douglas, C in C RAF Fighter Command, Tooey Spaatz and Monk Hunter. Officially the RAF handed over the squadrons to the new commander of the 4th Fighter Group, Colonel Edward W Anderson, who had come to Britain with one of the P.38 Groups. His deputy commander would be Lieutenant Colonel Chesley Peterson, who despite his rank and experience was still only 22 years old! The Wing Commander Flying would continue to be Myles Duke Woolley, at least for the time being. In due time the Americans would be complete masters of their own destiny.

Air Marshal Sir Sholto Douglas said at the parade:

"I would have wished that on this, my first opportunity of addressing all three Eagle Squadrons together on one station that my words should have been other than words of farewell. We of Fighter Command deeply regret this parting, for in the course of the past 18 months we have seen the stuff of which you are made, and we could not ask for better companions with whom to see this fight through to the finish.

"But we realise – as you too must realise – that your present transfer to your own country's air force is, in the long run, in the best interests of our joint cause. The United States Army Air Force's gain is very much the RAF's loss. The loss to the Luftwaffe will no doubt continue as before.

"In the 18 months which have elapsed since your first unit became fully operational, Eagle pilots have destroyed some 73 enemy aircraft – the equivalent of about six squadrons of the Luftwaffe – and probably destroyed or damaged a great many others. The actual official total of destroyed is, I believe, 73 1/2, the half being part of a Dornier shared with a British squadron and a symbol of Anglo-American co-operation. Of the 73 1/2 enemy aircraft destroyed, 41 have been claimed by the senior Eagle Squadron, No. 71 – a record of which they may very well be proud, but one which I understand, the other two squadrons are determined will not long remain unchallenged.

"It is with great personal regret that I today say 'Goodbye' to all you boys whom it has been my privilege to command. You joined us readily and of your own free will when our need was greatest and before your country was actually at war with our common enemy. You were the vanguard of the great host of your compatriots who are now helping to make these Islands a base from which to launch that great offensive which we all desire. You have proved yourselves great fighters and good companions, and we shall watch your future with confidence.

"There are those of your number who are not here today – those sons of the United States who were the first to give their lives for their country. We of the RAF no less than yourselves, will always remember them with pride. Like their fathers who fought and died with that American vanguard of the last war – the Lafayette Squadron – so will those Eagles who fell in combat ever remain the honoured dead of two great nations.

"And now I have some news for you. The Air Council, anxious to give tangible expression to the gratitude which we all feel for the great work you have done, is going to ask each of you to accept a small personal memento of your services to the RAF. The memento, I understand, will take the form of a medallion and, though it has not been possible in the short time available to have this medallion struck and ready by today, it is hoped that its presentation will be made in the very near future.

"I hope these emblems will serve as a pleasant reminder of your comradeship with the Fighter Command of the RAF – a comradeship which we have been very proud to share and which I, as your Commander-in-Chief, shall always remember with gratitude and affection.

"Goodbye, and thank you, Eagle Squadrons, Numbers 71, 121 and 133 of Fighter Command, and good hunting to you, Squadrons of Number 4 Pursuit Group, 8th US Air Force."

* * *

A fourth Eagle Squadron had in fact been planned. As usual pilots were recruited in Canada and trained at Glendale, California. After their training was completed, 22 pilots embarked for England on two ships.

It was at the height of the Battle of the Atlantic and the convoy was attacked by several U-boats. One of the ships sunk was that carrying twelve of the Eagle Squadron pilots. None survived.

When the remaining ships reached Southampton, the King and Queen were there to meet them and to express their condolences to the ten remaining pilots on the death of their comrades. Since these were too few to form an Eagle Squadron, they were posted in pairs to various RAF units. Only two survived the war, Dick Hoyer and Clair Waterburg, originally from Los Angeles but now living in England.

Chapter 8

The 4th Fighter Group, USAAF

IT WAS virtually business as usual after the handover of the Eagles to the USAAF and, specifically, the 4th Fighter Group of the US 8th Air Force. Most of the faces were the same – at least in 71 and 121 or, more correctly, the 334th and 335th Squadrons.

We continued to fly the Spitfire Vb, and Dixie Alexander and I badgered Don Blakeslee to let us do a rhubarb over France and we eventually got permission – provided we painted over the RAF roundel with the American star.

I don't know if you have ever tried to draw a five-pointed star, but it's not easy. Eventually, my crew chief said, "Sir, I have a star on this medallion my mother gave me. Perhaps you could copy that."

We leapt at this idea – we didn't know one star from another, anyway. But it's an interesting thought that, as a result, the first two US fighters to fly over occupied France were emblazoned with the Star of David!

We were also fitted out in bits and pieces with US uniforms. Many of us hadn't been all that keen to leave the RAF squadrons we knew and loved and transfer to the USAAF, and we secured the right to at least wear our RAF wings. This was to cause me some trouble.

I was stopped in Grosvenor Square one day by a US General, probably a West-Pointer.

"Major!" he barked. "You are improperly dressed! Who gave you permission to wear the wings and decorations of a foreign power on the uniform of a US Army officer?"

"Sir," I replied, "The President of the United States and King George the Sixth of England!"

He knew when he was beaten. He was also a Southerner.

"They're mighty purty!" he said.

The ranks, too, altered.

Squadron Leaders became Majors, Flight Lieutenants, Captains and Flying and Pilot Officers to First and Second Lieutenants. (Lootenants now, not Leftenants!) And virtually all the sergeant pilots were commissioned. The RAF ground crews remained, at least for the time being, so as to teach the new American ground echelon men how to service the Spitfires. The first US ground crews were those earlier assigned to the 50th Fighter Squadron, 14th Fighter Group, but their P.38s were not now coming in from Iceland, so they became the nucleus of the 4th's ground personnel.

The first operation following the transfer, came on October 2, 1942 – Circus 221. Duke Woolley would lead a diversionary sweep in support of the mission, between Calais and Dunkirk. 334 and 335 engaged several FW190s at 24,000 feet that afternoon. Oscar Coen, Gene Fetrow and Stan Anderson each claimed one destroyed, Duke Woolley and Jim Clark sharing another. Duke Woolley remembers this show:

"The weather wasn't awfully good on this day and as we had not expected to fly, some of the chaps had pushed off to London. Then, more or less out of the blue we were asked to run the Wing round Northern France to help divert the Germans from a bombing raid.

"I took what pilots I had on base and soon we were floating around over France, when down below I suddenly saw a squadron of aircraft in a similar four-man section that we were now flying. At first I thought they were 'friendly' but for some reason I questioned it and got up-sun of them. I called up and told everyone to stay up while I took my section down to take a closer look.

"I could see they were 190s. I got very annoyed that they were flying in a similar RAF-type formation and closing in, called the boys and told them to give me about 200 yards start, for I wanted the leader!

"I and my number two went down into the formation and I got right above the three aircraft behind the leading 190, then arrived behind the leader – a matter of about 10 yards. In fact I could look down to my left, right into the cockpit of one German just to the left of the leaders. I knew perfectly well that at that range I couldn't fire at him on the sight, I had to aim just up a bit – then gave him a two second burst, then broke away, calling for the others to come down.

"I created a little confusion amongst the Germans, for I'd hit the leader absolutely dead right. I blew both wings off, which began to flutter down and then the fuselage nosed forward. The rest of the Germans just paused a moment then the other chaps were amongst them and we shot down three more with some others damaged. We might have got some more but they all went downhill so fast when we hit them I had to reform the boys so as not to lose our precious height.

"Jim Clark, who had been my Number 3, had come down as I had attacked the leading 190 and opened fire. I could see his tracer missing the 190 as it began to disintegrate. However, back at base, I allowed him half a share in the Focke Wulf in order to encourage him. This it obviously did, for he was later to become a high scoring Lieutenant Colonel.

"When we got back and the boys who had been in London heard we'd been on a show and scored the first kills for the Group, they were pretty furious."

Because of this shared kill with an RAF pilot, the American 4th Fighter Group was to carry this half victory with it for the rest of the war, so that by the war's end, it still showed the "1/2" in its tally.

Several more missions were flown during October, the Group losing its first pilot on the 20th when Tony Seaman's aircraft developed engine trouble while on convoy patrol. Before he could get it home, the thing blew up in mid-air and he was killed. November saw a continuation of these operations, mostly led by Duke Woolley. Frank Smolinsky of the 335th bagged a 190 on the 19th while on the following day, on a Rhubarb, Roy Evans of the 335th caught and shot down a Fiesler 156, light observation plane near Furnes.

Don Blakeslee came back from the wilderness towards the end of November. Jim Daley and Mac McColpin were reassigned to the States so Don was called back to take command of the 335th Squadron.

Duke Woolley left in December, shortly to receive the DSO. From now on the 4th would be American manned and American led. Pete Peterson was now the Group Leader, leading them for the first time on 13 January, 1943.

With the coming of the new year of 1943 came new aircraft. The Spitfire had been good, but politics now demanded that the 4th fly not British but American fighter planes. During the month the first Republic P.47 "Thunderbolts" began to arrive.

The Thunderbolt, especially after the Spitfire, was huge. It weighed 15,000 pounds to begin with, against the Spit V's, 7100 pounds. Its armament consisted of eight .50 machine guns with 2,136 rounds, as against the Spitfire's two 20mm cannon and four .303 machine guns, with 60 shells per cannon and 400 rounds in each machine gun. Its speed too was different; 433 mph for the P.47, 369 for the Spit. In a dive, both aircraft of course would exceed these level flight figures, but with the P.47, it certainly moved when going "down hill".

For us at least there was no love affair with the P.47 as there had been with the Spitfire. One of the great shocks of the war for me was to get out of my sweet little Spitfire, and go over to the great, seven ton giant which was the P.47 Thunderbolt. After our Spitfires it looked like a Stirling 4-engined bomber!

We might have taken more kindly to it if we hadn't had hours of flying time in the Spit, or even if we had not been hoping to get the P.51 Mustang. The great 56th Figther Group under Hub Zemke thought the P.47 was the greatest fighter in the world. Indeed, many of them, like Gabreski, Dave Schilling, Bob Johnson and Hub himself, built up impressive scores with it; but then they had never flown any other plane in combat. I recall a visit from one RAF pilot at Debden. He climbed up on the wing and peered into the vast cockpit.

"Well," he remarked, "I know what the best evasive tactic should be. Just run around the cockpit and hide in one corner!"

However, with time and experience, we came to have a grudging respect for the big "Thunderjug". Certainly considering its size and weight, this fighter had an amazing performance, particularly at altitude. It was faster than the Spitfire V and, of course, in a dive nothing could touch it.

In fact, one of the greatest dangers was that it would get into a terminal dive from which it was impossible to recover. This once happened to me. The stick became rigid in my hands. My first reaction of course, was to throttle back the engine. Immediately the nose started to go back under and I had visions of the plane starting into an outside loop, which would probably have ripped its wings off. As this started to happen, I immediately opened up the throttle and slowly edged the stick back. It finally took effect and the nose came up. The "G" effect on coming out of that dive was so violent that I blacked out but came to as the plane soared upwards. When I landed we found that the strain of coming out had slightly buckled the wings but otherwise the rugged airframe had stood up perfectly.

I remember discussing the plane with Don Blakeslee:

"Well, Don, at least the 109s and 190s won't be able to dive away from us anymore. This plane will catch anything in a dive."

"Well," he replied, "It damn well ought to be able to dive; it sure as Hell can't climb!"

* * *

Don Blakeslee had his chance to test the Thunderbolt against the FW190 on 15 April, 1943, the day he scored his first kill while flying it, and his first with the 4th Fighter Group.

Pete Peterson was leading a fighter sweep in co-operation with Rodeo 204, and was steering the 4th near the Belgian coast. Two other US Groups, the 56th and 78th were in on the show.

After a sweep round Cassel, Don and his 335th, having got hooked up with two squadrons from the 56th, spotted three Focke Wulfs 6,000 feet below. Don winged over and dived, chasing one 190 all the way down to 500 feet, while scoring numerous strikes on it. Then, obviously realising how low he was and that he was not shaking the P.47 off his tail, the German pilot decided it was time to leave, but he'd left it too late. Even as he jettisoned his hood and began to get out, his fighter went into the ground near Ostend. Don's comment when he landed was, "Yeah, it can dive!"

Shortly afterwards, Pete and Bob Boock, who'd joined 71 Squadron just before the transfer, put two more FWs into the sea, but Pete's Thunderbolt let him down. His engine packed up and Pete had to go into the sea himself. He was 30 miles out from the English coast but an RAF Air Sea Rescue Walrus amphibian landed and picked him up safely. Sadly two pilots didn't make it back, both from the 334th. Richard McMinn was one. He was hit by a 190 and went down in flames in that combat. Then there was the veteran former Eagle, Stan Anderson. Stan, from Indianapolis, had joined 71 Squadron back in March 1942. He'd been in action over Dieppe and with the 4th he'd already gained three and a probable victory, and become flight commander. A promising career had now been cut short.

Just a month later, May 14, Don and Lee Gover got two more FW190s over Knocke, in a bounce on some FW190s near Hulst. The fight lasted nearly 20 minutes as the Thunderbolts fought their way to the coast and the Channel. Peterson got another 190 the following day, to bring his score to eight, with three probables and six damaged. For Pete his time was now running out. The "brass" wanted him Stateside, and they soon had their way. His natural successor was Don Blakeslee, whilst another former Eagle, Gil Halsey, from Chickasha, Oklahoma, took over the 335th. For the 4th Fighter Group, the legend of Don Blakeslee was about to begin.

The 4th's radio call-sign was 'Horseback", so Don was from then on, 'Horseback Leader'. He was proud of his RAF wings, which those of us who transferred to the USAAF were authorised to wear over the right breast pocket of our uniform. Our USAAF Wings we wore over our left.

He had a very independent attitude and was very blunt in defence of his convictions, which did not endear him to some of his superiors. The problem for them, however, was he got the job done, and you can't stop a man who is being successful at what he's paid and trained to do. But diplomacy wasn't part of his make-up. He wanted the best for his pilots and his Group and if he had any say in it, that's what he would get. His experience was already sound, having done a tour of duty with a Canadian Spitfire Squadron. It is suggested that he only allowed himself to be transferred to the Eagles so that he could avoid being tour-expired, with all the dangers then of being a flight instructor. But whatever the true reasons, the Eagles, the 4th and then the 8th Air Force had in him a natural leader.

Great air combat leaders were relatively rare; that is, the really true air tacticians who could quickly size up and then seize to good advantage a given situation as it developed. All the planning in the world counts for nothing unless someone can see what is going on and then direct his various flights and sections to the fighting. Blakeslee was that kind of man. Johnnie Johnson, for the RAF, between 1943 and 1944 was that kind of guy too. But for the 4th, it was Don Blakeslee.

One of the first problems for Blakeslee to overcome was the problem that the three Eagle Squadrons had never flown together. Each had been in different RAF Fighter Wings. Peterson had started the process of working the three units into a single team. Blakeslee continued the work. Then came the change of aircraft and another problem to be solved, but he did it and within a very few weeks, the 4th were fully in tune with their new Thunderbolts.

Another old Eagle was now in command of the 336th Squadron, Jim

DuFour – a mature 33 year old from Alameda, California. He had an interesting story to tell of how he joined the Eagles. He had tried to join the RCAF in Canada shortly after the war started but had been turned down. He then decided to join the Seaforth Highlanders but fearing his name might be known in Canada, joined up as James Crowley, a Canadian! Only when he'd done this did he request a transfer to the RAF in order to become a pilot and join the Eagle Squadron. Once in England he met a WAAF officer who commanded the WAAF contingent down at Ford in Sussex. Not wishing to be married under his false name, he had it changed back to DuFour. For some years the name of Crowley and DuFour appeared on the lists of former Eagle pilots. He had flown with 121 Squadron, becoming a flight commander, and was now a Major with the 4th.

* * *

On May 18, Duane Beeson shot down his first confirmed German, although another former Eagle was lost. Robert A Boock, brand new second lieutenant, went into the North Sea during a dog-fight off Knocke and Blankenburghe. From Springfield, Illinois, he'd been an Eagle since 8 September. Beeson had joined 71 Squadron three days earlier. I can still remember the first time I saw Duane Beeson. I was chatting to Jim Clark in the Mess.

"What do your new pilots look like?" I had asked him.

"Seems like they're robbing the cradles," Jim Clark replied. "Look at that one!"

I saw what he meant. Not only was Beeson shorter than most of the pilots, he had the face of a young inexperienced boy. I knew he had to be at least 18 (in fact he was going on 21), but he looked much younger.

"Hardly one to scare the Hell out of the Luftwaffe."

If I had looked a little closer, I might have seen a steely glint in his eye, but I had already dismissed Beeson as one of the many young hopefuls who, in the event, wouldn't be around very long. Sometimes guys looked like that. One couldn't say exactly why, it was just that with some guys you just felt they wouldn't make it. You couldn't tell them, of course, and you couldn't stop them flying. It was just one of those strange things. However, perhaps in Beeson, we see how wrong we "experienced veterans" could be.

Indeed, I couldn't have been more wrong about him. But then, I guess nobody else would have dreamed that this baby-faced boy would go down in history as the most aggressive, determined killer in the USAAF. In the short space of a year this fresh-faced boy from Boise, Idaho, had 19 air and five ground kills and was a Major. He was also the topscoring 4th Fighter Group pilot on the Thunderbolt, with 12 victories.

Not long after he made Major, he was shot down, like me, on a strafing mission, on 5 April, 1944, to become a prisoner of war.

Beeson, or "Bee" as we knew him, flew his "Boise Belle" throughout the summer and autumn of 1943, scoring modestly at first. In fact, by the end of that year he'd only scored six kills, five 109s and one Focke Wulf, but in the new year he really got into his stride, but perhaps a trifle over-confident. But then, ground fire could bring down the best of us!

We could have been excused for mis-reading Beeson's character. He was not like "Baby-Faced" Nelson, the brutal Chicago gangster, whose innocent looks belied his vicious nature. Among his friends, he was retiring, friendly and popular. It was only when he got into the air he became so dangerous.

Of course, all fighter pilots finally had to face three possible fates: death, German POW camp or, perhaps the most dangerous, return to the USA to become a flying instructor! Beeson got lucky – he became a prisoner! Like most of us who suffered the same fate, Bee's initial contact with Hitler's vicious Third Reich was a pleasant surprise. Instead of a concentration camp, torture, or even summary execution, he found himself received by a charming, fluent English-speaking "interrogator" who introduced himself as Hans Scharff. He then proceeded to give Bee the latest news of the 4th Fighter Group.

Finally he asked for news about four or five of Bee's friends. Bee knew they had been shot down but maintained a stoic silence. Scharff smiled. "Well, I'm sure they'd like to see you. Come with me."

Scharff led Beeson into a neighbouring room where he was warmly greeted by his missing buddies.

Fate has a strange sense of humour. Having survived some of the most dangerous missions of the war, emerging unscathed after being shot down over Germany, one would think Duane Beeson would have lived happily ever after, to a ripe old age, but that was not to be.

Hardly had he returned to the States after being liberated, than he developed a brain tumour, which within a few months was to prove fatal. Duane Beeson was also one of those fighter pilots who thought long and hard about his profession and how he could improve things. He worked for hours on his deflection shooting, studied methods used by other, former fighter pilots. He was one of the very few to keep both hands on the control column during an attack and actually press the gun button with his left thumb! He had big hands too.

He worked out a method of bouncing enemy aircraft and overshooting at speed in order not to slow down and be in danger of getting bounced himself. He certainly never had to worry about the enemy pilot he'd just attacked firing at him when he did overshoot – that German was usually dead, or certainly out of the action.

Like all the really good fighter pilots he got in close before firing. His camera-gun films showed just how close. They revealed close-ups of disintegrating German fighters and burning fuel tanks – split seconds before the film became obscured as German oil covered the camera lens!

He had the drive of two men, was fastidious and was painstaking in everything he set his mind to. In early 1944 he, Don Gentile and John Godfrey were in friendly rivalry for top scorers, which led, in its way, to the 4th's record-breaking achievements.

* * *

Brew Morgan went down on 21 May. Blakeslee led a Rodeo that afternoon and when several gaggles of enemy fighters were seen near Bruges, 335 stayed as cover squadron, while 334 made the bounce as 336 gave cover towards the French border. A tremendous dog-fight started but the 4th came off second best with three pilots lost for just one Me109 shot down. Brew was one of the missing, but it had been he who got the 109. He recalls:

"I think I was shot down on my 100th mission. I was the Squadron's Operations Officer and had the day off as I had a date with a Red Cross lady. But Blakeslee spotted me in the Ops shack where I was checking the flight schedule before leaving. He told me one of the flight leaders had gone sick and I should replace him.

"Once the fight started over Belgium I got separated. Our rule was to try and climb and rejoin the squadron or go low and head for home. With fighters behind me and lining up to shoot, I tried an attack by pulling a tight circle with partial flaps. I managed a shot but missed – then got hit in the engine.

"I dropped my flaps, undid the harness and prepared to bale out. Unfortunately I couldn't open my canopy. My ammo-belt-container doors on the wings were flapping and slowing me down further but I couldn't get the canopy open. Then a cannon shell exploded in the cockpit wounding me in the face, hands and leg. My instruments were all shot away except for the altimeter and speed indicator. I went into a slow spin and got hit again.

"At 400 feet I managed to pry open the canopy but by then I was too low to jump and too busy to get my harness back on. I was over water now and knew that I would have to ride it in. I hit the water at about 185 knots and was immediately thrown out of the plane. My next recollection was of being under the water, then inflating my Mae West. When I got to the surface, I jettisoned my parachute and began to inflate my dinghy. I thought that my number was really up when two ME109s circled me, then rolled in. I felt sure they were going to strafe me but instead they saluted me, then flew off." Brew was later picked up and taken prisoner.

The Group failed to score for the next month. Some pilots were beginning to feel a bit fidgety about the Thunderbolts, but that would soon change. Then on June 22, Blakeslee led a Ramrod to Belgium, supporting bombers. South of Breskens they saw the 40-odd B.17s of the 381st and 384th Bomb Groups coming out from Antwerp. For these two Groups it was their first mission – they lost four of their Forts.

A score of 109s and 190s were harrying the bombers, a couple of which were already streaming smoke and heading down. Leaving the 334th as top cover, Blakeslee led the other two squadrons down. Within five minutes the enemy fighters began to withdraw, having lost four of their number to me, Fonzo "Snuffy" Smith and Ernie Beatie (two).

Three days later, the Duchess of Kent arrived at Debden, attended by General Monk Hunter. She was there to present the original RAF Eagle Squadron crests to the three American successor units. In this way the three 4th Fighter Group Squadrons became the only USAAF squadrons to have Royal Crests, although Washington never officially sanctioned it.

* * *

Those Eagle pilots still with the 4th Fighter Group were now getting into their stride, passing on their skills and experience to the newly arrived pilots. These forerunners of the mighty US 8th Air Force were very much like the old Pathfinders of the old America, who set out to "blaze trails" across the wilderness, the wilderness now being occupied Europe and Germany.

However, not all former Eagle pilots transferred to the 4th Fighter Group. Some had gone home, some had stayed in the RAF – it had not been obligatory to transfer; they were after all in the service of the Royal Air Force primarily. A number had already left the Eagle Squadrons for service overseas, in the Middle East or Far East.

Chapter 9

Eagles on Malta

THE island of Malta in the middle of the Mediterranean, situated just 20 minutes flying time from German and Italian airfields on Sicily, was strategically placed between the Italian ports to the north and the German and Italian forces fighting the Allied armies in North Africa. In order to fuel and supply his armies, Field Marshal Erwin Rommel, commander of all Axis forces in North Africa, had to have ships from Italy sail to his North African ports. What stopped many of them were the Air and Naval forces based on Malta.

It follows, therefore that the Germans tried everything – except the one tactic that would have worked – invasion – to try and stop Malta operating. But to operate anything like successfully it had to defend its base, a task entrusted to the Malta anti-aircraft gunners and the British Royal Air Force.

Malta, often referred to as Britain's unsinkable aircraft carrier in the Mediterranean, was also known amongst the RAF fraternity, as the "fighter pilot's paradise". Not because of warm sunshine, blue seas and olive-skinned, beautiful women – although that was a consideration – but rather because the air was rarely free from German aircraft with unlimited air combat!

Inexperienced pilots were not wanted on Malta – they didn't live long enough. Some experience was needed, but so too were volunteers. Obviously the Air Ministry had to post certain men to Malta, but they were always pleased when pilots volunteered. So much so that, officially, nobody could deny a pilot who volunteered for Malta. A Commanding Officer who might well want to retain a good pilot in his own squadron had no choice but to forward the request, and, unless it was a case of inexperience, the man would soon be on his way. Only when he got there did he fully begin to understand what he'd let himself in for.

In 1942, as the battle for Malta was really hotting up, there were several Americans on Malta, or on their way. Many Eagle pilots were those who, having volunteered for the RAF in the first place, were now restless at not seeing the action for which they'd come and for which they'd been trained. In 1941 it was only really 71 Squadron who were in the thick of the air fighting over France. 121 were operational but not in the mainstream of things, and 133 had gone off to Northern Ireland. If they had come across the Atlantic to fight, then a fight they wanted.

Among the first to volunteer for Malta were Richard McHan, Jim Peck and Don McLeod of 121 Squadron, and Hiram Putnam of 133, in February, 1942. Another volunteer that month was the non-American flight commander of 133, "Tim" (H A S) Johnston. Within a few weeks they were joined by Reade Tilley, Fred Almos, Doug Booth and Norman Chap, from 121, and Fred Scuddy from 133.

There were a number of very individual squadrons on Malta, but with the losses in pilots and the serviceability of aircraft, pilots on occasion tended to be spread around. And they pooled aircraft. Whilst they kept their natural allegiance to their squadron, it seemed appropriate sometimes to feel more akin to the base where one generally operated. Luqa, Takali or Hal Far were the main airstrips but as the island was only about six miles wide by 11 miles long, one could expect in difficult moments to lob down anywhere.

Jim Peck and Don McLeod arrived on the island on 21 March, 1942, having flown off the British aircraft carrier HMS "Eagle", led by the veteran air fighter, Wing Commander E J "Jumbo" Gracie DFC – "Operation Picket 1". Deputy Leader was Tim Johnson. Of the 16 Spitfires that had been due to fly off the carrier, only nine did so as a Blenheim, scheduled to arrive and escort/navigate the others to the island, failed to arrive.

Peck, McLeod and the others knew they had "arrived" at 2.35 pm, shortly after touching down, having successfully covered the 700 mile trip from the carrier. At that time came the third heavy air attack on Takali within 24 hours, in the shape of 70 Ju88s with escorting fighters.

Officially, Peck, McLeod and Johnston were with 126 Squadron, and within a day or so they were in the thick of the action. There was no time to stand around on Malta! On their first day in combat, Peck and McLeod both destroyed Me109s, while Johnston damaged a Stuka. The next day Peck also damaged a Stuka, and Mac got his second 109. Towards the end of March Peck damaged a Ju88 but Mac was shot up on April 2, baled out into the sea but was rescued by a launch.

On Malta at this time was Laddie Lucas, who it will be recalled, was at Fighter Command HQ in England at the time 133 were lost over Cherbourg and Brest. Before that occasion he was flying Spitfires on the island. He remembers the Americans on Malta, and the formation of the American Flight within 126 Squadron:

"The American pilots, I remember, were a damn good lot; there's no doubt that they really were an absolutely super bunch. With those guys it was the "art of the possible." For most of our fellows it was the art of the impossible, but they were so positive that I admired them tremendously.

"It seems now that a lot of those guys were called 'Tex' – they all seemed to come from Texas or somesuch; there was 'Tex' Putnam who had been in 133 Squadron in England and had come out with us in a Sunderland Flying Boat. We had flown out from Mount Batten, and he had a great time taking the rise out of the Navy chaps, for it was just after the "Channel Dash" fiasco and the Navy types were pretty sick about all that, I can tell you.

"Tex, or Hiram, which was his real name – was a really super chap. He was a dark, swarthy-looking guy with a moustache; he came out with a supply of cigars which used to stink the bloody place out! He was excellent and a great friend. He went to 126 but was killed in April. He actually hit a wireless mast and they thought it was an accident but when they got to him they found he'd been hit by a cannon shell and was already dead when he pranged in.

"There was also Donald McLeod, known to everyone as "Mac". He'd been in 121 and had been around for some time and then went into 126. There was Jimmy Peck, who was another super chap, also ex-121, and had come out at the same time. He came from California. Jim and Don were like "Mutt and Jeff" – a pair together. 126 Squadron, when they got their aeroplanes, primarily operated from Luqa, not Takali, which is where we on 249 Squadron were, with 603, who came in April, taking off from the US carrier "Wasp" with the chaps of 601 Squadron.

"A lot of these Americans flew off the "Eagle" with Jumbo Gracie, and he went back to England to bring out another bunch. Jumbo was very thick-skinned and didn't care who the hell he was talking to, so Hugh Pughe Lloyd, the air boss on Malta, sent him back to get Air Ministry to send out more Spitfires. These arrived in April.

"Mind you, Jumbo flew on a reciprocal course at first. They maintained absolute radio silence of course. Suddenly an Australian pilot called him up and asked Jumbo when were they going to set course for Malta! It was only then that Jumbo realised he was heading all these Spitfires back towards Gibraltar!   Jumbo later became the Station Commander at Takali.

"Peck and McLeod I can recall particularly. Don was shot down at least once and these two were constantly ribbing each other. Don was large, fair-haired, flamboyant and garrulous, whereas Jimmie was dark and small. When Mac was shot down he did something to his throat and couldn't speak. Jimmie, when he saw Don all bound up, said, "Well, that'll bloody well teach you to keep on talking!" Jimmie was a first-class fighter pilot and got a DFC.

"Reade Tilley was another six-footer, tremendously gracious. He'd been in 121 too and was to get a DFC later. He made a real mark, very impressive. Then there was Richard McHan. We used to call him "Sunday" McHan, because he always was so smart, especially by Malta standards. Most of us looked terribly unkempt on the island – I recall that Screwball Beurling, the Canadian, looked an absolute mess; I could never get him tidy – he was all over the place . . . but McHan was always spruce, Sunday best! He was with us in 249 for a while. He had a real personality and was very amusing. He used to walk along the tops of those bastion walls of our Palace mess. It was a lovely old 15th century villa, with a superb marble staircase and hall. It had a terrace with great thick bastions from which he could look out and down on Takali, which was about a mile away. Old "Sunday" McHan – I can see him now, walking along these walls, and there was a 200 foot drop on the other side! Harry Kelly was another Texan, with a real deep south voice; it took him an age to get his words out. Tex Spradley, who'd been with me in 66 Squadron, not with the Eagles, had an extraordinary accent, even deeper than that of the deep south. He was always trying to piss-off over Sicily to have a squirt at them there and I kept having to restrain him.

"Doug 'Tiger' Booth, from New York, was another in 126. He was also a press-on guy who used to do mad things. Tim Johnson – an Englishman – was a flight commander on 126 but had been flying with 133 in Fighter Command. He got on marvellously well with the Americans and they were tremendously fond of him. He'd been in the colonial service before the war and could have stayed there but he came home and joined the RAF. There is no doubt that he was quite an exceptional person, a bit older than most, and he had, I know, a most unpleasant experience.

"He was always getting shot-up but this one day, he told me, he was coming back and as Luqa had been heavily bombed, he made a run over the airstrip to see if it was alright to land, when an unexploded bomb went off right underneath him. It shot his Spitfire way up into the air and he just couldn't believe it; he just had time to flick it over and bale out, his parachute opening just as he hit the ground!

"I think somehow the Americans responded to being commanded by Englishmen. There is no doubt that once the 8th Air Force was formed and they were all together they were a marvellous lot but initially I think they gained a lot by being commanded by RAF people. All the wing-leading that people like Don Blakeslee learnt flying with the RAF and with the Eagles, had been absorbed, and the intelligent ones were able to benefit a great deal from that association.

"With 249 Squadron we had the most extraordinary mix of people. In my time we had an absolute cross-section of the English speaking world. We had English, myself, Norman Lee, Daddo-Langois, and then we had the New Zealanders, Australians – an irreverent lot – Canadians, South Africans who were seconded to us for a while, Rhodesians, who were great, and then the Americans. And the Americans added something to it, I don't know exactly what it was. These Commonwealth people looked at them and thought, all these guys from the great USA . . . but the Americans responded to it all.

"Eventually they had what was termed the American Flight, in 126. It wasn't really like that but we had such an extraordinary set-up in Malta in the spring of 1942, when we had, relatively speaking, very few aeroplanes. These chaps were all Spitfire pilots, of course, although we still had a few Hurricanes. You should have seen their faces when they saw them. Thus, we had so few aeroplanes, we used to pool pilots from different squadrons and make up a composite flight, and the Yanks tended to keep together."

Of the second batch of pilots that Jumbo Gracie brought in off the "Wasp" in April, five were American. Reade Tilley, with 601 Squadron, had been with 121, of course, while in 603 Squadron there were Fred Almos and Doug Booth, also from 121. Two other Americans were not former Eagle;, they were Pilot Officer G Murray and Sergeant Walcott. Unfortunately, it seemed that Walcott had no intention of going to Malta, for no sooner did he take off than he headed south for North Africa, arriving over Algeria and force-landing his precious Spitfire south of the Atlas mountains. He later made contact with the American Consulate claiming to be a lost civilian pilot requiring repatriation to the States.

March and April were busy for most of the newly arrived Americans. Sunday McHan had arrived in a 95 Squadron Sunderland from Gibraltar on 21 February, being attached initially to the MNFU – Malta Night Fighter Unit. However, flying with Wing Commander W A J Satchell, Takali's Wing Leader, in a 126 Squadron Spitfire, he damaged a Ju88 on 15 March. In the same action was yet another non-Eagle American, Pilot Officer Howard Coffin from Los Angeles, who was one of the first Americans to see action over the island.

On the 26th, McHan's Spitfire was damaged in an attack on a group of four Ju88s but he got it back to Takali. In May he damaged a Macchi 202 fighter and continued actions until he was eventually shot down by an Me109 in early July, being burned and wounded when he baled out.

Doug Booth, who arrived from the "Wasp", flew with 603 and then 126. He gained two probable Me109s in fights in May and was shot up by another on the 15th and forced to crash land.

Harry Kelly damaged a Ju88 on 8 April, then destroyed one that same evening. He damaged a 109 on the 14th but was then himself shot down, baled out and rescued despite his parachute failing to open properly. He hit the sea which caused some bad bruising, but he survived.

Unhappily he was killed in action in July, the day before McHan was knocked out of the fighting.

Jimmie Peck was in the thick of all this action. During March and April he destroyed one Me109, probably another and damaged two 109s, one Ju87 and three Ju88s. Early in May the so-called American Flight was formed in 126 Squadron, which comprised Peck as flight commander, Don McLeod, Reade Tilley, Doug Booth, Fred Almos, Sunday McHan and Bruce Downs.

Peck continued his scoring in May, against fighters, with two 109s destroyed, a probable and a damaged, with an Italian Macchi also damaged. On 20 May came the announcement of his DFC. In early June he went back to Gibraltar to lead a batch of Spitfires back on HMS "Eagle". He bagged another Me109 in early July.

Two former Eagles were to end up as the most successful representatives of the three squadrons in England, Reade Tilley and John Lynch.

Reade Tilley was undoubtedly impressive. Not only was he well over 6ft. tall, he was incredibly good-looking. I remember walking down Piccadilly with him: almost every woman we passed turned to look at him. More importantly, Reade was also the perfect, charming gentleman, apparently innocently oblivious of his striking good looks.

Tilley had flown and fought with 121 Squadron in England, arriving on Malta in mid-April 1942 with 601 Squadron, having flown off the USS "Wasp". 601 had landed at Luqa, while the second squadron from the "Wasp" – 603 – landed at Takali.

In his first real action over the island on April 23, Reade's aircraft was shot up in a fight with Ju88s and Me109s, but five days later he got his own back, shooting down an Me109; then he joined the American Flight in 126 Squadron at the beginning of May. It was during May that he really got into his stride, destroying 109s on the 8th and 14th (two), plus a Macchi 202 on the 20th (which in fact was an Re2001). He also damaged three other 109s and a Stuka. That brought him the DFC.

In June he went back to Gibraltar, boarded the carrier "Eagle" and helped lead another force of Spitfires off the ship to the island, on June 9. Back in action during July, he shot down a 109 and a Ju88 on the 9th, and damaged two Mc202s and a 109. He finally left the island on August 17 with a score of 7 destroyed, one probable and 6 $\frac{1}{2}$ damaged. During his time over Malta, he had gained valuable experience both in air fighting and tactical thinking. In most air battles, although the "all-out" approach can bring a modicum of success it is the pilots who can size up tactical situations to the best advantage who are the most successful. Of his days on Malta, Reade Tilley recalls:

"There was a great deal of personal satisfaction achieved over Malta. The stalking; if some stupid clod comes by in front of you and you shoot – that's not very satisfying. But if you have to plan an action, with, say, bombers coming in from one direction, with their fighter escort working ahead of them and also behind them, the sun is to one side, so you have then to work out the best place to position oneself for the best advantage. Then, if leading a flight, perhaps divide the force, have some go fast to take care of the fighters while others go for the bombers, and if then everything works, you turn into the bombers, making a head-on attack, turning just at the right instant – you're well lined up, going straight at them. Then you fire, see pieces begin to fall off, parachutes dropping and so on, then this, I think was very, very, satisfying.

"Malta had its moments. One day we had a knock-down, drag-out, tooth and claw fight. There were some of our bombers that had gotten stuck on the airfield and the Germans were trying to destroy them. They put on a maximum effort all day long and the airfield was under constant attack. We were flying missions against the enemy as they were coming in and then we had to land while the field was still under attack! Then refuel and rearm the Spitfires while they were actually being strafed in the pens by the German fighters.

"I think the bravest thing I've ever seen was my ground crew on that day, up on the wing of my airplane, loading 20 mm shells and then with a form of bucket brigade of 5-gallon petrol cans of aviation spirit; passing them up, dumping the fuel in the tanks, all while under attack from the air. That took an awful lot of courage.

"When I finally landed, after about my third mission of the day, I saw this staff car drive up and out got Air Marshal Hugh Lloyd and Wing Commander Gracie, who were the top people there. They came running towards the plane, so I got real ready to be modest, because it had been a pretty rough day and only a few of us had got off so many times. So, there I was, ready to be modest, but they went right by me and up to the ground crew, started shaking hands with them and patting them on the back. I learnt a great lesson then; you don't have to be smart enough to be an Air Marshal to see real raw courage and recognise it."

Johnnie Lynch, despite his posting overseas in July 1942, didn't in fact reach the island until the end of October, flying in off the carrier "Furious", then serving with 249 Squadron. By then the main Malta battles were over, although the island continued to have some raids. Malta by this time, while still a thorn in the side of the Germans, was a little away from the main stream of the North African battle, which, following the Allied landings in Oran and Algiers, had moved west to Tunisia. Now Malta's fighters were taking an offensive role to attack the German's air transport system, or ranging over Sicily looking for the enemy. Sea convoys could no longer get through, so fuel and supplies were having to be taken to the battle zone by air.

Johnnie Lynch's first successes came on 11 December when he probably destroyed a Ju52 transport and shot down an escorting Me110 fighter. A few days later he helped to destroy three Ju88s. He became a flight commander and by March the following year, was CO of 249, so he was yet another former Eagle to command an RAF squadron.

During April 1943, Lynch was to score several successes, over German Ju52s, a Ju88 and an Italian Ca313, winning the DFC. A Ju52 he shot down on the 28th was reported as the 1,000th enemy aircraft shot down by Malta fighter pilots during the war. On May 10, he shot down two enemy floatplanes – a Cant Z.506B and a Fiat RS.14, then damaged an Me210 fighter. This brought him a bar to his DFC. In July he shot down a FW190, his final air combat victory. Soon afterwards he joined the USAAF, was promoted to Lieutenant Colonel, and continued the war in the Mediterranean with US forces.

* * *

Other Eagles who got to Malta were Leo Nomis, Arthur Roscoe and Nick Sinetos. Two of the former had seen action with 71 Squadron in England, Sinetos having been with 133. In fact, Sineto was actually taking off from the carrier "Furious" as the carrier "Eagle" was being torpedoed and sunk by a German U-boat.

"Chief" Nomis was with 229 Squadron on the island, having arrived in August 1942, being led in from the "Furious" by none other than Wing Commander Walter Churchill, former CO of 71. However, Leo didn't last long. Apparently, he was so keen to get into the action that he took off on an unauthorised flight to Sicily which incurred the wrath of the "brass". So on 14 September he found himself posted to Station HQ – "pending disposal". The "disposal" turned out to be a posting to the Western Desert, and the crack 92 Squadron RAF. Not so much a punishment as a reward!

"Art" Roscoe also arrived on Malta from the "Furious", with Nomis and Churchill, going to 229 Squadron. During September he managed to damage a couple of Macchi fighters, then destroyed an Me109 on 10 October during the big October Blitz. This was followed by two probable kills over 109s on the two successive days but on the 12th he was wounded in the shoulder and had to crash land on Takali. He received the DFC – the quickest recorded by an Eagle pilot, and had then to be evacuated back to England, via Gibraltar. If that sounded easy, it wasn't.

He was flown off the island in a Liberator along with 33 other passengers plus a crew of five. Ten of the passengers were civilians, including two children, the others RAF officers, some like Roscoe having been wounded on Malta, including the great George Beurling DSO DFC DFM, or others who were returning home for a rest.

The Lib arrived at Gibraltar in the midst of a violent storm, and low on fuel. The pilot overshot the runway and in attempting to go round again, stalled and went into the sea. The aircraft broke its back and sank. Eight of the civilians were killed or drowned, including the two children, while five of the pilots also lost their lives. Roscoe managed to escape from the smashed aircraft and despite his arm being in a sling, managed to get himself onto a wing, helped some of the others, and was finally rescued by boats from the shore.

* * *

Strangely enough there were a number of Americans on Malta other than those who had come via the Eagle Squadrons in England. One of the most successful was Claude Weaver, who flew with 185 Squadron. From Oklahoma City, Weaver had joined the RCAF, come to Britain and then been sent out to Malta as a Sergeant Pilot in 1942. He won the DFM after shooting down a number of enemy aircraft, including a Macchi fighter over Sicily, but he was then himself brought down and baled out. He evaded capture and later was able to return to Allied territory. Later, in England, he flew with a Canadian Spitfire Squadron, won a DFC but was killed in action in January, 1944.

Other Americans known to have been on the island were Pilot Officer Joe Lowry, Sergeants Vasseure Wynn and Joe Otis, flying with 603 Squadron, and Pilot Officer Ripley O Jones, from New York, who had previously been with 611 Squadron in England. Otis was killed not long after his arrival, trying to land a badly damaged Spitfire.

Lowry saw considerable action with 249 Squadron, while "Rip" Jones was killed with 126 Squadron in October 1942, diving head-on into a Ju88. He had 7 $\frac{1}{2}$ victories and had been raised to Flight Lieutenant.

Wynn, known as "Georgia" – he was from Dalton, in the State of Georgia – ended up a Major in the USAAF and was flying with the 4th Fighter Group and the former Eagles in England in late 1943, early 1944, being credited overall with six victories by the war's end. Of these he claimed 1 $\frac{1}{3}$ destroyed, two probables and two damaged over Malta, 2 $\frac{1}{2}$ destroyed with the 4th, plus two more on the ground.

Chapter 10

Eagles in the Middle and Far East

WHILE some Eagles had gone to Malta, a few had had postings to other RAF squadrons within Fighter Command. Others still had gone to other theatres of operation.

Among those still in Fighter Command, Nick Maranz had gone to No.1 Squadron RAF in mid-1941. He'd flown a few patrols and escort missions during June, flying Hurricanes, but had failed to return from a Circus Operation on the 21st to Desvres. He survived as a prisoner of war, going to the famous Stalug Luft III. He returned to California after the war.

Newton Anderson, former Chicago newspaper reporter, who had been with 71 Squadron, was the first to be given command of an RAF unit, taking over 222 Squadron in May 1942. He too was shot down on a Circus Operation to Hazebrouck the following month, but for him there was no happy ending. Newt has no known grave.

Another former Eagle of 133 Squadron, who would also rise to the dizzy heights of command with the RAF, was Jim Nelson. He did not transfer to the USAAF and in January 1943, commanded 124 Squadron for six months.

Undoubtedly for exactly the same reasons that some Eagle pilots volunteered for Malta, others requested overseas duty, in the hope of seeing a bit more action than they were seeing in Fighter Command.

Once Japan came into the war, there were also those who had begun to think the Eagles should ship out to the Far East, to get at the guys who had bombed Pearl Harbor! Four pilots in 71 Squadron certainly felt that a transfer to the Far East was the best plan, which is why Wally Tribkin, Mike Kelly, Eddie Miluck and Hal Marting put in a request to be sent to the Far East. Hopefully, they could then get themselves assigned to the Flying Tigers – the American mercenary pilots being recruited by the Chinese. However, by the time the postings came through, Singapore had fallen, and the four Eagles only got as far as the Middle East. Norman Chap in 121 Squadron was another who

volunteered for overseas duty and ended up in the Middle East with
the others, and so did Bob Mannix, of 71. Hal Marting and the others
had heard as early as February 1942 that the Eagle pilots would be
transferring to the US Army Air Corps, which is why none of the four
– Hal, Ed, Tribkin and Kelly – felt disloyal in leaving to get at the
Japs. Having decided, they put their requests into 11 Group HQ,
Uxbridge, had them approved and sailed for Durban at the beginning
of April 1942.

The four arrived in Durban, South Africa, on May 18, left again a
month later, finally arriving in Egypt via the Suez Canal, at the beginning
of July, going to the Kas Farite camp. Just over a week later they were
sent to No. 239 Fighter Wing, west of Cairo. On the last day of July
postings came through to front line squadrons, Marting going to 450
Squadron – mainly of Australians – while Tribkin and Miluck went
to 250 Squadron, both of which flew the American P.40 Kittyhawk
aircraft. Both Squadrons were based at LG (Landing Ground) 91, south
of Amriya and to the east of El Alamein.

Ed Miluck was very lucky on 21 August, flying as one of a section
of four Kittyhawks covering 112 Squadron in a recce of the central
battle area. They were jumped by three Me109s and Miluck and Flight
Lieutenant N Hancock both had their aircraft holed. Ed was lucky
because the 109 that ventilated him got in as close as 75 yards before
the pilot fired!

Wally Tribkin was in a fight just a month later, September 20. Again
the squadron was covering 112 when some 109s tried to bounce them.
Tribkin and another pilot went after two Messerschmitts. Wally chased
one right down on the deck but finally had to leave it, although he was
certain it had been damaged. Later a 109F crashed, its pilot captured.
As Wally was the only pilot to make a claim for a 109F he received
the credit. The German pilot turned out to be Feldwebel Krummlaut
from II/JG27. Tribkin, with two other pilots who'd fired fleetingly at
the 109 later attended the interrogation of the German NCO.

Miluck got his chance to score on the first day of October. A German
raid was reported on its way, the pilots of 250 scrambling to intercept
them near Lake Maghra, in company with the Shark-mouthed P.40s
of 112 Squadron. Ed Miluck recorded in his diary:

"'Stukas at 9 o'clock!' the radio spluttered and I began to sweat.
They were coming straight out of the west – eighteen of them, with

a dazzling sunset behind them. ... we climbed instinctively to get in position for attack.'Messerschmitts coming down!' The sweat really began to pour. It looked like a warm and sticky do.

"Half our flight started for the twenty Messerschmitts and soon it was a shambles up there and a massacre below – so damned many planes buzzing about, I kept wishing my 50-calibres were shotguns. The Stukas began jettisoning their bombs and that was a delightful sight.

They were directly over their own lines. I think I damaged an ME109 as he overshot me and climbed past my nose and I also managed to make a head-on attack into a Stuka. The bullets sparked against the motor but I had to turn away before I saw what happened, as tracers were streaking past my wings from behind.

"Returning to the shambles, I overtook a Stuka diving for the ground and helped him on his way with all I had left. It must have been enough; he hit with a hell of a thump. When I looked around again, five or six Jerries were burning in the air and the rest were limping off. The score: six Stukas destroyed, six probably destroyed, many more aircraft damaged, and we'd forced them to bomb their own troops.

The twelve kites of 250 Squadron RAF, by some miracle, were intact, without a single bullet hole in a fuselage."

The Stukas came from III/StG.3, escorted by the 109s of JG.53.

Marting didn't get off to a great start, having to go into the RAF Hospital in Cairo early in August. Then, on 17 September, while taking off, his aircraft caught in the slipstream of another P.40 and when his aircraft ground-looped, the undercarriage collapsed, but he was unhurt. A couple of days later they moved to LG.224, where he went down with a cold and a sore throat so was again grounded.

Hal Marting knew of his friend's success, as both squadrons were in close proximity – indeed, Hal stayed with Ed and Wally on the night of the 8/9th October, finding then that both units were due to make an attack on a German airfield the next morning. Much to his disgust, Hal did not fly on the first mission, which was the one on which all the fun was had.

Daba airfield was found to be under water, which is why the Allied fighters decided to work it over. Both sides were over-optimistic on their claims although the RAF afterwards referred to this day's work

Squadron Leader Pete Peterson was shot down over Dieppe but rescued. Seen here being collected by Oscar Coen (in front cockpit) in a Miles Magister, 19 August, 1942.

Spitfire Vc of 133 Squadron, aircraft usually flown by the CO, S/Ldr E H Thomas (MD-C, BM260).

Gus Daymond, Red McColpin and Jim Daley. Each had received the British
DFC flying with the Eagles. Seen here on the day the Eagle Squadrons became
the 4th Fighter Group USAAC.

Don Blakeslee's P.51 – WD-C. No frills, no kill marks, no name, but everyone
knew it was his plane.

Pilots of 121 Squadron at Rochford, June 1942. Ozzie Osborne shows the others how it's done. Left to right: "Snuffy" Smith, Jim Sanders, Don Young, Osborne, SL Williams, Pat Padgett, Gene Fetrow, Sgt Vance, Gunner Halsey, Frank Boyles, Sel Edner, Jim Daley, Jim Heppel, Barry Mahon.

Pilot Officer Joe Kelly, 71 Squadron. Note Eagle Squadron crest with British and American flags in the eagle's claws.

The Eagles become the 4th FG – Debden, September 1942.

In early 1943 the Spitfire made way for the big Republic P.47 Thunderbolt.

Wing Commander Myles Duke Woolley led the Eagles when they became the 4th FG. With him are Stan Anderson and Brewster Morgan.

Duke Woolley and Pete Peterson, on the occasion they both received the American DFC. Duke was the first RAF fighter pilot to be so honoured.

Art Roscoe, saw action with the Eagles, on Malta and later commanded a Spitfire Squadron in Sardinia.

Some of the 56th's pilots; Frank Gabreski (34), Bob Johnson (28), Bud Mahurin (21), Landry (5). On wing: Walter Cook (6) and Dave Schilling (33).

Lord Trenchard visits the newly formed 4th Fighter Group at Debden. l to r:
Ben Bennett, Tiger Booth, Jim Goodson, Vic France, Dick Brayley, Duane
Beeson, Lord Trenchard, Black-Snake Peterson, McGrattan, Mike Sobanski.

Lieutenant James A Goodson seated in his P.47, 1943.

as "The Daba Prang." That night Miluck was to record in his diary: "Due to recent heavy rains and resulting sticky mud, Kesselring got caught with all of his Me109s concentrated in a small area on several 'dromes. The entire RAF went into high gear at dawn and hasn't let up yet. Where the fighters and day medium bombers left off the night bombers took over. Every field in the El Daba area had been bombed, dive-bombed and strafed.

"On our first show, we just bombed. On the other three, we bombed and then strafed. On the second, we were attacked by several 109s and I squirted at one for a hell of a long time. When the next one came by, I remembered to turn on my gun switch and did much better!

"Wally tangled with a dozen Macchi 202s and Me109s but escaped with four cannon slugs in his cockpit and minor holes in fuselage and wing. When he crash-landed on the field, the poor kite sighed and collapsed.

"So did Wally."

Hal Marting and his squadron moved to LG.175 later in October. Hal flew a successful dive bombing sortie against a rail line and railway station – his 500 lb bomb scoring a hit on the rails. The next day he successfully bombed and strafed some trucks and tents on a German emergency airfield.

It was not all fun in the desert! As Ed Miluck recorded:

"Bloody flies! Not to mention the body lice, variously known as mobile dandruff or fuzz bunnies," or a couple of days later;

"A miserable morning with an ever-increasing wind stirring the damp dust and black sand clouds covering the horizon. Gulped a gritty breakfast of beans, bacon, bread and jam, plus a cup of tepid coffee."

* * *

By this stage of the war in the Middle East, there were other Americans in evidence, the USAAF having arrived to support the Desert Air Force Squadrons. One of these was the 57th Fighter Group, which comprised the 64th, 65th and 66th Fighter Squadrons, flying the latest P.40 variant, the 'F' – known as the Warhawk. This Group began operating with 239 Wing in October, especially on October 20, when yet another strafe of the Daba airfields took place. Hal Marting scored a victory on this day, as he recorded in his diary:

"Tuesday – LG.175. Took off at 0830 escorting 24 bombers. We were top cover and US 66 was leading as close escort. The bombing was beautiful, the best I've ever seen and three large fires were burning on the 'drome as we left. On the way back we were attacked by six or seven 109s and Macchi 202s. The first one seen, came up behind PO Winn and I turned into him and fired from about six hundred yards, closing down to four. My No.2, Prowse, saw my shots hit and the Macchi went into the ground about a mile behind. It was a lucky shot as three of my guns stopped and I only used 100 rounds altogether. FL Clark damaged three 109s and was badly shot up himself. Winn had one or two holes in his tail. We had no losses and mine was the only confirmed victory."

By now the mighty El Alamein offensive, planned by Field Marshal Bernard Montgomery and his staff, was about to begin. The see-saw battles that had raged across North Africa since 1940 would at last begin to turn in the Allies' favour, especially with the expected invasion of Oran and Morocco in Operation Torch, scheduled for November.

Hal Marting, Wally Tribkin and Ed Miluck knew that the offensive was about to begin, for rumours about it had been around for days. On 22 October, the squadrons were briefed for a major attack on the morning of the 23rd as the offensive, preceded by a tremendous artillery barrage, would begin soon after dark on the night of the 23rd. But by that time, Marting would be a prisoner.

He did in fact fly the early mission on that fateful morning, once again going for the El Daba airfields with bombs and machine-gun fire. The Wing formation approached the target from the sea, diving to 5,000 feet to drop their 500 lb bombs. It was some time later that he was able to complete his diary entry for that morning, but when he did so he recorded:

"Took off at 0700 to dive bomb El Daba 'dromes. Was leading top cover of six and we were top squadron. Bombed okay but in climb afterwards was left by the rest of top cover; not getting full power from engine. Attacked four Me109s which were climbing up between me and the formation. First one went down in flames. All my guns stopped when attacking the second so dived to the ground and started home alone. 109s didn't follow.

"Over the front lines was hit several times by light flak and last one, an explosive, hit the engine which quit after a few seconds. Belly landed in front of 62nd Italian Infantry, barely getting over their mine fields. Was taken prisoner by the Wops, questioned four times and given over to the Germans that evening who questioned me again and put me in transit prison camp at El Daba."

Hal never did get to put in his claim for the 109 he shot down. 109s from JG27 and JG53 had scrambled to intercept the P.40s, II/JG27 having Uffz. Jurgens crash-land after battle damage. Perhaps this was the pilot Hal had shot down. As well as 450 Squadron there were aircraft from 112, 250 and 3 RAAF. Some of the pilots saw a P.40 following a 109 down, and records noted that this P.40 pilot had not returned. That was Hal.

Hal's friend Ed Miluck noted in his diary that Marting was missing but then, when the barrage began, recorded:

"9.45 pm. Bags of excitement, everyone waiting for the fun to begin. What a bright, full moon tonight, by which to kill – or be killed.

"10.00 pm. Kee-rist! All hell has busted loose. Fifty miles to the west the horizon is filled with the man-made lightning of heavy artillery. As far back as this, the ground shakes and the tent walls quiver when the bombs fall."

Hal Marting might have missed the El Alamein show, although it is not recorded how much he witnessed from the German side of the lines, but he had not finished with the war. In fact he was eventually taken to Greece by the Germans, but from there he escaped and eventually turned up back in Cairo, via Turkey. For his escape and return, Marting received the British Military Cross.

* * *

Miluck and Tribkin kept up the Eagle offensive in 239 Wing during the days following the start of the El Alamein drive. Tribkin and another pilot took off before dawn on the last day of October and flew 20 miles behind the enemy lines on a freelance strafe. They went via Lake Maghra, up to the Gulf of Kanayis, turning before reaching the sea to fly south-east along a track with telegraph poles along one side – a sure sign of enemy activity. Sure enough they came across some enemy transport and went down on them. When they flew off they left one staff car and two trucks burning, with a gun carrier and a score of other vehicles damaged.

Miluck obviously had a great sense of humour, reading through his diary. An entry on this same last day of October records:

"In the excitement of an attack by Macchi 202s on a long range strafe at Sidi Barrani, miles behind the lines, the CO of 450 Squadron was shot down by his No.2. He force-landed OK, but is a hell of a long way from home. Guess I'll buy my No.2 drinks."

(The luckless CO – Squadron Leader J E A Williams DFC, from New Zealand, was taken prisoner and ended up in Stalag Luft III with Gordon Brettell. Williams, like Brettell, took part in the "Great Escape" and, also like Brettell, was among the 50 men shot by the Gestapo.)

Wally Tribkin got a Macchi on November 4, as Ed recorded:

"Wally shot down a Macchi 202 – one of five which attacked the squadron – but was later attacked by two more and had to do aileron rolls down to the deck before he could shake them off. What shook him was to find himself on his back at 400 feet, going down like a bomb. He dusted the deck, pulling out."

Norman Chap, who'd come out from 121 Squadron, was flying with 250 Squadron now. His last day on earth was November 7, 1942. That afternoon, 12 Kittyhawks had flown out to strafe the Sollum-Sidi Barrani road, but met four low flying Ju52 transport aircraft trying to sneak in from Crete. Three were shot down in flames, Norman Chap getting one of them. On their return flight they ran into a bunch of Stukas and Me109s and in the subsequent scrap, Chap went down in flames.

Wally Tribkin was out of the fighting temporarily, following a silly accident. A petrol can, too near a fire, exploded, sending burning fuel over his face, head and back. He was rushed to Cairo hospital bemoaning his fate, but at least he was not seriously injured.

Miluck was seeing all the well-known places of the desert war as the advance proceeded. All knew now that the Americans had landed at the other end of the Med, so the push forward was gaining momentum. During November he saw Gambut, Gazala, Tobruk, Benghazi ...

His sense of humour comes through again in a diary entry for December 19, when the CO asked for four volunteers to go on a special dive-bombing operation behind the lines:

"Somebody tripped me up as we fought to get out of the door, so I volunteered with the three pilots who fell on top of me. My kite had a big 500-pound bomb underneath when I got to it and I checked all the instruments carefully but couldn't find anything wrong, even on the third try. We climbed in and I over-primed the engine but it started anyway – even when climbing the damn thing wouldn't miss once, not even when I turned off the gas.

"By the time we reached the target I was sweating something awful. There was so much flak and black smoke that it was like diving into a thunder cloud. I dropped my bomb from 19,000 feet . . . in that way I could watch the others and give a good report to the CO if we hit anything!

"About this time, I noticed that someone was following me. I waved gaily and turned to watch him but when he started shooting at me I became worried and told my leader to call him off or I'd get sore. He called back and asked, "Where are you? . . ." – "In my plane, stupid!" I said. He then asked what my position was and I answered, "I'm sitting down. If I could get on my knees, I'd pray." I saw by this time he wasn't coming up after me so I dived for the formation, the fellow behind following me down and even bringing some of his friends.

"My leader saw us coming and yelled, "Look out – Messerschmitts!" but I laughed and said, "It's only me, silly boy," and waggled my wings. He wasn't much of a leader, because he began trying to follow the fellow behind me and they must have thought it was a game because they followed me everywhere I turned and did the same things I did. What a time we had before we got rid of them and turned for home!

"When we were over our own lines, the leader called and told me to slow down and get back into position. "You're my No.2," he said, "and are supposed to watch my tail." "Sure I am," I said, "but I'm doing it through my rear-view mirror. That way I can watch both our tails."

He said some nasty words, so to humor him I let him catch up; we were almost home anyway.

"When we landed and gave in our reports, the CO said to me, "Damned good show, Lieutenant. Clever of you to lead those planes into the trap.""

By Christmas, Miluck and Tribkin had reached the required 200 operational flying hours to end their tours. Both were very relieved to have come through this momentous time in the desert air war unscathed – if one discounts Wally's petrol burns! By the end of December, both men had been notified of their transfer to the US Army Air Corps and informed they were on their way back to the States. Miluck, who was later to change his first name to Michael, flew 110 combat missions in all, and back in the USA he became a fighter instructor, ending up a Major. He later saw service during the Korean War.

Wally Tribkin also returned Stateside. In 1944 he returned to Europe to fly operations with the 404th Group, 9th Air Force, but was killed in a jeep accident in Belgium that November. Sadder still, Hal Marting didn't see out 1943. He was flying a P.40 in South Carolina, on 20 September, taking some films to be developed, but crashed and was killed.

* * *

While these Eagle Kittyhawk pilots were seeing action, there were a couple more former Eagles in the thick of the desert war. Robert L Mannix, from Daytona Beach, Florida, having left 71 Squadron in September 1941, ended up in the Middle East, via the USA, and was posted to 127 Squadron RAF in mid-1942. 127 flew Hurricane 11b cannon-armed fighters, out of LG.92, within 244 Fighter Wing, RAF, a landing ground not far from where 250 and 450 Squadrons were operating.

Bob Mannix was in a fight with Me109s from JG27, after a scramble on July 8. In the subsequent dog fight, Mannix forced a 109 off his CO's tail, while the "Boss" – S/Ldr C O J Pegge – was shooting down another. Mannix became a flight commander.

On the 27th, 127 were flying top cover to fighters of No.1 SAAF Squadron on an anti-Stuka patrol over the Alamein Line, when they spotted some Ju87s but then saw more than a dozen Me109s above and in the sun. These – they were from JG27 – then dived making individual passes on the 127 Hurricanes, but Mannix managed to get behind one that was attacking another pilot, and opened fire. A five-second burst badly damaged the Messerschmitt, part of its tail being seen to be shot away, but the important thing was that the 109 broke off his attack on the other Hurricane.

August contined in this vein, then in early September, Bob may have shot down one of the top Luftwaffe aces in the desert. It was on the 6th that 127 Squadron flew top cover to Hurricanes of 7 USAAF and 274 RAF Squadrons flying an armed reconnaissance, looking for ground supply convoys. 127 were suddenly attacked by a dozen Me109Fs. Once more it was the pilots of JG27 who made the bounce, and they were successful.

Two pilots of 127 went down, plus five of the South Africans, one being the CO. 274 Squadron lost one. However, in the air battle, two 109s were shot down by 127 Squadron, Mannix getting one, Sergeant W J Malone a probable. JG27 lost two pilots in this action, one being Oberfeldwebel Gunther Steinhausen, who just moments before had shot down one of the Hurricanes as his 40th victory. Just short of his 25th birthday, Steinhausen had been with I/JG27 since the spring of 1941 and had become one of the great aces of the North African campaign. He was promoted to Leutnant after his death and the announcement of the award of the Knight's Cross was made in November. It is uncertain which of the RAF pilots shot him down, although it could well have been Bob Mannix, as his victory was confirmed, whereas Malone, given only a probable, may in fact have shot down the second German pilot, Hans Benthin, who was later taken prisoner.

At the end of October, Bob Mannix was given command of No. 33 RAF Squadron, which also had Hurricanes. With the El Alamein offensive now very much underway, 33 Squadron found themselves moving about quite a bit as they changed landing grounds as the advance moved forward. On November 2, Mannix led his Squadron for the first time, providing top cover to 238 RAF Squadron, getting into a brief scrap with some 109s who were escorting Stuka dive-bombers. The next day he flew a ground strafing operation, which was led by the Wing Leader, Wing Commander Johnnie Darwen.

Ed Miluck had noted in his diary about Bob getting 33 Squadron, but with reservations about the Hurricanes. Bob had apparently confided to Ed that you could always tell where a Hurricane had taken off because of the furrows in the sand where the pilot's heel had dragged!

By 18 November, Mannix was just about getting settled in to his new command and responsibilities. Operating now from LG.101, situated to the south east of Mersa Matruh, a first-light show had been scheduled for that morning, Bob Mannix leading off his men at 7 am. The targets would be found on the road south of Benghazi.

Heading in low along the road, the Hurricanes found four German trucks which they left shot-up, then, spotting a nearby landing ground, they attacked and shot up a Ju88, while another Junkers, seen in the air, was brought down by one of the sections. While thus engaged, the Hurricanes were seen by six Me109s – yet again from JG27. It was now 8.20 am. The 109s came screaming down on the Hurricanes, Mannix being caught, hit and shot down by Leutnant Willi Kientsch.

Kientsch would become one of the most successful pilots of II Gruppe, JG27, gaining 52 victories in the desert and later in the Mediterranean and in France. He would win the Knight's Cross and Oak Leaves, as CO of the Gruppe's 6th Staffel, before being killed in a flying accident in Belgium at the beginning of 1944. For the Eagles, however, they had lost yet another of their number and the RAF a valuable squadron commander.

* * *

Leo "Chief" Nomis had been posted off Malta for his unauthorised flight over Sicily. As mentioned in the previous chapter, his "punishment" had been a posting to the crack 92 Squadron of the Desert Air Force. He joined them in mid-November 1942, with the Alamein push in full flood.

He began operations with this famous Spitfire Squadron, which had been through Dunkirk and the Battle of Britain, and then joined the Biggin Hill Wing in 1941, prior to coming out to North Africa. One of its star fighter pilots at this time was Neville Duke, who would emerge as one of the highest scoring fighter pilots of the desert war. Nomis's CO at this time was Squadron Leader J M Morgan.

Leo was to bag two enemy fighters on successive days in January, 1943 – the 7th and 8th. On the first date, the squadron had moved forward to Hamraiet landing ground to do Readiness, only to have themselves bombed three times during the day by Me109 fighter bombers. During one of these attacks, 92 got themselves into the air and engaged the Jabo 109s. They found the Messerschmitt pilots – they were of II/JG77 – were prepared to stay and fight, which many 109 pilots had been reluctant to do in recent weeks. The CO claimed one shot down and Nomis another, with a third damaged, but 92 lost two Spitfires as well, although both pilots survived.

The next evening, after another day of Jabo attacks on Hamraiet and the battle front, Nomis was one of five pilots scrambled, and vectored towards Tamet. They found a lone Me109, which Nomis engaged and after a tough fight, he shot it into the sea.

Not long afterwards, like Miluck and Tribkin, Leo Nomis was informed of his transfer to the USAAF and left for Cairo and the States. By one of those strange twists of fate, Nomis was later to fight with the Israeli Air Force against the Egyptians – flying a Messerschmitt 109!

* * *

Finally there were the couple of Eagles who managed to get right out to the Far East, to fight the American's personal enemies – the Japanese. One was John "Red" Campbell, another, Don Gaffene, of Los Angeles, both from 121 Squadron. Sinus problems caused Campbell to try for a warmer climate, and both men found themselves transferred to 258 RAF Squadron, where they met up with Art Donahue, the fourth US pilot to be in the original 71 Squadron although he left soon afterwards.

With the war in Russia not going well for Stalin's troops, Britain had contemplated giving some air suport to them in the fall of 1941, and two or three fighter squadrons had been ear-marked for the southern area of that theatre of operations. However, en-route by sea, via Freetown, the Japanese war had begun. 258 was one of the en-route squadrons re-assigned to the Far East, getting off at Freetown, then flying overland to Khartoum. But by then, only Campbell and Donahue were on their way, for Don Geffene had been interned in "neutral" Spain.

While ashore at Gibraltar, the pilots had flown some patrols around the Spanish coast, in case they could spot long range Focke Wulf Kondor bombers that liked to attack Allied convoys. On one sortie, Geffene's engine failed, causing him to make a forced landing in Spanish Tangiers. Campbell had caused a bit of an international incident by strafing the downed fighter to make certain any "friends" of Spain wouldn't get hold of it.

Campbell and Donahue eventually reached Singapore by a very circuitous route, on 29 January 1942. Just over two weeks later, Singapore fell, but Campbell had shot down a couple of Jap aircraft, and so had

Donahue. The remnants of the RAF fought their way out via Java and Sumatra, and those who were not killed or captured eventually got back to India. Red Campbell, after shooting down a Zero over Palembang, was himself shot down but baled out. After evading capture for some days he was eventually taken prisoner, thereby starting three and a half years as a guest of the Japs. He was the only Eagle pilot so "honoured".

Meantime, Don Geffene had escaped from his internment but too late to catch up the Squadron. When he did finally report in, the remnants had reformed at Colombo. Don then went to 30 Squadron, also based in Colombo, at Ratmalana.

It was at the time the Japanese were still free-ranging across the Indian Ocean and Colombo was the natural defensive position for the eastern coast of India. The Japanese made an attack on the island on Easter Sunday (the 5th). Despite some erroneous claims by the RAF defenders, the Japanese Navy planes made a successful raid and shot down a number of the defenders. Don Geffene was one of the Hurricane fighter pilots caught by the Navy Zero fighters and killed.

Chapter 11

Personalities and the P.47

BY THE summer of 1943, the British people knew only too well that the Yanks were "over here". The mighty 8th US Air Force was now pouring into the country by sea and by air, as America's tremendous military and industrial machine went into full gear.

The size of the 8th Air Force was beyond the imagination of many. It was often an awe-inspiring sight to see wave after wave of four-engined B.17 and B.24 bombers, forming up over East Anglia, Lincolnshire or Cambridgeshire, before turning finally towards the North Sea or the Channel to hit targets in France, Germany or the Low Countries. Still a major force and influence was the 4th Fighter Group at Debden.

Don Blakeslee was still Deputy Commander to Edward Anderson, and in August of that year, the three squadrons were commanded by Oscar Coen, Gil Halsey and Jim duFour. It is a fact that, in the main, former Eagle pilots were to command two of the three squadrons until the spring of 1944.

There is no doubt that the experience the former Eagles brought to the Group made a tremendous difference to the performance of the younger pilots arriving from the US. For instance, on 28 July, Gil Halsey had led a Ramrod to Germany for the first time, the Thunderbolts range extended by the use of 200 gallon belly drop tanks. The mission was as withdrawal cover/escort for bombers returning from Emmerich.

Near Leerdam, the Group spotted a group of B.17s under attack from enemy fighter. Halsey sent 335 Squadron over and in front of the bombers, the 334th to starboard, while 336 went to port. There must have been over 500 German fighters, but the Group, in a massive, whirling dog-fight, claimed three Me109s and six FW190s, losing just one pilot, who baled out. Duane Beeson got his third that day and other ex-Eagles – Leon Blanding, Carl Miley, Lee Gover and Frank Boyles each got one.

Unhappily, former Eagles still operating with the 4th would be amongst the continuing casualties. Henry Ayres was the pilot who baled out that day – ex-133 – to go into captivity.

I walked into the bar of the Officers' Mess at Debden later that day, after returning from a gruelling 8$\frac{1}{2}$ hour mission. My only interest was in quenching my thirst and relaxing, but even as I downed my drink, I became aware of the grin.

I put down my empty glass and saw that the grin belonged to a small, blonde character who seemed to be welcoming me to the bar as if he owned it. Considering that he was obviously a new arrival and I had been flying in the Squadron for a year, I felt this was a bit of a cheek. What's more, I wore the two silver bars of a Captain, so I gave him a rather cold stare.

I thought this would put him in his place, but he took it as an invitation and bounced up to me with an outstretched hand.

"Swede Carlson, Sir, from Red Bluff, California!"

I looked at the grinning, impertinent face and considered how to put him in his place, but the broad grin and his obvious delight at being there won me over.

"Welcome to the 4th Fighter Group, Lieutenant."

"It's a great honour to be here, sir!"

The next day, I took him up to check him out. I told him to stay on my wing and then set out to give him the roughest ride I could. It was standard procedure. No new pilot had even been able to stay with me before, but after a series of aerobatics and wild manoeuvres, the Swede was still exactly two feet off my wing, where he had been all along.

As soon as I landed, I checked his records and found that he had over 1000 hours of flying time, mostly as an instructor, which was much more than most pilots in the squadron. He had consistently made a nuisance of himself with every officer he had come across, regardless of rank, in order to get into combat; but at the age of 24, he was considered too old and, what was more, he was a very good instructor! But Swede Carlson was a very determined man, as I was soon to discover. He not only got into combat, but he got into his choice of Group, the famous 4th.

On this first mission, he showed himself to be not only a first-class pilot but an excellent wingman. We were bounced by about 20 Me-

109s. Carlson didn't shoot any down, but he protected the tail of his No.1 to enable him to shoot one down.

"Good show!" I said after we landed.

"Oh, it was great! Everything I've always wanted – almost!"

"Almost? What was missing?"

"What I'd really like is to fly on your wing."

"Well, it's time for my wingman to move up to a No. 1 position, so if you want to be my wingman, you've got it!"

I didn't realise at the time that such a casual decision was to save my life three days later.

It was one of those days when all hell broke loose. We picked up the bombers just as they were making their target run. At the same time, we saw the black specks out in front of them, about 100 FW 190s preparing to make a head-on attack. There was nothing for it but to try to break them up before they got to the bombers. They hit a bomber or two, but we were able to deflect most of them from their target.

They swerved round and down to come up on the last group of bombers from below. We followed and were soon engaged in violent dog-fights right down to the ground. I was lining up on a 190, watching flames licking his side when I heard "Blue Leader, break left!"

Almost at the same time, I heard the crump as I was hit.

I whipped into a tight turn and saw the 190 behind me. I tightened my turn, but started to stall and with a damaged plane I was in no position to out-turn him. Then I heard the Swede:

"OK Goody – I've got him!"

My attacker was suddenly hit by a hail of bullets and a P-47 pulled up beside me. In it was the Swede, grinning from ear to ear and giving the thumbs-up sign.

My plane had been hit in the wing and tail so that, although the engine was still running, the airspeed was well below normal. I told the Swede to head for home – I knew he would be low on fuel and might not make it if he stayed with me.

"I reckon I'll stick around for a while" was the only response I got.

He nursed me back across the Channel and we landed on the South Coast with fuel gauges on zero.

When he was finally shot down strafing an aerodrome early in 1945, the squadron thought he was gone until they heard him on the radio directing their attack. Pierce McKennon asked, "Where are you?"

"I'm on the ground, Mac, but my radio's still working!"
The mass of Germans converging on Carlson's plane must have been furious. Not only had their airfield been destroyed but the last plane shot down whilst the Swede was directing operations was that of Hauptmann Hoffmann, their CO. Maybe one reason he didn't get torn limb from limb is that I'm quite sure that when they got to him, the Swede would be grinning from ear to ear.

In August, Don Blakeslee began to lead the Group regularly, although still only Deputy CO. Indeed, when Colonel Anderson left on 20 August, to become CO of the 78th Fighter Wing, Chesley Peterson returned to head the 4th. It was obviously the right decision, and Peterson had as good a reputation with the 4th's pilots as did Blakeslee, but it was little reward for Don at this stage, especially as just four days earlier, Don had led a successful Ramrod close escort mission to Paris.

On that show, the Group had made rendezvous with the B17s at 28,000 feet, coming in behind the bombers as enemy fighters made a head-on attack against the Forts. 334 made the first bounce, and then everyone joined in. The running fight lasted for forty minutes, from 9.20 to 10 am, beginning before they reached Paris, then over the city, and continuing on the way back to the French coast. The eventual score would come to 18 German aircraft destroyed for the loss of just one – Joe Matthews – another former Eagle with 121 Squadron. Yet he evaded capture and got back before the end of the year, claiming a victory too. It was not until Joe got back to put in his claim that the Group realised that on that August day they had equalled the record for kills in a single mission with their arch rivals, the 56th Fighter Group, who operated out of Halesworth, Suffolk, commanded by the great Hub Zemke.

Among the scorers on the Paris show was Jim Clark, now a flight commander in the 334th, who got two FW190s, Roy Evans (an Me109) – formerly of 121 Squadron, who had just taken command of the 335th, Ray Care (a 190 for his third kill) who would later command the 334th, Dufour, CO of the 336th, and former Eagles, Howard Hively, (a 190) Jim Happel, (a 190) Snuffy Smith, (a 190) Don Young, (1$^{1}/_{2}$ 190s), Frank Fink, ($^{1}/_{2}$ 190), Joe Matthews, (a 190), and one Jim Goodson (two 190s).

James A Clark, from Westbury, Long Island, New York, was tall, handsome, with blue eyes, and came from a wealthy family background. Flying was in his blood for his uncle, Tom Hitchcock, had been in the Lafayette Flying Corps in WW1 and scored two victories before being shot down and captured in 1918. Tommy Hitchcock later escaped and got into Switzerland. After that war, Tommy became an international sportsman and polo player. During WW2, he was in England with the US Airforce, often visiting Jim at Debden, but was then killed flying a Mustang, the day before Jim was married. Jim himself was a very fair man, perhaps too fair, for he once refused promotion to captain and also thought a DFC award had not been earned! He had an old head on young shoulders, being just 20 when he joined 71 Squadron in June 1942. But that didn't stop him scoring a dozen air and five ground victories, as well as being Deputy Group CO in 1944.

Howard W Hively – known to everyone as "The Deacon", came from Ohio and Oklahoma, joining 71 Squadron in July 1942. He had been studying for an engineering degree before the war. His victory on the 16th was his one and only for 1943, but he was to score heavily in the following year, to end up with 12 air and three ground kills. He was also lucky to survive, for on one occasion he went down into the Channel but was rescued by an RAF Air Sea Rescue Walrus.

* * *

There was a lull in the 4th's scoring after the huge success on the Paris mission, but the Group had other things on its mind, for one thing, the arrival of a new fighter – the P.51 Mustang. Don Blakeslee flew in the first one on 25 September, 1943, Oscar Coen and Jim Clark immediately giving it the once over in the air. It seemed to them a great little fighter.

Meanwhile the Thunderbolt remained their aircraft, and with it they broke back into the scoring on October 8, on a Blakeslee-led Ramrod to Germany. Of the six German fighters shot down that day, while effectively protecting the B.17s on their way back from Bremen, Duane Beeson got two Messerschmitts to bring his score to five, while Roy Evans got a 190 to equal Duane's score. These two were the first 4th Group aces of the war. Also scoring on this mission was Lieutenant "Kid" Hofer.

Ralph Kid Hofer was from Salem, Montana, and was known as "Kid" not only because this was his middle name, but he looked young too. He was a fighter and looked it. A "fighter" in fact he was, having won a boxing title in 1940 in the light-heavyweight class of the Golden Gloves Tournament. He also played football in a Chicago League team, and was often seen on the airfield at Debden in his old football jersey – Number 78. Although not an Eagle pilot, he, like several other high scoring pilots of the 4th, owed much of their success to the tuition and experience imparted to them by those who had been brought up in the school of hard combat, classes of 1941–42, with the RAF.

He joined the RCAF almost by accident. Having taken a trip to Detroit he thought he'd pop across the Canadian border for a look at Ontario. At the border the immigration officer said he supposed Ralph wanted the RCAF recruiting office like so many before him, then pointed out the building across the street. Hofer had never been near an aeroplane in his life and until that moment had never even thought about them. Before he really knew what was happening, he had gone into the building, signed up and was soon on his way to flight training. It had been as simple and as easy as that.

When he eventually found himself in England and with the famous 4th Fighter Group, he was in his element. The simple way of doing things seemed the best, even down to scoring his first victory, on this October day – for it was his first combat mission! First kill on a first mission was not unheard of, but it was rare. Soon a number of crosses began to appear on his aeroplane, which was also adorned with a flying jackass in boxing gloves with the words "Salem Representative" on it.

The "Kid" could also be a bit rebellious when he wanted to be. Not long after his first victory, he took a trip to London, only to be picked up by Military Police for not wearing his Lieutenant's "bars" on his trench coat, and then failing to have on him his identity card. But, as was later recorded, "As usual, he managed to talk his way out of it!"

On one occasion in his tour with the 4th, he was trailing a German fighter, pumping shells into it, when his fuselage fuel tank ran dry, causing him to lose speed. Switching over to his wing tanks he tried to catch up with his quarry, only to see another Mustang slide in and take up the attack. Hofer immediately yelled for the pilot to "Break!", which he did, thinking someone was warning him of a German on his tail. Hofer then nipped in and finished off what, after all, had been his victim in the first place!

One evening a P-47 landed with a large Alsatian dog and no sign of anyone else. The plane dived ahead of us, pulled up into a perfect loop and ended up behind us. "Duke's getting real good at flying!" said Hofer as we drove back to dispersal.

"Any fool can do a loop," I said, "but how is he on instruments?"

"Great!" said the Kid.

After we dropped them off, Ralph Saunders, a new boy, could restrain his curiosity no longer.

"Sir, did he have that dog on his lap?"

"Yeah," I said sourly.

"That's fantastic!" Then, sensing my mood, "But I guess you dis-approve."

"To get enough room, he leaves his parachute off," I said.

That was the Kid. Another pilot to get his first kill that fall was John Godfrey – a Messerschmitt 109F – on a Ramrod to Germany, led by Selden Edner (now CO of the 336th) on 1 December. It was the Group's only victory that day.

John Trevor Godfrey, from Rhode Island, was 21 when he joined the Group. He wore RAF wings on his right breast. He had not been in any of the Eagle Squadrons, but he'd been trained by the RCAF and RAF. He had joined the RCAF after running away from home – and a wealthy family – to join the Montreal Regiment, but his father brought him home. However, the young Godfrey still wanted action and adventure and not the college education his parents had planned for him. Finally and reluctantly they agreed that he could apply for the RCAF but if he failed to get in, he promised to give up his ideas and go to college. Fortunately for the USAAF, but not for the Luftwaffe, he was accepted.

After training in Canada, he came to England, in the knowledge that his brother Reggie had been killed when his ship had been torpedoed by a U-boat on his way to England as an aircraft technician. Completing his training with the RAF, he then transferred to the USAAF, dropped his RAF sergeant rank for that of a US Second Lieutenant and reported to the 4th on 22 September, 1943. On his P.47 he had painted – "Reggie's Reply"

* * *

Just a week or so away from Christmas 1943, my old pal whom I'd met on my first day with 133 Squadron, Don Gentile, got his first victory since his Eagle days. He, in company with Norley and Vermont Garrison, found a lone Ju88, when returning from a Ramrod support mission to Bremen, which they shot down. All three men were to have distinguished flying careers, as did Willard Millikan who got a 109 on 20 December for his second victory.

Donald Salvadore Gentile, from Piqua, was 21 when he joined 133 Squadron in June 1942. He loved speed, had a great liking for fast cars, and then took flying lessons, which eventually led him to have his own Aero-Sport biplane which his father bought for him. He began to terrorise the neighbourhood with his low flying once he'd got his licence, but he was unable to gain entry into the Air Force because of his low college grades. Frustrated, he persuaded his parents, who were Italian immigrants, to let him volunteer for the RAF.

He sailed to England on the same boat as Jim Clark, where both became instructors for a time, but Gentile quickly tired of that and by more low flying got himself posted, which is what he planned, ending up with the Eagles. He was just getting into his operational stride when 133 were lost, and, but for the grace of God, he might well have been lost too. He was down as spare pilot and wishing someone would drop out on take-off.

He was good-looking, with a Clark Gable moustache, swarthy complexion and a winning smile. He won a lot of ladies over and scored a lot of victories – over the Luftwaffe! Don Gentile's startling good-looks were misleading. His handsome features, black wavy hair, dapper moustache, and tall athletic build gave one the impression of a suave, debonair playboy.

Nothing could have been further from the truth. Most of the other pilots in the Group were hard-drinking, fun-loving, hell raisers. True, there was an unwritten, unbroken rule that nothing was ever allowed to impair combat readiness or efficiency but off duty it was "wine, women and song", with never a thought for the morrow. If our lives were to be short, they would at least be merry ones!

Not Gentile! He came from a small town in Ohio and he had the values of a small town boy. His parents had known hard times both in Italy and in the States and the lessons they had learned, they had passed on to their son. While most of the other pilots ended up broke by the end of the month, having spent everything on gambling, drinking or just having a good time, most of Gentile's pay was regularly sent home to be banked for him by his parents. By the time he returned home he is said to have had close to $8,000 in his account. The flesh-pots of London were of little interest to him, so he spent most of his time on the base. I saw him take an occasional drink and even politely, if awkwardly, escort the occasional girl whom his buddy, John Godfrey had found for him, but his concentration never deviated from his main concern: to prove himself!

The dedication was undoubtedly influenced by his Italian immigrant background; but also by his strong Roman Catholic convictions. He never missed Mass if he could help it. I'm sure he saw his religion as part of his constant goal.

This was never more strongly demonstrated to me than one morning as I was driving to dispersal and picked Don up as he was coming out of the Chapel. By this time, his determined aggression had already resulted in his building up quite a score of victories.

"Do you go to the Chapel before every mission?" I enquired.

"Sure," he replied.

"You pray to God to protect you?"

"No, no; I pray for Him to give me another kill." was his reply. "I asked him for two today. Don't you ever pray for a kill, Goody?"

"No," I said. "I leave it up to Him. After all, the German and his family are probably asking God to protect him". Don looked at me in amazement.

"But God would never do that!" he said.

It was obvious that he was convinced that the Almighty was just as anxious to see Don build up his score as Don himself. He may have been right – Don shot down two that day!

Don Gentile reached ace status on January 14, on a freelance sortie led by Selden Edner – now a Lieutenant Colonel and deputy Group Leader – over France. The Group got eight on that mission, Gentile going head-on into two FW190s, forcing them to break away. He then turned and shot them both down. However, he then got into trouble with another 190 which seemed to be piloted by one of the German "experten", for he had a real hard time trying to shake the German.

Even his calls for help could not be answered, for although some pilots asked where he was, Don was too busy and too rattled to answer. However, the 190 pilot, whoever he might have been, ran out of ammo, as did Don, so both broke off. After that, Don felt he had been up against the best and could now cope with anything the Luftwaffe threw at him.

It was when Gentile tied up with Johnny Godfrey that he came into his own. Of course, the timing was right too. By then the 8th Air Force had enough fighters to give strong protection to the bombers all the way to the targets and back. The German fighters had continued their attacks, of course, but by now they were always outnumbered. We also noticed that the general quality of their pilots seemed to be suffering as they brought in less experienced pilots to replace their losses.

Louis H Norley was known as 'Red Dog' Norley. None of us knew his Christian names, and if we had, we wouldn't have used them. 'Red Dog' was what we called him and Red Dog was what he was. It wasn't just his red hair, it was that his whole rough, tough, happy, hard living, hard drinking, hard fighting, down-to-earth, open character, was summed up in the name Red-Dog.

He came from Conrad, Montana. In the air, he was as aggressive and tough as he was on the ground. He rapidly became a flight leader, and then squadron commander of 335 Squadron, and later still, the 334th.

Under most Group Commanding Officers, this might never have happened. Not only did he lack the social graces, he had no university education. But we were blessed with the greatness of Don Blakeslee, It was true that Don had no more higher education than Red-Dog, but that wouldn't have influenced him. I'm sure that Blakeslee neither knew nor cared about the level of education of his officers. What he immediately recognised was their strength of character – or lack of it.

I don't believe I have ever met a stronger character than Blakeslee himself, so that probably made it easier for him to recognise the same qualities in others. In the case of Red-Dog, this recognition coincided with a warm friendship, but Blakeslee was just as capable of promoting an officer with whom he was not particularly close. He was simply able to keep his friendship quite separate from his appreciation of the man.

Like so many others who had survived hundreds of combat missions,

Red-Dog was killed on a training sortie, having been shipped back to the States as instructor. By then, he had over 550 combat flying hours and had also seen some service in Korea. He was also a Lieutenant Colonel when he was killed, on 1 August, 1967, at Oakland, California. He had scored a dozen combat victories and wore the ribbons of the DFC and clusters and Air Medal with 13 oak leaf clusters under his silver wings.

Another great character was Willard Millikan. It would he hard to imagine a more underprivileged childhood than "Millie's". His father and mother were trying to eke out an existence in the parched desert of Iowa during the worst of the Drought and the deepest depression the State had ever known.

A desperate situation was made worse by the character of Millie's own father. It may have been the years of poverty and frustration that drove him to it, but any money his father was able to scrape together went on drink. It therefore fell to Millie to support the family, working during school holidays and after school itself. As if that wasn't bad enough, not only did Millie's father not help, he added enormously to the problems. He was one of those men who became violent and belligerent when drunk. He would attack his wife and when Millie went to her defence, the father would turn on him too.

The father, by all accounts, was a powerful man and at first both Millie and his mother took terrible beatings. The young Millikan, however, met this problem with what became his usual courage and determination. He started to build up his young body through physical exercise and sport. Gradually he became strong enough to hold his own in his own home, and at the same time, became the local hero as an outstanding baseball player.

Normally, one would have expected Millie's scholastic activities to suffer under the pressure of his problems at home, but one would have been wrong. He worked as hard at his studies as he worked at everything else giving priority to his work at school and for a very good reason; he had an over-riding ambition.

It was typical of Millie that his sights should be set high but, even today, his goal would be considered unrealistic. In those days, for an impoverished Iowa farm boy, it was simply ridiculous. Not, however, for Millie; he was convinced that he could, and would, become a pilot in the United States Air Force.

Apart from the more obvious obstacles, no candidate was even considered unless he had a university degree. Millie started off bravely enough, but the burden of supporting his family was enough even for his broad shoulders. All he could manage in preparation was an occasional flying lesson, but they probably helped when the big opportunity opened up. When the war started in Europe, and the Commonwealth Air Training Scheme started in Canada, it was the answer to all Millie's problems and ambitions.

At least it should have been, but Millie always got things the hard way. I think he tried too hard. It meant so much to him that he could never relax; and sometimes in flying you have to relax. As usual, he persevered and became one of the few that graduated as fighter pilots. By the time he got to England and completed his Operational Training, the US was in the war and the Eagle Squadrons had become the 4th Fighter Group. But he got his RAF Wings and was RAF trained.

When he arrived at Debden, he was assigned to my Squadron – 336. He did well. Between September 1943 and May 1944 he shot down 13 enemy planes plus two more destroyed on the ground. He was even acting CO when I had to go to Italy for some weeks, and while I was away, he was shot down and taken prisoner. But before that, he had made the team, made the war, and made the grade.

Vermont Garrison, from Kentucky, ended the war with eight air and one ground kills to his name, so was one of the 4th's aces. The trouble, I guess, was that he ended the war in a POW camp in Germany. He was also in the 336th, and was lost to flak on March 3, 1944, minutes after getting his last two air kills. He might have been a higher scorer if his luck had held, but he had to wait for the next war to add to his tally.

That was in Korea. Flying with the 4th Fighter Wing, in an F.86 Sabre, he shot down 10 Russian Mig 15s to become an ace of the 4th in both conflicts. Not bad for an old guy of 37.

* * *

The air war over Germany, fought by the US 8th Air Force Bomber and Fighter Commands, supported by RAF Fighter Command, became a deadly affair towards the end of 1943 and early 1944. Vast armadas of B.17 and B.24 bombers would, almost daily, head across the North

Sea to pound German industrial targets, escorted by US and RAF fighters.

The problem in the early days was that the fighters did not have the range to escort the bombers all the way to the more distant German targets. In any event, the American bomber force had been convinced that their heavily armed bombers could fight their way through to any target with the minimum loss. The RAF had thought that way too in 1939–40 and soon been taught that life wasn't that easy or simple and went over to night bombing. The Americans, however, were brought up with their daylight doctrine, in order to use to advantage their Norden bomb-sights for precision bombing, so fought to improve their fighter performance in order that the bombers could have protection to German targets and back.

The P.47's range had been extended by the use of externally hung drop tanks which took them a fair way in, and relays of fighters could take them to Germany and get them back, unless the penetration was just that bit too far. RAF Spitfires too could, with long range tanks, take them or help bring them back from the German border, so both fighter forces helped each other in this way.

But once out of range of the P.47, the German fighters had the bombers to themselves and it was then that a real knock-down fight between the bomber's air gunners and the Luftwaffe pilots of the German Homeland began.

The bomber Groups from the various Air Divisions flew in boxes, each bomber helping to protect its box. There were high squadrons, middle squadrons and low squadrons. With anything up to 13 guns on a B.17, to attack a box of, say, 20 bombers the Luftwaffe pilot had a fair proportion of the 260 .50 calibre guns firing at him. It took a certain bravery on the part of the German pilots to press home an attack against that fire-power, but they did.

If they could plan it they would try to make head-on attacks, where the Forts and Libs were more vulnerable. Most of the guns were designed to fire rearward. A frontal attack could knock out engines and, if on target, kill or put out of action both the bomber's pilots. Pilot armour was at their back, not in front. Pilots quickly took to wearing protective body armour – bullet-proof vests, although a direct hit by a 20 mm shell didn't "bounce off" too many vests!!

But it still took skill and daring to go head-on into a formation of

B.17s, where the closing speed was terrific. It took just seconds to bore in, aim, fire and half roll to break away and down, or break upwards. In either direction the fighter would then come under fire from the rear-firing gunners, but he was a fast and fleeting target. By late 1943, Boeing was bringing out the B.17G – which had twin .50s in a chin turret designed to help combat the head-on attacks.

When the B-17G started to come on stream, General Tooey Spaatz sent one over so that we could practise formating on it and adjust our speeds if necessary. Several of us checked out on it so that we could get an idea of what it could and couldn't do.

In the midst of this programme, we got back late from a mission one day and had an enormous problem: we all had dates in London that night and we had missed the only train that would get us there in time.

"No problem!" I decided. "We all pile into the B-17, fly down to an airfield near London and take the Underground!"

Off we went. Then we ran into another problem. Every airfield we called up for permission to land said "Sorry – we can't take a thing that size in here!" Meantime the weather was worsening and the cloud thickening fast. Then through a gap in the clouds, I suddenly saw a runway beneath us. I felt that would do nicely, and I couldn't call them because I didn't know what airfield it was – it was a new one – so I just went in and landed.

I taxied up to the control tower, we all piled out and asked a startled little man who had appeared, "How do we get to London?"

"There's a truck over there just going – if you run, you'll catch it!"

We piled into the truck, got to London and arranged to meet next morning at the Crackers Club.

Next day, after a few cups of coffee, someone suggested, "Shouldn't we be getting back?"

"I guess so. Where was that airfield?"

Nobody knew.

There was nothing for it but to embark on a programme of somewhat embarrassing telephone calls to all the RAF and USAAF bases in the London area.

"This is Major Goodson, USAAF. I'm sorry to bother you, but we have misplaced one of our airplanes. It has four engines and the USAAF star on the wings and fuselage. Do you have it, by any chance?"

The answer we received, particularly from the RAF, was usually unprintable.

The reaction of General Spaatz when I finally plucked up courage to phone him was calm but foreboding.

"Just lemme get this straight, Major. This B-17G is the largest plane in the world. There is only one in the UK – and you've LOST IT?"

* * *

When the bombers were escorted, the US fighters had to protect their charges against all manner of attacks and ploys. It was all too easy to get carried away in a fight and be pulled away from the bombers and go after Focke-Wulfs or Messerschmitts. It took strong leadership to ensure that pilots, especially the inexperienced guys, didn't go beetling off all over the sky, and leave the bombers unprotected. It also took men like Don Blakeslee and Hub Zemke to keep control of the battle and bring their fighter pilots into the right positions to protect their charges. They also sent fighters ahead to try and break up the German fighters massing for a head-on pass. One advantage the Germans had was that, with the time the bombers were over Germany, quite a number of fighters could engage, land, rearm and refuel and be back up to height again when the bombers were on the return trip. But the defending fighters did much to protect them.

In any event, the bomber crews still took terrible beatings. One had only to see them coming back to base, with engines knocked out, perhaps trailing smoke, a wheel hanging down, huge holes blasted through wings, fuselages or tails, to guess at the battles they'd fought. Rarely did a red flare not arc up from at least one bomber as it came into the airfield circuit, denoting wounded on board and the need for immediate medical aid.

The Luftwaffe not only used cannon and heavy calibre machine guns in their attacks, but as the battles continued, larger calibre weapons came to the fore, and air-to-air rockets, bombs, and even heavily armed and armoured FW190s, whose pilots were tasked to bring down at least one bomber each time, if not by gunfire then by ramming.

We in the fighter Groups desperately needed more range in order to take the bombers to every part of Germany. We just had to be able to go with them. Fortunately there was a plane on its way and eventually we and the other fighter Groups would get it. That fighter was the Mustang.

Chapter 12

Mustangs and Memories

As THE year of 1943 came to an end, so too did some of the 4th's way of life. Don Blakeslee took command on 1 January, 1944, when Pete Peterson was sent to the 9th Air Force as Combat Operations Officer.

Colonel Donald Blakeslee was more than the Commanding Officer. He was the Group. He had helped to create it. He had flown more than 1000 combat hours with it. He had imbued every pilot in it with some of his indomitable independent spirit. Indeed, had it not been for that spirit, neither Blakeslee nor the leading Group of the war, officially credited with 1016 enemy aircraft destroyed, earning its motto, "4th but First", could have done what they did.

It may be thought that the Generals were taking a bit of a risk. They knew that Blakeslee had joined the Eagles to avoid being taken off combat duty for a rest after completing his tour of duty with the RCAF; this meant that he had far more experience than any pilot in the Group. They knew he was the pilot's choice, and that morale slumped every time he was passed over for the job. They knew that he would lead the Group with aggression and brilliance in the air, but they must have had grave doubts as to whether this dashing young hell-raiser could carry with dignity the responsibility of a full colonel. They must have known he would be his own man and fight to the end for the things he believed to be right. But the Eighth Air Force Generals, like Jimmy Doolittle and Tooey Spaatz, had been fighter pilots themselves. They picked him anyway. We were lucky with our generals.

I've heard many speeches from great men when they took over their new commands. Some were amusing, some were corny, some were pathetic, some were maudlin, some were patriotic, some were magnificent; but Blakeslee's was the most eloquent – and typical. He simply climbed onto the bar, drew himself up to his full height of 6ft.3in. and bellowed, "Tonight, the drinks are on me!"

But Blakeslee was also imbued with the basic discipline of the RAF. His final speech, at about 1 a.m., was just as typical as the first: "All pilots will report for briefing at 6 a.m.!"

Almost immediately, Blakeslee confirmed to the generals that he was no "yes man". He began a determined, non-stop campaign to get the P-51 Mustang for his Group.

Somehow the 4th had never really seemed to settle with the Thunderbolt. Perhaps it was due to the old Eagles having had Spitfires, and the Mustang, although different in many respects, did perhaps have the look and feel of the old Spit.

There was also the problem of Group victory scores. Hub Zemke's "Wolfpack", the 56th, had now shot down over 300 German aircraft, whereas the 4th – who had been the premier Group in the ETO, was still trying for its 100th! Then Blakeslee wetted the appetite of the pilots when he was ordered to fly lead to the newly arrived 354th Group of the 9th Air Force, in order to "show them the ropes." They were equipped with Mustangs, and as Blakeslee refused to stay overnight at the 354's base, he would fly "his" Mustang back to Debden each evening, so that the boys could drool over the lovely sleek lines of the new fighter.

The others all had their good qualities, but they also had their weaknesses. The Hurricane lacked speed and power, the Spitfire lacked the range, the P-38 Lightning lacked manoevrability. The P-47 Thunderbolt lacked speed in the climb and could be out-manoeuvred by the German fighters.

Only one WWII piston-engined fighter outclassed both its adversaries and its allies in every respect. That was the P-51 Merlin-engined Mustang. It was faster than the Me-109 and FW190 at almost any altitude and could also out-climb and out-dive them.

I have heard Spitfire pilots claim to have out-turned the Mustang, but the Mustang pilot probably didn't use the trick I once played on an Me-109.

Over Berlin, flying a P-51D, I bounced a 109 about to dive onto the B-17s. He immediately turned into me and we were very soon in a tight turn with him gaining on me slightly. As I looked over my shoulder and saw his nose gradually moving up to get in a deflection shot at me, I felt the Mustang start to stall. I immediately dropped my right hand onto the well-placed flap lever and let down 5 degrees of flap. Right away, I was able to start out-turning him. He was soon forced to break out of the circle and dive for home. I wasn't able to catch him, of course. The same flap that had enabled me to out-turn him held me back in the dive until it was retracted, by which time he was well out of reach.

But the outstanding feature of the P-51 was its amazing range. With the P-47 Thunderbolt, we had to endure the agonising experience of escorting the bombers to the limit of our range and then turn for home, although we could see the Me-109s and FW-190s up ahead of the bombers, waiting for us to leave before they dived in to wreak havoc among the now unprotected bombers.

With the Mustang, we could escort the bombers to any target they could reach and even carry out the "Shuttle raids" described later in this book.

These extraordinary achievements were accomplished by suspending two 108-gallon droppable fuel tanks, one under each wing, in addition to the internal tanks which filled every bit of space.

It was a credit to North American Aviation's President, "Dutch" Kindelberger, and to Ed Schmued, the German designer, who had left Germany for the States just before the war, that the plane could take off with such a load and still have such excellent performance.

However, many other players had a part in the drama of the Mustang. Although North American gets the credit for designing the plane with its low-drag, thin, laminar-flow wing, it was the British, in the form of Sir Robert Self, who headed up a British buying team sent to the U.S.A., who actually commissioned and bought the plane.

The Mustang at that time was powered by an Allison engine with no supercharger. It could therefore be used only at low altitudes and initially the RAF used it mainly for photo reconnaissance.

It took another Englishman, Ron Harker, Chief Test Pilot of Rolls-Royce, to give the plane what it needed. It was by chance that Ron flew a Mustang when he saw one at Duxford. He was warned that it was useless above 10,000ft. and when he landed, they waited for him to confirm the plane's deficiencies. They were wrong.

"This will be the best fighter plane in the world," he said. "All it needs is our Merlin engine."

The final word on the P-51 Mustang was probably uttered by Field Marshall Goering at the Nuremberg Trials. When he was asked at what point in the War he had realised that Germany could never win, he replied, "When we saw Mustang fighter planes from England escorting

US bombers over Berlin."

The Group very nearly lost Blakeslee on 7 January. During a With-drawal Support mission, the bombers had been to Ludwigshaven. Near Hesdin in France, a dozen FW190s came down on the bombers, hoping to pick off any stragglers. The P.47s attacked and a dog-fight began.

The fight went all the way down from 24,000 to 3,000 feet, Blakeslee getting one but then three latched onto him, pumping lead into his Thunderbolt until it looked like a sieve.

I was leading the flight next to him and because I had seen him roll over into a vertical dive, I was able to follow him with my wingman, Bob Wehrman. Even I couldn't quite keep up with him. Don shot down three, but I saw more 190s coming in on him.

"Horseback Leader, break right! I'm coming!"

He turned into them, but before I could get closer to him, I saw flashes on his plane.

"Keep turning, Don. I'll get him!"

"He's getting me! Where the hell are you?"

It was only seconds. It seemed like an hour. Finally, I was able to close and shoot the 190 off his tail. Blakeslee's plane was badly hit, but he kept attacking. He shot at another 190, but was hit by another before I could shoot it down. I zoomed past the stricken 190 and finally caught up with Blakeslee. His plane was covered in oil. He couldn't see through the windscreen, so he opened the canopy.

"I can't see, Goody – I'll have to fly on your wing."

I pointed him in the right direction, but then had to leave him to break into more attacking German planes. When I was out of am-munition, I turned into them and drove them off by bluff.

When we finally crossed the Channel and I had guided Don onto the long runway at Manston, I ran over to his plane to find that both it and he were covered in black oil. We later counted sixty-four 20mm cannon shots in the plane.

"I'm sorry, Don," I said.

"Yeah! Where the hell were you?"

"Well, at least you made it!"

Then I realised that throughout the whole engagement, there was only one thing uppermost in my mind; not my own safety, not the destruction of the enemy, but giving cover to Blakeslee and not letting him down.

He didn't say much at the time, but he recommended me for one of the highest decorations. In that area, I have been fortunate, but the greatest honour for me will always be Blakeslee's "Thanks, Goody, you saved my ass!"

Every man who served under him would have felt the same.

Blakeslee's kill also made him an ace, but few would have known about it for Don would never have said so. He never did make a fuss over his own score. Just to shoot them down was enough. He didn't go in for fancy artwork on his Thunderbolt either. He had no time for what he called the "prima donnas", who he felt were only interested in building up their own score and he hated the Press attention they received. He didn't feel it was part of the job. There was no colourful Walt Disney character, or some such emblem on his engine cowling, along with a name, whether it be the name of a sweetheart or something that the plane's owner felt represented his own personal character. There was none of the "Boise Bee" – Duane Beeson, or "Shangri-La" – Don Gentile, or "The Deacon" – Howard Hively. And there were certainly no black crosses or swastika markings to denote victories on his plane. All that was needed for him and the other pilots to see was just plain WD-C, and everyone knew where the Boss was. The only bit of "colour" was the white nose paint work, but then all the 4th's aircraft had white engine cowlings, and a white band round the tail fin.

* * *

Blakeslee kept up his bombardment of General Bill Kepner for the Group to have Mustangs. He must have been seen to weaken, for Don kept on. The General liked Blakeslee – some others didn't – but he was worried about taking the 4th out of the line in order for them to convert.

"The 4th has the key role on every escort mission. With the losses the bombers are taking, we just can't afford to take the 4th out of combat at this time to check out a new plane. That would take weeks!"

Finally, Blakeslee asked, "How long COULD you take us out of combat?"

"No more than 24 hours."

"That's all we need!" said Blakeslee.

Kepner looked incredulous, but Don was serious.

"Most of our boys have combat experience in Spitfires. This plane's not much different. I can have them checked out in a day!"

The Group got Mustangs.

Apart from Blakeslee's P.51, the only others the boys got their hands on initially were three that were flown in on February 14 – Valentine's Day – and it was certainly the start of a love affair. Blakeslee told his pilots they should check out on the Mustangs between missions, and that anyone who couldn't hack it ...., well there were still plenty of Thunderbolt Groups they could be assigned to!

Early February saw the Group fly its last Thunderbolt missions, led by either Blakeslee, Edner, Goodson or Jim Clark. They shot down eight on the 10th, the 334th notching up its 50th, four on the 20th and three on the 21st and 22nd. The 20th saw the start of "Big Week" for the 8th Air Force, when they attempted two things to help the pre-invasion planning: smash Germany's aircraft industry and destroy its operational aircraft in the air.

In that week over 350 German aircraft were claimed by the 8th – mostly overclaimed by numerous B.17 and B.24 gunners, but the factories and airfields had been bombed, and, despite the claims, enemy fighters were destroyed. In the midst of Big Week, the 4th took its day off – and went over to Mustangs.

That happened on 23 February. A big batch of P.51Bs were delivered to Debden and the old Thunderbolts were shipped out. So fast did they go that the 335th Squadron had to borrow some of the 334th aircraft in order to fly missions on the 24th and 25th. Sel Edner led both these shows. On the first mission, another Withdrawal Support from Germany, one FW190 was shot down and the Group's last P.47 pilot was lost – Joe Sullivan.

The next day saw the final P.47 mission for the Group, a Penetration Support do, between Sedan and Stuttgart. Soon after the "Jugs" joined with the bombers over Sedan, five FW190s were seen making a head-on attack on the B.17s, getting one bomber. Don Gentile, Vermont Garrison and Glenn Herter got three of the 190s, before four more were bounced – Duane Beeson and Pierce McKennon getting one each. These were the last P.47 kills for the 4th, which brought Beeson's score now to 12, Gentile's to six and McKennon's to a modest four.

Equipped with the Mustang, we could at last cover the bombers

Hal Marting (centre) also flew P.40s in the Desert Air Force. Brought down, he was captured but managed to escape and return to his unit.

The Terrible Twins – John Godfrey and Don Gentile.

Mike Sobanski – 4th Fighter Group.   Pierce McKennon – 4th Fighter Group.

Bob Mannix flew with the Eagles in England and then saw action in
North Africa. Eventually he commanded 33 Squadron RAF but was
then killed in action. Note the insignia on his flight jacket, the
American and British flags with the words "Nuts to Nazis" written
across them.

Mike Miluck saw action with the RAF in the Western Desert flying P.40 Kittyhawks.

Don Blakeslee after the award of the American DFC – he already had a British one!

Duane Beeson – 4th Fighter Group.

Jim Clark – 4th Fighter Group.

John and Don pose in front of a red nosed Mustang, with its red and white checkerboard marking.

Don Gentile's pranged Mustang "Shangri-La" which he bellied in right in front of the press – and Don Blakeslee!

Kid Hofer with his "Salem Representative". Note that in addition to his aircraft kills, he has claimed a train and two sailing ships.

The boys letting their hair down in the Debden Mess. Rear: Ingold, Red-Dog Norley, Fred Glover, Don Blakeslee and Benjamin the I.O. of 336 Squadron. Front: Pierce McKennon and Deacon Hively.

Visit by Mr Lovett, US Secretary for Air. l to r: Don Blakeslee, General Bill Kepner, HQ 8th AF Fighter Command, Jim Goodson, General Jesse Auton, CO 65th Fighter Wing, Mr Lovett.

Blakeslee tells General Bill Kepner what it was like to fly the Shuttle mission to Russia and Italy, July, 1944.

Swede Carlson – 4th Fighter Group.

Red-Dog Norley – 4th Fighter Group.

Leader of the rival 56th Fighter Group – Hub Zemke.

Lieutenant William G Spencer, 334th Squadron, 4th FG, 1945.

Kid Hofer and Jim Goodson. Goodson had just scored his 30th kill.

Colonel Don Blakeslee, CO of the 4th FG.

Wee Michael McPharlin, 71 Eagle Squadron. Killed in action on D-Day, 6 June 1944.

Bill Spencer with his P.51 Mustang, 1945.

Eagle Squadrons Memorial Plaque – RAF Debden.

4th FG Insignia and Eagle Squadron patch.

anywhere they went. For the first time, the carnage over the target area was over and the bomber crews had some hope of completing their tour of duty.

On almost every mission, the 4th was involved in combat. At the height of the so-called 'Battle of Berlin', we were flying missions almost every other day and each mission lasted about eight hours. This did, however, give rise to another problem, which frustrated one young man who thought he was entitled to the Purple Heart.

The Purple Heart is one of America's top decorations, awarded to those who have been wounded in combat.

Most of the glorious deeds which have merited this coveted medal have been well documented; one has not. It was not exactly a glorious occasion, but I think it should be recorded, if only to illustrate the important fact that war is not always a story of daring deeds, of glorious victories or desperate defeats. Usually it is dull, dreary and soul-destroying, but occasionally it is alleviated by short flashes of comedy; tragi-comedy, perhaps, but enough to raise a wry smile. Such was the case of the pee-tube.

Almost all fighter planes in WW11 were equipped with a pee-tube. In Hurricanes and Spitfires, with a range of under three hours, they were not often used, but as range increased, so did the importance of the pee-tube, until with the P-51 Mustang with an endurance of $8^{1}/_{2}$ hours, it became a crucial piece of equipment.

It was not easy to use. The pilot had to undo his harness, then his parachute, then the flies of his flying suit, his trousers, his underwear. He then had to fish around under the seat for the pee-tube and insert it in such a manner as to avoid unpleasant accidents, and all this whilst he was keeping formation, navigating, keeping an eye out for enemy aircraft and flying the plane.

For some, this didn't seem too difficult. I remember one Southerner drawling: "Hell, ah've peed on Paris, ah've peed on Brussels and ah've peed on half the cities of Germany!"

For others, however, it was such a bother they preferred to suffer for the duration of the trip.

However, Burroughs (his name has been changed to avoid embarrassment) thought he had found the perfect solution. With the aid of an athletic support with a metal protector cup, a can opener and a great deal of ingenuity, he ensconced himself in his cockpit and painstakingly inserted the pee-tube into the athletic support so that when the need arose no further adjustment was necessary; all was in a state of permanent readiness.

Unfortunately, like many an inventive genius before him, he over-looked one factor. All went well until the Squadron reached 30,000 feet. First, Burroughs was aware of a blast of cold air on his nether regions. This should not have surprised him, since he should have known that the outside air at that altitude was probably some thirty degrees below zero. However, he was lulled into a false sense of security when the cold blast seemed to subside, to be replaced by a not unpleasant numbness.

His combat report does not record how long it took him to realise he was in serious trouble. When he did, he made a dive for home and, more importantly, for lower altitude, since no amount of pulling and tugging would release him from his self-made trap. As anyone who has suffered from frozen appendages knows, the freezing process is relatively painless, whereas the thawing-out process is accompanied by excruciating pain.

When he landed back at base he was in agony. His mood was not improved by the unsympathetic amusement displayed by the onlook-ers. This was increased when he was examined in hospital, since the enormous swelling which followed the thawing-out process was the subject of endless ribaldry.

However, his spirits reached the depths of despondency when I, as his Commanding Officer, delivered the final blow. Looking back now after fifty years, I wonder if I wasn't too hard on him.

I turned down his application for the Purple Heart for wounds received in combat.

* * *

Although these eight-hour missions were exhausting, no-one's en-thusiasm ever waned. Pilots fought to get on each operation.

The reason was simple: Blakeslee was on almost every mission. Each pilot had only one thought in mind – not to let down Don Blakeslee. The new pilots put their faith in him; old hands like those of us who commanded the squadrons and often led the Group knew instinctively what he wanted; we were always where he wanted us and he was always where we knew he would be.

When Blakeslee said "Horseback here – I'm going in", he knew he would be covered. When any of us took our squadron into the attack, we knew we were covered. The disciplines of the RAF were ingrained in him.

Everyone knows that fighter pilots are a special breed: devil-may-care, aggressive, hell-raising, macho extroverts. True, they may have come from different social backgrounds and their parents may have been preparing their sons for something other than a military career. The Depression and shortage of ready cash may have obliged some to take on temporary jobs not usually associated with flying. The actors and directors of Hollywood who knew the young make-up artist, Gus Daymond, would never have dreamed he would become a leading fighter ace and top Air force Commander, and Snodgrass and Zimmerman, Undertakers and Embalmers, of Le Grand, Oregon, never thought their young apprentice, whom we were to call "Pappy" Dunn, would ever make a good undertaker, let alone a fighter pilot.

Pierce McKennon, however, was in a completely different class. There was no doubt in the minds of his parents, and indeed, of some of the greatest musical experts, that the young McKennon would become one of the world's finest classical pianists. He was undoubtedly a child prodigy and with the amount of practice and expert tuition that were the dominating feature of his early life, he would certainly have become world renowned as a brilliant musician.

In fact, that was the way it was going, and although Pierce did occasionally rebel by breaking into jazz or boogie-woogie in the middle of Debussy's "Claire de Lune", as far as anyone knew, he was as enthusiastic about his musical career as anyone else. This illusion was shattered in 1941 when Pierce disappeared without trace. He resurfaced some weeks later in the RCAF as a trainee pilot. He was 18 years old. When he transferred to the USAAF in 1942 he arrived at Debden to join the 4th. I remember him as he was then, thin, dark, quiet, even self-effacing.

He had been with us some time before any of us heard he could play the piano. Then we had one of our dances, and since we had no band of our own, a local ensemble of civilian musicians were brought in. In those days, even the top English dance bands were years behind their American counterparts when it came to playing modern music, and the local talent was far from being "top" of anything.

After an hour or so of uninspired playing which threatened to put the damper on the entire evening, the "band-leader" announced a 15 minute break. The next thing we knew, an explosion of brilliant jazz filled the room. Pierce McKennon was at the piano. Fortunately someone at some time recorded some of his playing and my friend Dick Konsler got hold of a tape which he sent to me. Even today, even the experts agree that Pierce's boogie-woogie ranks with that of the 'Greats'.

From that evening on, Pierce was always being asked to play and he usually agreed. One night I came back to the base at about 1am. Walking through the deserted Officer's Mess, I heard the familiar sounds of Mac's boogie-woogie and found a small group of pilots listening to him. I told them to call it a day, since the latest weather forecast indicated improvement, so there was bound to be a mission next morning.

"How about one last request for you, Goody?" Mac said. "What'll it be?"

"Rachmaninov's 2nd Piano Concerto!" I said facetiously and headed for the door. I was stopped dead by the crashing chords of that great piece of music. Since then, I have heard it played by the world's greatest pianists. It may have been the liquor, it may be nostalgia, but none of them ever affected me as Mac did that night.

One would not expect someone obviously so capable of such sensitivity to become Commanding Officer of one of the leading fighter squadrons in the US Air Force, but that is what Mac achieved. In his quiet way he earned the respect and intense loyalty of all his men.

When the Germans developed their jet and rocket fighters, the only way we could catch them was to go down and strafe them on their airfields. The curtain of flak thrown up made such attacks extremely dangerous but it was the only way we could finally destroy the Luftwaffe.

It was on a strafing attack on an airfield near Berlin on 18 March, 1945, that Mac's plane was hit by flak. He was far too low to bale out and, with no power left in his engine, he had only one chance; he simply bellied-in on the middle of the enemy airfield. His radio was still working so he ordered his squadron to get out of the flak and head for home.

"See you later, fellows! Thanks for everything.'

For once his pilots disobeyed his orders. They screamed down to strafe the German soldiers and vehicles converging on the stranded Mustang pilot. Immediately the Germans turned and ran for cover.

At the same time, Mac's wingman, Lieutenant George Green, had dropped his wheels and was about to land out of a steep turn. He taxied over to Mac's stranded Mustang – called "Ridge Runner" with its rows of black crosses on the cowling – leapt out of the cockpit, threw his parachute on the ground, and, bowing from the waist, told Mac that his carriage awaited!

Mac didn't hesitate. He leapt out of his wrecked fighter, ran to Green's and clambered in, closely followed by Green, who sat on his lap. Escorted by the rest of the gang, they made their way back across Germany, Holland, and home, a trip of some 1,000 miles. They had to fly high to avoid the murderous flak, so they shared the oxygen mask, switching it back and forth between gasps.

Mac also had a very clear idea of priorities – HIS priorities. Bill Spencer told me that during the occupation of Germany, Mac was driving down the road in a jeep in the snow when the windscreen wipers packed up. He took out his .45 and shot out the windscreen. That solved the problem of seeing where he was going, but the snow came in and it got rather cold. To get round this, Mac simply stopped a German car, took it and left the owners the jeep!

Mac, like Don Blakeslee and some of the others, was eventually rotated back to the States. Don always told me: "You were lucky! You got shot down and became a prisoner of war – we had to become instructors!"

He was probably right. The accident rate was high in training schools. Like Red-Dog Norley, what the mighty Luftwaffe couldn't achieve was accomplished by students. In Mac's case, the youngster in the front cockpit panicked and froze on the controls and Mac didn't have the strength to overcome him and pull the plane out of the dive. He should have bashed him over the head with a fire extinguisher, but maybe that wasn't Mac's style.

There was a funeral after the crash. I only hope they played boogie-woogie as well as Bach!

Mac officially has 12 air and 8 ground kills with the 4th, the DFC with four oak leaf clusters, Air Medal with 16 clusters, Purple Heart, French Croix de Guerre and around 560 combat hours. Even the lucky escape on March 18 didn't curb his ardour for ground attack as he destroyed more planes on the ground in April. They nearly got him again on April 16, a 20 mm shell splinter smashing through his canopy to wound him in the face, but he got back. June 18, 1947 was the date of the passing of this musician and fighter pilot from Fort Smith, Arkansas.

* * *

The Group's first Mustang mission had been pencilled in for February 26 but bad weather caused a postponement. Mike Sobanski's luck was doubly out for, to Blakeslee's disgust and anger, Mike got confused on landing, and, thinking his wheels were up when he'd already lowered them, pulled them up and made a very nice wheel-less landing! As the Group were also having several teething troubles with the Mustangs at this time, an air of uncertainty pervaded as to whether the old P.47 wasn't such a bad kite after all.

The Mustangs carried red paint work on the plane's spinner rather than the old white cowlings of the P.47s. The red noses would soon become well known amongst the Luftwaffe pilots.

Two days later came the first mission. Jim Clark led a freelance sortie, the Mustangs taking two 75-gallon drop tanks under their wings for extra range. Several aircraft aborted with mechanical problems but the rest found only empty skies. Some went down on an airfield near Soissons, where Cowboy Megura, Duane Beeson, Vermont Garrison and Bill Smith blew up a lone Ju88 that was preparing to take off.

I led a Target Support mission on the 29th, but again the Luftwaffe stayed away and six Mustangs turned back with troubles. As the P.51 had effectively doubled the Group's range of operations, the pilots were getting a little jittery, for it meant they could be further away from base when they got trouble.

Edner led the next mission, on March 2, to support returning bombers. Six enemy fighters put in an appearance to make head-ons at the bombers, 336 going after them, Vasseure Wynn (ex-249 Squadron on Malta) and Glenn Herter each claiming one. The Group's Mustang score had started.

Berlin was on the 8th Air Force's agenda for early March 1944, and all the boys in the 4th Fighter Group wanted to be in on that. March 3 saw just a target support mission for bombers returning from the Big City, but the Mustangs, troubles or not, were there, picking up the B.17s near Neumunster. They brought them back to the coast before leaving them near Terschelling Island after fighting their way through a host of enemy fighters.

Don Gentile got two, Millikan, "Swede" Carlson and Garrison, one each, and Pappy Dunn an Me210. Garrison, as already recorded, then fell victim to flak and had to wait till Korea to score again for the 4th. Pappy Dunn too had problems, his engine was losing power and he felt he could not get home. A bomber crew who heard his call for a course home gave him 270 degrees and he later found himself over Cherbourg with no radio, little fuel and a rough engine. He decided to try for Spain, broke cloud to find a big fat Heinkel 111 bomber in front of him. He used the last of his gas to shoot it down, then baled out – eight miles from the Spanish frontier. He ended up in a POW Camp.

The other loss to the Group that day was Glenn Herter, who had got the first Mustang kill just 24 hours earlier. He was lured down after a low flying decoy, bounced and killed.

We never knew that "Pappy" Dunn's real name was Philip, we just called him Pappy. In 1941, when we were still in the RAF, most of us were 18 to 20 and although we never discovered his real age, he may well have been approaching 30; a most advanced age for a fighter pilot in those early days. Of course, when he volunteered for the RAF he probably knocked quite a few years off, but they needed pilots badly and Pappy could fly, having log-books to prove it.

The route he had followed to become a fighter pilot with the RAF and later the USAAF had been a devious one. His original ambition was to become a medical doctor, and indeed, he was in medical school when his studies were interrupted by a condition which was to recur frequently in his efforts to become a doctor; he ran out of money! He therefore took advantage of his limited medical knowledge to obtain employment with Snodgrass and Zimmerman, embalmers and funeral directors, of Le Grand, Oregon.

Oregon, in the northwest corner of the USA, was one of the closest States to that other northern territory of the US – Alaska, and Alaska called on Oregon for many goods and services. One would not normally expect the services of a funeral parlour in Le Grand to be required in Alaska but one would be wrong. In Alaska, the long, hard winters presented a problem for undertakers, in that for much of the year the ground was frozen to such a depth as to make grave-digging impractical. In those days, cremation was not yet popular, so under-takers simply postponed burials until the spring thaw at which time funerals would take place, en-masse.

This sudden surge of business at one time was inclined to over-whelm the limited local industry, so places like Le Grand would send the more expendable members of their staff to help out! Since Pappy fell into that category, he found himself in Alaska, where, once more, he had sufficient income to allow himself to continue his flying lessons, with a view to qualifying as a commercial pilot, for which the demand in the rapidly developing Alaskan aviation industry was growing.

As the spring boom dried up, so did Pappy's financial resources, and his flying career was once again interrupted. Help, however, arrived from an unexpected source; Hitler attacked Poland, and Britain and France went to war. This meant that Canada was at war too, and was chosen as the training ground for RAF and RCAF pilots.

Pappy not only had flying hours to his credit, but was soon on the spot, log-book (probably in expanded version) in hand! The RCAF accepted him gratefully. When Pappy got to England his one ambition was to join the other American volunteers in the RAF Eagle Squadrons but, probably because of his dubious age, he was made an instructor. He finally got his transfer to the USAAF, and then came to the 4th late, but not too late.

Pappy was delighted to be part of the famous Group and cheerfully accepted the fact that he stuck out like a sore thumb. It was not just that he was much older than the other pilots; he was different in almost every respect. Most of us were over 6ft, Pappy was about 5ft. 5ins. Don Gentile, Jim Clark, Johnnie Godfrey, Kid Hofer were outstand-ingly handsome, with full heads of luxuriant hair and the others were not far behind. Pappy's round face was homely and his hair was thinning, to say the least.

Even his performance as a fighter pilot was less than spectacular. On the charts on which we recorded victories, Pappy's name stayed at the bottom with no claims of enemy aircraft destroyed or even damaged, although he once claimed one German "scared"!

I remember one hectic mission when the Group was involved in dogfights with over a hundred German fighters. As the pilots landed, they reported their experiences and claims to the Intelligence Officers, but some were missing and Pappy was one of them. It was only when we had almost given up that Pappy's plane came into the circuit and landed. His report on his mission went something like this:

"One minute I was flying along with the Squadron in Blue 4 position. The next minute, I'm still in Blue Four position, but all the planes around me have black crosses on them. I thought I'd just sneak away rom them, but soon they were coming at me from all angles. I broke nto a tight turn. They were still all around me. I tightened the turns even more and flipped into a spin. Spins have always scared the hell ut of me and I've fought to get out of them as soon as possible. Not this time! I just sat in that spin happy as a clown.

"I finally pulled out at a few thousand feet, hit the deck and headed for home."

The Intelligence Officer wanted something more specific to report. "Are you claiming a victory?"

"Hell, yes!" said Pappy. "I made it back!"

* * *

Despite the fact that the 4th had only switched over to Mustangs a week before, and were still having teething troubles with the new planes, the Group were assigned to escort the bombers all the way to Berlin, on 4th March, 1944.

The 4th would fly directly to the German capital city to give target support, after making rendezvous with the bombers over Kassel. 238 Forts from the 3rd Bomb Division were assigned the task (B.17s of the 2nd Division failed to form up due to weather) although no more than 60–70 were effective over the target. In a fight, the 4th shot down four but lost two.

The next day Blakeslee led a Target Suppport mission over France, the Group claiming eight victories, but lost Steve Pisanos. After getting two Me109s, Steve had to force-land. He hit the ground half in and half out of his P.51, but he survived, evaded, and was back with the Group in September.

Everyone loved Steve Pisanos. He had the natural, out-going charm of the Mediterranean and with Steve it was more than skin-deep; he was a thoroughly nice guy. For me there was something else underneath the easy friendliness, something which was not immediately evident. Steve was living proof of the fact that, with determination, one can achieve the most improbable goals.

As a young, impoverished boy in Greece, Steve announced to his parents that he was going to become a pilot. Since they had neither the means, nor even the inclination, to take this announcement seriously, they just laughed at him. They shouldn't have.

To take flying lessons in Greece at that time was not only difficult, but far too expensive for even the combined resources of the Pisanos family. To apply for pilot training in the Greek Air Force, one had to be a university graduate, another goal out of reach for Steve and his family.

Steve therefore managed to work his way from Athens to New York, where he got a job as a pantry boy. He earned $15 a week, $12 of which he spent on flying lessons. Eventually, the hotel manager loaned him the rest of the money necessary to acquire a CAA flying licence.

Normally, this would have enabled him to get a job as a pilot, but the Depression was still on and many qualified pilots with more experience were out of work. More important, Steve was not an American citizen, and for this reason he couldn't join the US Army Air Corps, even had he the necessary educational qualifications, which he hadn't.

At this point, Fate came to Steve's aid in the form of Adolf Hitler. Suddenly, Great Britain was at war, and the Empire Air Training Scheme was soon organised in Canada. They were desperate for men who could fly, so when Steve turned up in Toronto they took him in, without asking too many questions about his education or nationality.

He had actually applied for American citizenship, so the RCAF treated him like all other American volunteers and, at his request, when he got to England, he got posted to the Eagle Squadrons.

When the Eagles transferred to the USAAF, Steve moved too, though he was still officially a Greek citizen. I well remember when his US citizenship finally came through. Over the bar in the Officers' Mess was a large sign: "All drinks tonight are on Steve Pisanos – American!"

A rather pedantic Administration officer was puzzled. "If you've been a Greek citizen until now, how come you got into the US Air Force?"

Steve's charming smile was broader than usual when he replied, "Two reasons – first, they needed me, and second, I lied."

I remember the day Steve went down. It had been a mission to Northern France. On the way back, we strafed an airfield and Steve was hit. I told him to try and make it and we'd stay with him, but eventually he said, "It's no good, Jimmy, I can't make it, I'm going to have to belly in."

But he wasn't finished. He managed to avoid capture and join the French underground in Paris. When the first American troops entered Paris, they were surprised to be greeted by a charming character with a broad smile who introduced himself as "Steve Pisanos – American!"

Today, he could introduce himself as Colonel Pisanos, DSC, DFC with oak-leaves, A.M. with oak leaves, followed by a string of foreign decorations. He could, but he wouldn't.

It was on this show that two huge four-engine Focke Wulf 200 Kondor aircraft were caught in the air and shot down by roving P.51s, Snuffy Smith getting a half share in one. The next day it was back to Berlin, the Mustangs coming back to Debden with claims for 13 enemy fighters but they had lost four. Berlin again on the 8th, and another big scrap, with 16 fighters shot down, this time for the loss of just one, but it was yet another former Eagle, Sel Edner.

Sel was leading the Group as he had done several times over recent weeks. He became separated from the others, lost his wingman and failed to get back. Luckily, news came through later that he was a prisoner. Of the 16 claims, Gentile and Godfrey claimed three and two respectively, with a sixth shared between them.

Gil "Gunner" Halsey, former Eagle and until now, CO of the 336th Squadron, ended his tour on this day, being rotated back to the States. I was promoted to Major and given command of the unit. The two stars of the 336th, Gentile and Godfrey, now came under my command. Both the Squadron and the Group would soon be adopting new tactics to get at the Luftwaffe fighters.

We were now fully equipped with P.51 Mustangs which not only had the range to protect the bombers over any target in Germany, but had superior performance over the Me109 and FW190. Perhaps the most important consideration on a more strategic level, was the knowledge that the invasion of the European Continent was coming up and it was essential to eliminate the Luftwaffe as a viable fighting force. Until then, top priority in our Group had always been the protection of the bombers and when the German attackers dived for the ground, we returned to take care of our "big friends". Now, however, in 336 Squadron, I decided that, provided the bombers were under no immediate threat, we could afford to become more aggressive. What developed was a flexible system of attack whereby one Flight of four planes would break off to attack any German aircraft trying to fly away, followed by a second Flight of four, who would provide cover. The other two Flights of the Squadron would either follow on down, or stay up to continue the escort, depending on the situation at the moment.

It was natural that the attacking Flight should be led by Don Gentile, with Johnny Godfrey as his wingman. Two reliable pilots would complete that Flight and to give further protection, the second Flight was usually led by that pillar of strength, Millie Millikan. Most of Millie's 13 air-to-air victories were shot down right off the tail of one of our planes. So it worked. In no time Don Gentile and Johnny Godffrey were leading aces with about 30 confirmed victories each. Don's were mostly air-to-air kills, as Johnny was more often his wingman, and Johnny built up his score after Don had rotated back to the US with ground kills.

Gentile and Godfrey became known as the "terrible twins" of the 4th. They flew as an element but not like the usual leader and his wingman. With the skills both had developed, the two adopted a more open, more fluid fighting team game. By tacit agreement, when a situation developed, the leader would be the pilot who was in the best position to attack, the other man would slide in to cover and protect the one attacking. If during the combat the situation changed, then the second man would take the lead, the former leader becoming the wingman and protector.

This fighting team really got together during March and April, 1944, helping to make them the best months for the Group. Kid Hofer too got into his stride in March through May. Beeson and I added dramatically to our scores, and even the Boss, Don Blakeslee, more than doubled his score during this period.

Losses of course, occurred. Beeson ended his string of successes on April 5. He had just shared the destruction of a JU88, then went down to strafe the enemy air base near Gardelegen, Germany. Hit by ground fire he baled out to be taken prisoner. Vic France, another former Eagle, had scored modestly, bringing his score to five air and five ground kills by April 18. On that day, as a flight commander with the 334th, he chased an Me109 at low level, misjudged it and went into the ground and blew-up.

The Eagles were getting fewer.

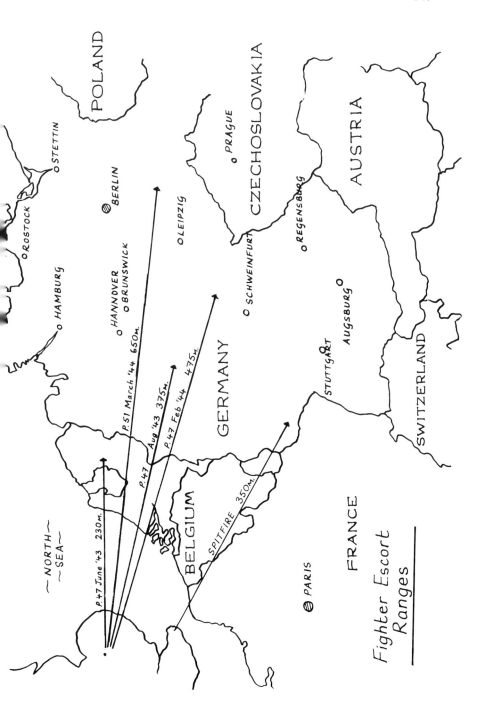

POLAND

CZECHOSLOVAKIA

AUSTRIA

O STETTIN

O PRAGUE

○ ROSTOCK

● BERLIN

CZECHOSLOVAKIA

O LEIPZIG

O REGENSBURG

O HAMBURG

○ HANNOVER
○ BRUNSWICK

O SCHWEINFURT

AUGSBURG O

STUTTGART

GERMANY

SWITZERLAND

P-51 March '44 650m.

P-47 Aug '43 375m.

P-47 Feb '44 475m.

P-47

SPITFIRE 350m.

BELGIUM

FRANCE

~NORTH~
~SEA~

P-47 June '43 230m.

● PARIS

Fighter Escort
Ranges

Chapter 13
Shoot-downs and Shuttle Missions

AT THE time of D-Day – June 6, 1944, the three 4th Fighter Group Squadrons were still being commanded by former Eagles, but only just. Mike Sobanski, leader of the 334th, was killed on D-Day so the post went to Deacon Hively. The 335th was commanded by Jim Happel (ex-121) while I still had the 336th.

D-Day was hard for the Group. Mike Sobanski, born in America, but living and studying in Warsaw, Poland in September 1939, fought long and hard to get to the West to fight, having been wounded in Warsaw. Finally he got to America due to his citizenship. He joined the Air Corps, became a pilot and ended up with the 4th. He'd gained six victories, two DFCs, three Air Medals before being being killed on the evening of June 6.

Mike was my room-mate at Debden, so I knew him pretty well. What's more, he was my friend. The friendship started when we were training together in Canada.

Mike and I had one thing in common from the start; we were the only two who had actually experienced War. Whilst I was splashing around in the wreckage of the ATHENIA, Mike was crouching in the rubble of Warsaw as the Germans bombed the city. Out of it came a solemn vow: never again would Mike Sobanski lie helpless in the rubble and dirt. He would be up in the air, in the driver's seat, looking down on the people on the ground instead of being one of them. He was going to be a pilot.

When his home was destroyed, it took months for him to get through Poland, Czechoslovakia, Hungary, Rumania and Istanbul, to finally stand at the door of Harry Bruno's apartment in East 57th Street, New York City.

Harry Bruno had flown with the British Royal Flying Corps in the First World War. Harry's wife was Polish and Mike's mother had been her best friend. This rather tenuous connection resulted in Mike turning up at the Bruno's apartment in New York. When he arrived on the

Bruno's doorstep, he immediately announced that he intended to join the RCAF and return to England to continue the fight against Germany. He had come to the right man. Harry was a friend of Billy Bishop, the Canadian World War I pilot hero, and, in 1940, in command of the Empire Training Scheme in Canada.

Harry had spent his life in aviation, from building a glider to his career in the RFC. Back in the USA, he became an aviation public relations consultant and he knew every important aviation figure in the world. He asked me when I met him after the war, "Who was the first man to fly the Atlantic?"

"Charles Lindbergh," I replied.

"No, he was about the 26th. The difference was that I handled his public relations!"

When Mike turned up and joined the RCAF, Harry asked me to keep an eye on him.

So Mike found himself, together with me and several thousand other young hopefuls, in the vast Royal Canadian Exhibition area in Toronto, now converted into the largest military induction centre in the world. The Empire Training Scheme was probably the most important factor in achieving victory in Europe. In a remarkably short space of time, an enormous training system was set up capable of turning out thousands of aircrew every month. All across Canada, training centres and airfields sprang up, converting Canadian, British, Australian, New Zealand, South African, Rhodesian – in fact all Commonwealth civilians into pilots, navigators, bomb aimers and gunners. In addition, they trained a goodly number of volunteers from the United States and other countries. Mike, therefore, was not the only foreigner, and, like the others, he soon mastered enough English to get by. He never attempted to master the English way of speaking, always retaining a strong, deep, Polish accent.

We trained together and ended up in the Eagle Squadrons together and Mike was one of the most heartbroken when we had to exchange our beloved Spitfires for the P.47 Thunderbolts. On the day the last Spitfire was due to leave, Mike and Bob Messenger took off for one last flight. Before they landed, every police force in England was calling the base. They thought at least fifty planes had gone wild and were attacking everything in sight. In fact, the planes were Spitfires and it was Mike and Bob saying goodbye with a beat-up to end all beat-ups.

They came screaming down in vertical dives, levelling off at the last minute to flash past farmhouses at less than roof-top height, screamed under bridges, clipped the tops off trees and broke the glass in every greenhouse for miles around. They were lucky to get off with being confined to base for a month!

Each night after a mission, Mike performed a solemn rite. In a large, black-paged photograph album, he painstakingly printed in white ink the events of the day, wherever possible illustrated with photographs. It covered every aspect of his service life: the planes he had flown; the people he had known; missions he had accomplished; combat reports. One night, he seemed to be taking longer than usual.

"For God's sake, come to bed. We've got an early briefing tomorrow. You can do that any time!"

"No, this is important. It's alright for you guys. Every time you shoot one down or get promoted or decorated, it's in your local newspaper. My friends and family in Poland don't know where I am or what I'm doing.

"As far as my people know, I just ran away. That's why this is important. I'll show it to them after the war".

"I'm sure your family don't think you goofed off!"

"No, but they don't know I'm a Captain in the leading fighter group of the US Air Force. Besides, there's the girl I'm going to marry, Maria Vnug. I want her to see all this."

"If it's that important to you, maybe you should give me her name and address, just in case."

"No", he said with conviction. "I know I'm going to survive this war. I know!"

In the dark morning hours of 6 June 1944, Mike and I dressed for our parts in the invasion. As I waited at the door, he put his precious album on my bed, together with a scrap of paper. It bore a name and address in Cracow, Poland. It was the last time I saw him.

Immediately after the end of the war, I saw for myself what the Germans had done to Poland and remembered Mike's words:

"Poland has always been attacked by Russia to the east and Germany to the west. Both aggressions have been brutal and vicious, but we Poles know that, of the two, the eastern enemy is by far the worst."

I sat in a drab café in Cracow looking at the confusion, misery and fear pervading post-war Poland and I understood.

The girl had been hard to trace and it had been harder still to persuade her to meet me. When she finally came into the cafe, she was ill at ease. She recognised me easily enough by my clothes and came to my table. She shook hands coolly and didn't return my smile. Her English was poor, so we spoke in German. Almost her only comment was "Don't speak German so loud."

Apart from nervousness, she showed little emotion of any kind as I told her Mike's story. I explained how he had wanted her to know about it and went through his album for her page by page. Before I had even finished, I saw that she was looking around. She obviously wanted to leave. I closed the book, stood up and handed it to her. She shook her head.

"Es ist alles vorbei – it's all over!"

"Yes, and we won!"

"No," she said. "You won your war. We lost ours."

She handed the book back to me and turned and left.

The 4th lost 11 pilots on D-Day. One had been Ed Steppe, Sobanski's wingman. His last words were to Mike, calling – "Watch out behind you, White Leader!" Another to go down was Mike McPharlin.

The 4th flew six missions on this famous day. They shot down four of ten FW190s they found in the landing pattern at Evreux airdrome, during a sortie to Rouen led by Deacon Hively, looking for ground targets. All the big names led missions on D-Day – Don Blakeslee, Jim Clark, Happel, me and Deacon Hively.

Wee Mike McPharlin also went down on the Sobanski mission. He had come a long way since being shot down over Dieppe and attempting to paddle home full of benzedrine. He was now a Major, flying with the 339th Fighter Group, operating out of Fowlmere, but on D-Day was flying with the 4th's 334th Squadron. He was heard over the R/T to say that he was aborting the mission. His left magneto was out and his motor was running rough. He was not seen or heard of again. A sad end to a former Eagle.

Surprisingly the Luftwaffe hardly showed its face over the invasion area, whereas the Allied High Command had thought that they would react in some strength. That they didn't was good news for the Allies, but it did show how poorly off the German airforce was now, and how the confused situation of D-Day itself baffled the Germans into not knowing if this was the real invasion or just a diversion for the expected attack in the Pas de Calais area.

In fact, although the 4th flew long and hard from D-Day onwards, it did not find any enemy aircraft until 20 June. They were found not over the beach-head but on a Withdrawal Support Mission to the bombers going for Politz, Germany. This, in fact, was the first Group mission to Germany since the invasion, all recent missions having been flown over France and Normandy in support of the landings. Jim Clark led the mission.

Near Greifswald Bay a bunch of 25 enemy fighters were seen heading south and the 334th put a section down on a group of five Me109s which were then seen to turn towards the Mustangs. Two 109s were shot down and then a big dog-fight developed and more Germans were shot down. It was then that I spotted a number of aircraft on Neu Brandenburg airdrome and led the 336th Squadron down.

It had occurred to me some time early in 1944 that dog-fighting in the air might get you into a fight with one enemy aircraft and with an enormous amount of luck you might shoot it down, two if you're really lucky – and then you came home. On the other hand, on the ground there were all these airfields with perhaps 20 or 30 planes on them and if you had the guts to go down through the flak and get at them, then you might destroy any number in one attack. So it seemed to me that was the way to do it.

Therefore, since we wanted to take out the Luftwaffe, and this was a top priority immediately before the invasion, I became a great advocate of hitting the Luftwaffe on the ground. Admittedly it was much more dangerous because by that time the German airfields were defended by a curtain of flak. But I still felt this was the way to destroy their airforce.

Years later I discussed this with Mordechai Hod, who commanded the Israeli Air Force in 1966. He listened very carefully to my theories and he agreed with me. In the six-day war, the Israeli fighters destroyed the Egyptian Air Force on the ground on the first day!

Normally we were escorting bombers, of course, but when we were relieved by the next batch of escort fighters and we took off back to base, I always took my outfit down to the ground, coming back low, looking for enemy airfields – spread out in battle formation – and if we spotted one we'd go in and take out any planes we found on the ground.

Our tactics were to get as low as possible – right down in the weeds. I studied low-flying and knew just how low I could get. I've flown back with the tips of my propeller bent because I'd hit the turf, but we needed to get low in order to avoid the flak by flying underneath the defensive fire.

We were very fortunate with our Generals in the American Air Corps, because they agreed with our tactics. Bill Kempner, for instance told us, 'As far as I'm concerned, an airplane destroyed on the ground is just as much destroyed as an airplane destroyed in the air.' – and, of course, he was right. So we hit them on the ground and that's where the Luftwaffe was destroyed.

Over Neu Brandenburg, I had shot down a 109. I saw him go into the ground and start burning, but out of the corner of my eye I glimpsed something else. It was almost an unconscious recognition; a short, stubby profile, a cariacature of a plane hidden in a revetment on the perimeter of the airfield.

I pulled up higher. As I turned, I saw it clearly. It was an Me163 rocket fighter.

I tightened my turn to line up on it, but by now I had to cross the airfield. Much worse, I couldn't hug the ground as usual; I had to be high enough to aim over the protective walls of the revetment which were covered with sandbags and camouflage.

So far, there had been no flak, but the moment I started across the airfield it started. The bright balls of fire came sailing up, seeming to move slowly until close and then whizzing by. There were the little black clouds of heavier flak, with exploding flashes inside them. They were mostly above me.

Automatically, I was taking evasive action, weaving and jinking, stomping one rudder and then the other, skidding and side-slipping, so that the fireballs passed underneath or behind. But I always kept my eye on the target and soon my shots were slamming into the prototype as I steadied the plane.

At the same moment, I felt the plane shudder. I heard the crump and smelt the explosive. I felt a numbness in my right knee and knew I was hit. But it was the plane I felt for. She was like a stricken warhorse. She tried to respond but the life-blood was ebbing. I tried to hold her up, but as I sensed her start to stall, I gently eased the stick forward. And so, tenderly and sadly, I nursed her down until, as softly as I could, I let her settle on the rough ground. As we hit the ground I cut the switch. We bumped and skidded to a halt. Suddenly, everything was quiet.

I slid back the hood, undid the seat harness and the chute and started to climb out. My right leg didn't seem to be working. I looked down. There was a lot of blood and the brown cloth of my pant leg was torn and shredded. I saw too that there was a gaping hole in the floor of the cockpit.

I hauled myself out and stood for a moment on the wing. I looked at my name and the thirty-two swastikas representing the official victories. I patted the side of the plane.

"Two more now, old friend – not bad! We went out on a high note."

There was an incendiary device to stick in the fuel tank to blow up the plane, but by now I saw the rest of the squadron coming in above me. I waved to them to shoot up old VF-B and limped off into the nearby woods.

* * *

So another Eagle was down. There were fewer old Eagles about now. The longer one managed to stay in combat, the greater the chance of becoming a casualty. The odds worked both ways. Experience could help one's chances of survival of course, but you can't keep flying missions and miss all the flak, or miss all the fighters.

Gene Potter, who'd been with 71 Squadron, was now a Captain with the 368th Fighter Group, but was killed in action over Normandy in July 1944. Wally Tribkin also failed to survive 1944 after his successful tour in the Middle East. He returned to the ETO to fly with the 404th Group, 9th Air Force but was killed in a jeep accident, in Belgium, that November.

Former 121 pilots, still in action, also had their losses. Bill Daley, by the summer of 1944, was Deputy Commander of the 371st Fighter Group, 9th Air Force, along with former Eagles Eric Doorly and Dale Taylor. On 10th September 1944, a runaway P.47 smashed into Daley's plane on the airstrip at Coulommiers, France, killing him instantly.

Jim Peck, ex-121 and then ex-Malta, had risen to command a squadron only to die in a P.38 Lightning accident in Christchurch, New Zealand,

12th April 1944. Ben Taylor would also die on active service in England, 22nd December 1944.

Two former 133 Eagles to die in the last year of the war lost their lives far from England and their native homeland. Fred Scuddy, who had also been in 121, died in India in June 1944, while Cecil Meierhoff was killed in action flying a Thunderbolt in the Pacific, on 22 July 1945. The Eagle's influence was felt everywhere.

But the 4th were now short of another two great flyers and fighter pilots – Gentile and Godfrey. Don Gentile had left, tour expired, back in late April 1944 after collecting the DSC, DFC with clusters, and several Air Medals, not to mention his 22 air and six ground victories. Godfrey left too, in order that both men could do a tour of the US to raise Bonds and generally show the flag.

It was decided to use the occasion of the "terrible twin's" departure for a big public relations operation. It was typical of Gentile that he insisted that his best friend and wingman come with him to share the glory. The PR people apparently liked the idea, so it was arranged and everyone was happy. Everyone except the Group Commander, Colonel Don Blakeslee.

Blakeslee was brought up in the strict discipline of the RAF. For him it was the Group that counted and the prime task of the Group was to protect the bombers. For Blakeslee, there was no room in the Group for what he called "prima donnas", pilots only interested in building up a personal score and seeking publicity. I was inclined to think there was room for both the aggressive types, and the solid reliable ones. I must admit, I would never have guessed that the insecure, shaken young man who first introduced himself to me as Don Gentile back in September 1942, had become the leading ace of the US Air Force. All I can say is that I did recognise that both he and Godfrey were brilliant flyers. Unfortunately, the one time Don Gentile's ability as a pilot let him down was partly my fault. Even more unfortunately, it took place in front of the top brass of the US 8th Air Force, the entire US Press Corps in England – and Don Blakeslee!

The occasion was Gentile's departure for his hero's tour to the USA. After the photos and interviews, it was decided that he should fly one low pass over the field so that the press could get photos and film of Don actually flying his famous plane, which he'd named Shangri-La, with its strings of black crosses on a white scroll under the cockpit, and Don's Fighting Eagle cartoon character, with its boxing gloves on a yellow circle. He was encouraged to come in as low as possible to give them a good chance of a shot. He'd asked me, 'Goody, you're the expert on low flying. What's the secret?' Without taking it very seriously, I had replied, "Well, you go as low as you dare, and then go just one foot lower!' Don apparently did take it seriously and indeed, might have got away with it, were it not for the fact that our airfield at Debden is not perfectly flat. The ground rises towards the centre in a sort of hump. As Don brought his Mustang in low, heading across the field towards the assembled crowd, the tips of his whirling propeller caught this higher ground and the plane belly-landed ignominiously in front of everyone. Worse still, it was right in front of Don Blakeslee, who immediately had Gentile grounded.

The fact that this would, to say the least, put a dampener on the meticulously prepared hero's tour to the States made not the slightest difference to Don Blakeslee, who turned a deaf ear to all entreaties from friends, foes and superiors. So Don and Johnny went off on their tour, were duly received by General Hap Arnold, the USAAF's Chief of Staff, and duly idolized by the American public who took the handsome young heroes to their hearts.

Don stayed on in the States until the end of the war. After a brief trial at civilian life, he went back into the Air Force where he felt more at home. He had a charming wife, three boys, a statue of himself in the centre of Piqua, Ohio, his effigy in his uniform in the Air Force Museum, in fact everything a man could want. In February, 1951, the jet fighter he was flying on a training flight plunged to the ground and exploded, killing Gentile instantly.

Johnny Godfrey also had everything a man could want – for a while. After his hero's tour of the States, he came back to the 4th Fighter Group, probably hoping to join his old buddies and pick up where he had left off. If so, he was disappointed. His old buddies had either been shot down, like me, or shipped back to the States, tour expired. What's more, the Luftwaffe didn't like to come up much anymore. The boys were also starting to meet jet-engined Me262s which our planes could hardly catch at the best of times. As a result, Johnny took to destroying the enemy on their airfields, and, like me, got shot down, not by the murderous curtain of flak, but by his own wingman! Johnny went in so low, his inexperienced wingman lost sight of him and continued his attack, unaware of the fact that Johnny was right underneath him. Johnny's plane flew into the hail of bullets, but, by some miracle, Johnny himself escaped serious injury and joined me as a prisoner of war in Stalag Luft III.

After the war, Johnny lived a charmed life. Idolised as a war hero, the handsome, highly intelligent charmer fell in love with and married Joan, a beautiful wealthy girl with whom he had three fine boys. He joined his father-in-law's highly successful lace business, eventually taking it over and developing it into an even more successful operation. His success and wealth led him into politics where his ability brought him further success as a Senator and an offer to become State Governor, an honour which he declined, preferring to devote his efforts to the family business. He had private planes, a racehorse stable, a hunting lodge and any other luxury he wanted.

At the height of his success and happiness, he contracted incurable sclerosis. In a couple of years he was dead, at the age of just 37. But he never gave up. He fought to the last and tried everything. At the end of his autobiography, "The Look of Eagles", completed just before he died, he wrote – 'I have reached the end. Joan and the children know that I never gave up; that I fought hard, even against this unconquerable disease. And I know that I have won a victory.'

One of Johnny's last desperate searches for a cure took him to Germany and to the clinic of Doctor Boss. I was working in Germany at the time and Johnny naturally got in touch with me. I immediately drove down to Southern Germany to see him. It was a shock. It was hard to believe that the emaciated, flabby, inarticulate body on the bed was the incredibly handsome 6ft 2" athlete of only a few years ago. He knew he only had a few more weeks to live, but the last thing he wanted was sympathy. On the contrary, instead of me giving him comfort, it was he who gave me strength. He could barely speak and I had trouble understanding the words he struggled so hard to form. 'It's OK, Goody. Life is for living, living to the full. If you've done that, death isn't so sad. And, by God, we've lived life to the full.' I looked at the wasted figure on the bed, thought of the golden Adonis of just a few months ago, and thought of an ancient Greek saying – 'Call no man lucky until he's dead.'"

* * *

The 4th Fighter Group, with it's few remaining Eagles, continued to fly missions throughout the rest of 1944. If taking their Mustangs to Berlin had been a milestone, so had the momentous shuttle mission to Russia, led by Don Blakeslee. On 21st June – in the Group's briefing room, it must have been a heart-stopping moment when the curtain was drawn back to show the red ribbon of the projected course for Operation Frantic – the first shuttle mission. From Debden the ribbon stretched out over Germany to Ruhland, on to Leszno, Poland, to land at Piryatin, Russia. Blakeslee would take no less than 16 maps with him in the cockpit.

The boys were not to fight unless absolutely necessary, nor would they drop their tanks unless forced to do so. The mission was all show and propaganda, but to be so it had to be successful and they had to get the bombers through. It would not look good if the 4th left a trail of gas-less P.51s scattered across Germany.

Forty-five Mustangs of the 4th, together with 16 from the 486th Squadron of the 352nd Group headed out just before 8 am. Ahead of them they had roughly seven hours of hard flying and for the leaders, hard navigation. Just over three hours later they made rendezvous with B.17s of the 3rd Air Division, over Leszno. Their target was an oil plant near Berlin. The Luftwaffe failed to make any sort of attack on the formation until 12.40 pm, by which time the aircraft were near Siedlce, Poland. Perhaps the enemy fighter pilots were waiting for them to return, but to their surprise they just kept on going east.

The 20 or so Me109s and FW190s which did intercept over Poland were engaged by the Mustangs, Captain Frank Jones of the 335th and Lieutenant Joe Lang of the 334th each claiming one. The 335th lost one pilot – Frank Sibbett. For a while Kid Hofer was also listed as missing, but he turned up later, having chased a 109, lost his way, and landed at Kiev. Whether the Russians at Kiev knew anything about the American Shuttle Mission is not clear, but probably not. There must have been some surprised faces when an American fighter landed amongst them – especially when they met the Kid! Hofer wasn't flying his famous "Salem Representative" on this mission, for he had fallen out with his CO, Deacon Hively, over some inoculations, and very nearly didn't fly. In the end Deac sent him off to fly with another squadron and so Lieutenant Preston Hardy flew Hofer's plane to Russia.

Blakeslee finally brought his Group into Piryatin airfield at 2.50 pm – right on schedule. They had covered 1,470 miles, escorting the B.17s for the last 580 of them, having crossed the Russian front lines just an hour earlier. It was a great achievement for the 4th Fighter Group and for Don Blakeslee.

There was another 4th loss on this historic day, but it wasn't a pilot but a crew chief. It just so happens it was my crew chief, who had been in one of the B.17s and was unlucky enough to have been assigned to the only B.17 lost on the mission – from the 452nd Bomb Group.

My crew chief was Staff Sergeant Robert Gilbert, and he went down the day after I was captured. I guess he felt out of a job so he volunteered to be part of the ground crew team who would fly to Russia in the bombers to help service the Mustangs on the "other side".

I recall an earlier occasion, when I had returned from a ground strafing mission in which my Mustang had been badly shot up by ground fire and I desperately wanted it repaired quickly in order to fly on another mission I knew was scheduled. Looking at Gilbert's face as he examined the damage, I offered to help him out. After all, I had got the plane all shot about! I guess he knew me better than I did, for he just turned to me and said, 'Major, let's strike a deal. You don't ask me to fly fighter missions, and I'll not ask you to help me service your plane!' I thought that was fair enough!

Anyway, Gilbert was on the B.17 headed out for Russia the day after I was shot down, and he was in the only bomber to be lost on that show. He flew as a waist gunner, as did the other enlisted men from the 4th who went out to help with the plane maintenance. When those 20 or so fighters attacked them, his B.17 was hit and set on fire and moments later he was parachuting down with the others. Luckily he was picked up by some Poles and for the next five weeks he lived with some Polish partisans who eventually passed him to the Russians. From here he was later flown to North Africa and by mid-August was back at Debden. I often wonder if he thought about our conversation standing next to my battered P.51, when he said I should fly and he should do repairs, whilst he was dangling at the end of a parachute over Poland!

* * *

After a few days in Russia, during which the Germans tried desperately to night bomb the Fortresses on Poltava airfield – and Deacon Hivey and a Russian General drank each other under the table – Blakeslee finally led part two of the shuttle mission – not back to England, but on to Italy!

On the 26th June, the Group went out on a Target Withdrawal Support show from Piryatin, across to Drohobycz, Poland, then down to Italy, landing at Lucera. The boys made rendezvous with the bombers east of Lvov, Poland, escorting them down to the Yugoslavian coast where they were relieved and they headed across the Adriatic, to be greeted by fellow pilots of the 15th US Air Force. Only four pilots didn't make it. One was Kid Hofer, and three others had been forced to abort back to their Russian base.

They flew out again on the 29th, still with orders not to engage the enemy unless engaged themselves. But that sort of order didn't stop Hofer and he was soon chasing aircraft all over the place. Both he and his wingman ran short of fuel in consequence, and Hofer then overshot Italy altogether, finally lobbing down in Malta, while the wingman crash-landed on a beach in Sicily! A couple of days later, while still available in this part of the world, Blakeslee led the 4th to fly in company with two Groups of the 15th Airforce on a Sweep to Budapest, Hungary. Forming up over Lake Lesina, the Mustangs then headed for the target, encountering between 75 to 80 Me109s. This time the boys were not restricted and the Germans too were found to be very aggressive, so a huge dog-fight ensued.

Deacon Hively got one but another shot him up, blowing off his canopy which caught his head and eye as it went. Grover Siems shot the 109 off Deac's tail, but Siems was then hit and wounded. Despite his own dazed state, Deac got two more 109s, and both he and Siems got back to Foggia. In all, the Group claimed eight 109s shot down – even Don Blakeslee got one, but lost five Mustangs, while the 15th lost one. One of the missing was Kid Hofer.

He was last seen, aggressive as ever, over the centre of Budapest, climbing up to engage a gaggle of more than 20 Me109s. Later his body and wreckage of his Mustang were found at Mostar, Yugoslavia. There has been speculation that Erich Hartmann, Germany's ace of aces, may have shot down Hofer on this 2nd July. But there is no hard evidence of this, nor that Hartmann was even engaged with Mustangs on this precise date. Like many things, it would be a nice story, but . . . Back at Debden, they knew before anyone else. And they knew the exact time. Duke, the big Alsatian, leaped up and let out a series of soulful howls and then went and lay down in the empty revetment where his master would never park his plane again.

After another local mission to Arad, Roumania on the 3rd, Colonel Don led his Mustang pilots home via a mission to Beziers, France on the 5th. Arriving finally back at Debden, they were greeted by General Bill Kepner, who gave Blakeslee and the Deacon a seven day furlough, while everyone else just got the next day off. All the beer that night, however, was free! The 4th Fighter Group, with an ex-Eagle pilot leading them all the way, had flown 6,000 miles, over ten countries and flown nearly 30 combat hours.

* * *

The 4th Fighter Group continued operations for the remainder of the war, but when Blakeslee left at the end of October, much of the old Eagle temperament left too. Which is how it should be; the Group and the pilots were now virtually all American trained, the old RAF days had finally gone.

Leon Blanding, former 121 Eagle, had been wounded back on 8th August and only Deac Hively was still around, commanding the 334th.

It was perhaps typical of our Group that one of the most successful leaders and the one who was there to the end should be known as "The Deacon", remembered not only for his victories in the air but as a comedian on the ground.

His nickname came not only from his somewhat gloomy expression and drooping moustache, but mainly from his brilliant portrayal of a country preacher. I don't remember which came first, but no-one on the base could remember him as other than Deacon Hively.

It is one of the great tragedies of the war that details of every mission are recorded in the individual log-books of each air-crew member and are also meticulously recorded in the archives of the US Air Force but, so far as I know, no written record exists of the brilliant preachings of the Deacon.

They were delivered in an appropriately sonorous voice, interspersed by many shouts of "Hallelujah!" and "Praise the Lord!" from his enthusiastic audience.

We were gathered in the bar after an eventful mission from which not all of our planes returned, and the Deacon was one of those missing. His crew-chief was still waiting for the return of the plane with the picture of a deacon on the cowling, a Bible in one hand, the other raised in blessing, when finally a pale figure came in. It was the Deacon. He collapsed on the bar and ordered a drink.

"Deacon! You made it!"

"What happened, Deac?"

After knocking back his drink, the Deacon climbed onto the bar and began:

"The Deacon is back! Praise the Lord!"

"Praise the Lord!" came in a chorus from the crowd around the bar.

"The Deacon is saved! Hallelujah!"

"Hallelujah!" shouted the chorus.

"Gather round, my children, and listen to the words of the Deacon, cos' the Lord hath saved the Deacon! Praise the Lord!"

"Praise the Lord!" from the growing crowd at the bar.

"Now gather round, children, and hearken to the words of the Lord, Praise the Lord!"

"Praise the Lord!"

"Now it came to pass that the birdmen of the 4th took off to give some succour and protection to the bombers carrying chastisement to the enemies of the Lord in the land of the Hun. Those who had planned their pilgrimage are called Intelligence Officers and they swore it would be a piece of cake and then went back to the bar.

"But the hosts of the enemies of the Lord came up and fell upon the birdmen of the 4th, spreading death and destruction and lo, the Lord's humble servant Deacon Hively found himself alone among a mighty host of enemies.

"So the Lord's humble servant, Deacon, called upon the Lord: "Oh Lord, why hast thou forsaken me? Speak to thy humble servant Deacon, and counsel him and give him succour!"

"And lo, the Lord spake unto his humble servant Deacon and said, "Deacon, hearken thee to the word of the Lord. Get thine ass out of there as fast as you damn well can."

"So the Deacon did his nut trying to get away from his enemies, but there was always one shooting at him.

"So he called again unto his Lord: "Lord, one of mine enemies is on my ass and I can't shake him off!"

"And the Lord replied: "Fear not, Deacon. That is just because he's a good pilot and you're lousy!"

"Lord, please get me out of this mess and I'll try to get out of the next one on my own!"

"And lo, the Lord hearkened unto the Deacon and the Deacon is back. Praise the Lord!"

"Praise the Lord!" chorused the congregation.

But the Deacon had another side to him, far more serious than playing a comic preacher in the Mess. His steady, reliable performance as a leader in the air led to his becoming Commanding Officer of 334 Squadron and deputy commanding officer to Blakeslee on the great shuttle raid to Russia.

Deac was one of the few 4th Group pilots to be rescued from the sea. Another had been Bob Hobart, but he had succumbed to his immersion shortly after rescue, on 5 April, 1944. The Deacon's experience began on 15 June, 1943, long before he had shot down his first Geman.

The boys had flown from Tangmere that day to escort Forts over France but on the way back, Deac's Thunderbolt started to get hot and trail smoke. There had been a brief skirmish with enemy fighters, but nothing much to speak of. Perhaps it was just engine trouble. Pierce McKennon spotted the problem too and formated on the smoking fighter, giving it the once over.

"I think you'd better get out of there, Deac," Mac had called.

"I've been thinking about it, Mac, but it looks awful wet down there; maybe I can hold on for a little while longer."

"We'll follow you down, don't worry," said Mac.

"OK," said Deac, reassured, "but I'm going to wait for a while, if I can." Looking down again, he continued, "That's one helluva step!"

The P.47s were at 27,000 feet, so the sea was indeed a long way below them, but the old Thunderbolt was starting to get hot and Deac told us afterwards that his feet were warming up nicely. Like it or not, he was going to have to go.

He slid back the hood, undid the straps, rolled the Jug over but he couldn't bring himself to drop out and held on tight. Finally, with smoke and flame round his feet and down to around 7,000 feet, he kicked the stick forward and out he went, seeing for the first time the line of bullet holes near the wing root where some Hun fighter pilot had got in a long range shot that had done the damage.

As his parachute opened and with still some way to go before he'd
hit the sea, Deac decided to have a cigarette. They'd all get wet and
wasted anyway. Fumbling under his parachute harness, he managed to
get one out and actually light it! Then he began to unload all the heavy
stuff from his pockets – lighter, cigarette case, knife, the beautiful
pearl-handled .38 revolver his Dad had given him, although not before
he'd fired off the six rounds, just for the hell of it.

He crashed down into the water, fought the release mechanism, and
then fought even more hard to get into his dinghy. The water was
freezing, even for June, but he finally made it. The P.47s were still
overhead, but to be certain, Deac fired off a couple of flares, nearly
hitting Jim Clark's fighter, but later it transpired that none of the pilots
had even seen the flares and had totally lost sight of Deac when he
hit the sea. However, he had to be down there somewhere and they
were busily getting off a fix for the Air Sea Rescue boys.

Then they had to go. Fuel was running short, so Deac was alone
in the Channel – a very rough Channel. Some time later he heard the
sound of an aero engine and looking up spotted an RAF Walrus amphibian
circling. Their experienced eyes found him. He was lucky that it was
an ace crew from 277 Squadron, RAF, crewed by two of the best ASR
boys in the business, Tom Fletcher and Len Healey, along with Sergeant
Green. They had been out looking for a lost RAF Typhoon pilot, got
the call and had found Deac's dinghy. It was too rough to land,
although this did not often stop the ASR boys, but they knew a rescue
launch was on the way so just stayed around and helped guide the boat
to him.

In fact Deac was 277 Squadron's 101st live rescue, and as fate
would have it, the 100th was another former Eagle, now with the 4th,
Ed Beatie of the 336th Squadron. Ed had splashed down into the North
Sea just four days earlier, on the 12th , and been picked up by a Walrus.

I guess Pete Peterson had been the RAF's most famous Eagle rescue,
when Pete had gone down after a mission when his P.47 developed
engine trouble. He'd gone down 30 miles out from the English coast
back in April 1943 but 277 Squadron and their Walrus amphibians had
got him out and back in less than an hour.

So Deac survived his ordeal, and like many others who were rescued
from the sea, went on to make a name for himself. Had it not been
for the rescue guys, he would have just been a name on some memorial

tablet somewhere, as another aviator – missing in action.

Deac went on to be credited with 12 enemy aircraft destroyed in the air and 3 on the ground, putting him among the top twenty or so scorers in the USAAF.

* * *

Don Blakeslee had found himself grounded after a Penetration Target Withdrawal mission to Hamburg on the 30th October. He had been expecting the order to come for over a year. Hub Zemke, boss of the 56th Fighter Group, had failed to return that same day, ending up as a prisoner, and the top brass didn't want to risk Don any more. Don handed over the Group to Lieutenant Colonel Claiborne Kinnard Jr.

Don Blakeslee returned to the US with the DSC and oakleaf, the Silver Star and bar, DFC with seven clusters, British DFC, Air Medal with clusters, over 500 combat missions and 1,000 combat hours. Just a month earlier he'd got another award – he married Leola Freyer on September 18th. With Hub Zemke he had been, and remains, one of the two finest fighter leaders of the US Air Force in World War II.

He was also a character in a class all of his own. Some twenty-five years after the war, I found myself sitting next to a three-star General at a formal dinner. The General turned to me and said, "I know, of course, that you commanded 336 Squadron of the 4th Fighter Group back in World War II, so you must have known Don Blakeslee."

"Of course," I replied enthusiastically. "Where did you know Don?" I shouldn't have asked.

"You see this scar?" said the General, pointing to an old but nonetheless distinctive mark on his chin. "Well, shortly after the war I was a young second lieutenant on a base where Blakeslee was the Commanding Officer. One night when I was Duty Officer, I heard loud voices coming from the Officers' Mess and thought I should investigate. That was my first mistake. No sooner had I stepped into the Mess when a booming voice yelled, "Take off your goddam hat in the Officers' Mess!" I turned to Blakeslee and saluted. "Excuse me, sir, I am the Duty Officer and as you know, the Duty Officer always wears his hat, even in the Officers' Mess."

"I should have realised," the General continued to me, "that Blakeslee had been brought up on the rigorous rules of the RAF, which made no concessions to Duty Officers or anyone else in the sanctity of the Mess, but I didn't. That was my second mistake."

"I told you to take off your hat in the Mess!" repeated Blakeslee.

"I went over to where he was sitting with some of his old 4th Group officers and made my third mistake by starting to repeat my reason for not doing so. The next thing I knew was when I woke up in hospital with a broken jaw!"

"The man" was what Blakeslee was, and under his leadership the 4th Fighter Group was moulded in his image.

He was also very proud of his RAF wings and his British decorations and it may be that, in the post-war Air Force, these reminders of Blakeslee's meteoric rise from a kid who was only just out of high school and starting a job, to full Colonel in three years was resented by some senior officers who had graduated from military academy and followed a less colourful and much slower career.

Certainly, his independent attitude and blunt defence of his convictions did not endear him to many of his superiors. He retired from the Air Force in 1965, still a Colonel, but still flying at the head of his command, which is probably the way he wanted it.

Diplomacy was never part of Blakeslee's make-up. He was a war-time pilot. He led by example, not by orders. He commanded obedience by the strength of his character, not the rule-book. He earned the admiration and loyalty of his men by his loyalty to them.

He had no time for those who would treat him as a hero. He didn't need them. He was the typical, ideal fighter commander, but he was, above all, every inch a man.

Chapter 14

When Eagles Come to Rest

MARCH 1945 had ended with an interesting operation to Hassel-Berlin, Norley again leading one group of Mustangs. On this occasion, three Russian P-39s (an American fighter given by the US to the Soviets) for some strange reason bounced the Mustangs. Shots were exchanged, but no real damage was done. However, Ken Foster of the 334th Squadron went down with engine trouble. He later got back and had a good tale to tell:

"I was flying Cobweb Green No. 3 on an escort mission to Hassel, 31 March 1945. Returning from target, my engine failed and I crash-landed near Ommen, Holland, at about 1030 hours. Upon landing, several Dutch people surrounded my aircraft, smiling and shaking my hand, saying they were Hollanders.

"About 100 yards from the aircraft, a chap on a bicycle waved to me, saying in English that he would help me and telling me to go up to some nearby woods and he would try to come later. I started towards the woods and encountered another farmer, asking him in sign language about this other chap. He replied by writing N.S.B. in the sandy soil. I didn't understand, and I could have saved myself much trouble had I known.

"I continued on to the woods and around noon the man who spoke English and two boys came near my hiding place, calling for me. I answered and they said they had clothes for me and gave me a couple of slices of bread. They said they would return later and moved on. At 3 o'clock, one of the boys returned, leading another man. They were all smiles, and motioned for me to follow them. I did. Upon entering a clearing the man pulled a gun on me and disarmed me.

"He took me back to the scene of the crash and turned me over to the Wehrmacht, who in turn took me to Ommen. At Ommen, I was thoroughly searched and all was taken with the exception of my escape maps, which they missed. Next morning I was moved by truck to Havelt, 5 miles north of Meppel, under guard of four men, and put into a single cell.

"That evening, Easter Sunday, I was questioned by an officer who asked my name, rank and number and then asked what the Americans thought of the Germans. Being a bit shaken by it all, I refused to tell him, not being certain how the reply would be taken.

"Near my cell window was an air-raid shelter, and Dutch boys and girls used to roll cigarettes out of some vile tobacco and hand them to me. There were six mean dogs chained nearby and they always set up a clamour. One day, a guard shot at one of the girls to scare them away. They didn't scare easily.

"Among all these people at the air-raid shelter was a boy who spoke English. He asked me to write him a letter. I told him I was an American pilot, and asked if he could help me escape. Later in the day he returned, asking for identification, and I gave him a dog-tag. He returned about 6 o'clock, handed me a worn hacksaw blade and a note saying he would be waiting for me at the air-raid shelter after 9 o'clock.

"He sat outside and watched while I started to saw the $3/4$ inch thick bars. I worked on the bars of three different rooms in the next three days, and by then two rooms had the bars half-sawn. On Thursday, I was interrogated and returned to another room where two other chaps were. They were a Norwegian and a Dutch lad flying in the Royal Air Force. After we had satisfied each other all was O.K., I revealed my hacksaw and we started to work on the bars again all afternoon. At four o'clock, we had the bar sawn through, leaving a small piece to hold it together. In the evening at 6 oclock, we were given the usual half loaf of bread and 3 chunks of meat, which was to be supper and breakfast. We made 2 sandwiches for each man.

"At 10.30, we broke out of the jail and tramped across country, crossing innumerable irrigation ditches and, after trying three farmers, found one who took us in at 4 o'clock in the morning and hid us. We hid up in a straw mow and the farmer's children didn't know we were there. In 2 days, he contacted the local underground, who provided us with civilian clothes and some tobacco. He provided us with news of the war and paid the farmer 50 guilders (£5) for hiding us and feeding us. For a week, we could hear the Germans and Allies blowing up bridges, and shelling and machine-gun fire all round us.

"On Friday the 13th, a girl came for us and said the Canadians had taken Meppel. We went to the local town, where the Underground agent was acting as Mayor, and saw the flag raised for the first time in five years. At Meppel, we met the Canadians and had supper, staying over that night. Next morning, we hitch-hiked down the convoy route to Nijmegen and reported at a Canadian ex-PoW camp. They flew us to Paris after cleaning us up and a short interrogation.

"After 3 days in Paris, I returned to the squadron April 21."

By the Spring of 1945 the Group's tally of enemy aircraft destroyed topped 1,000. New pilots were arriving all the time as the old and bold either became tour expired or lost. Among the new boys was Bill Spencer, from Boone, North Carolina, who joined the 334th in January 45. He was to fly 22 combat missions in the last months of the war, and flew several on the wing of his CO, Red Dog Norley. He remembers his first mission:

"On my first mission we were over occupied territory when we began to let down through a thick layer of cloud. As we broke through we soon spotted a train in a station and dived to strafe it. There was no flak going in as I guess we caught them on the hop, but as we pulled up and away the sky quickly filled with tracer and black puffs of exploding shells.

"On another mission I was flying wingman on a bomber escort. Looking down we spotted an Me262 jet as it raced in from below a box of B.17s, pulled up, fired into an engine, then turned over to go back down. My leader was down and after it, with me trying to keep with him as well as secure his tail in case other 262s were coming after us. I could see my leader firing but I did not see the 262 again as I had my eyes glued on the Mustang ahead of me. That was some chase.

"I saw several 262s in those last weeks, as well as one I could easily have shot down. We were flying along in open battle formation with me on the extreme right. I suddenly spotted this 262 come hurtling up and throttle back, then it seemed to format on us about 500 yards off to the right. It would have been the easiest thing in the world just to pull out and side-slip behind him and give him a burst, but it had been drummed into me that a wingman never left his leader, no matter what. I tried to call up the others, but discovered that someone had his finger pressed down on the radio button, so I could not get through to anyone. Just as I was considering what to do next, the German must have looked across at us and either seen us for the first time, or finally recognised that we were Mustangs and not 109s. Before I could even think of doing anything else, the pilot had put on the coals and headed up and away at a great rate of knots.

"One of our pilots, Paul Burnett, had an amazing escape during a mission on 16th April, 1945. We were led by Norley on a Penetration Target Withdrawal Support and strafing mission to Rosenheim/ Gablingen airdrome, Germany. After rendezvous and escort to some B.24s we left to shoot-up Gablingen, which was crammed with aircraft. We destroyed over 40 while another part of the Group, led by Colonel Woods, hit three fields near Prague. In all the 4th got over 100 aircraft destroyed that day, although we lost eight Mustangs. Not all the pilots were killed, and Burnett was among the lucky ones.

"He got hit in the strafing attack and apart from superficial damage, he had both his trim tabs blown down and jammed. The only way he could fly straight and level was by keeping the stick well back and the moment he relaxed that, the nose of the Mustang went down. He was pretty low and had no way of climbing to gain bale-out height. So he flew on for a while but knew that eventually he would have to bale out. He finally decided he would undo his straps, turn upside down and drop out and hope he had enough height to deploy his 'chute. So he undid the seat harness and radio lead, turned the P.51 over but as he fell, somehow got caught up by his parachute harness. The Mustang was heading down now as he tried to get back into the cockpit. Then he felt a burning sensation to his right arm and shoulder, finding a fire had started which was burning his jacket and harness. With an extra effort he kicked himself free, the flames having forced open his parachute pack. As the 'chute deployed, so his feet hit the ground. Boy, was he one lucky guy!"

The war was drawing to a close. Any Luftwaffe aircraft seen in the air was quickly a target for the roving fighters of the 8th Air Force. The policy of finding and hitting German aircraft on the ground was still a priority. One of the last missions of the war, flown by the 334th Squadron of the 4th was that of 16 April, recalled by Bill Spencer. It was very successful in scoring against a non-flying enemy force.

It was led by Red-Dog Norley, 16 April, 1945. Officially it was listed as the Squadron's 411th operation of the war, of which 288 had been flown with Mustangs. The mission was a Penetration, Target and Withdrawal Support sortie for B.24 Liberators who were going for Rosenheim. Norley took off with five sections of four Mustangs at 12.55 pm heading in across Ostend at 1.35 pm at 14,000 feet. They made rendezvous with the Libs 115 miles to the southeast of Stuttgart an hour later, having climbed to 16,000 feet – a thousand feet above the heavies.

The Mustangs escorted them to the target which was bombed visually with good results at 3.30. With no opposition and relief fighters arriving, Red-Dog led his fighters away from the bombers at 4 pm near Ulm, heading for the enemy airfield at Gablingen, north of Augsburg. They arrived just after 5 pm and worked it over for 40 minutes with impressive results:

Pilot		Rounds fired	Claims
Major Norley	White 1	?	2 FW190s destroyed
			1 Ju52 destroyed
			1 U/I TE destroyed
			1 U/I TE damaged
Lt G A Denson	White 2	1470	2 FW190s destroyed
			1 Me410 destroyed
			1 He177 destroyed
			1 Me410 damaged
			1 U/I TE damaged
Lt R A Dyer	White 3	1504	1 FW190 destroyed
			1 Me109 destroyed
			1 U/I TE destroyed
			1 Me410 damaged
			1 FW190 damaged
			1 Me109 damaged
Lt C W Harre	White 4	1555	1 Me109 destroyed
			1 U/I TE destroyed
			1 Me109 damaged
			1 U/I TE damaged
Lt W J Dvorak	Red 1	1387	2 U/I TE destroyed
			1 U/I TE damaged

			1 Me109 damaged
Lt W D Antonides	Red 2	1435	3 Me109s destroyed
			1 FW190 destroyed
			1 Me410 destroyed
			1 U/I SE destroyed
			1 U/I TE damaged
Lt M J Kennedy	Red 3	1160	1 U/I SE destroyed
			1 Ju88 damaged
			1 Ju87 damaged
Lt P E Burnett	Red 4	?	1 U/I TE destroyed
Lt J W Ayres	Blue 1	1700	1 Me109 destroyed
			1 U/I TE destroyed
			1 FW190 destroyed
Lt A R Bowers	Blue 2	1577	2 Me109s destroyed
			1 Ju88 destroyed
			3 Me109s damaged
Lt K G Helfrecht	Blue 3	1760	2 Me410s destroyed
			2 FW190s destroyed
			1 He177 destroyed
			2 Ju88s damaged
Lt R H Buchanan	Green 1	1500	1 FW190 destroyed
			1 Me410 destroyed
			2 FW190s damaged
			1 Me109 damaged
Lt W O'Bryan	Green 2	?	3 U/I TE destroyed
Lt M W Arthur	Green 3	1271	$^1/_2$FW190 destroyed
			1 Me109 destroyed
Lt W G Spencer	Green	4710	$^1/_2$FW190 destroyed
			1Me109 destroyed
			1 FW190 destroyed
			1 He177 destroyed
Lt D G Lowther	Purple 4	1655	1 U/I TE destroyed

* U/I = Unidentified
* TE = Twin-engined aircraft

As Bill says, Paul Burnett failed to return. He was flying Red 4, in Lieutenant Dvorak's section. Dvorak heard Burnett call that he had been hit during a strafing run, and later he was heard calling over the R/T so it was thought he was trying to head for friendly territory with a damaged fighter. Otherwise, apart from a few bullet holes in five Mustangs, there were no other losses.

In the event, news soon arrived that Burnett was safe. He had crash landed near Kaiserslautern and was picked up by US troops. When he returned he made the following report:

"I was flying the position of Red Four. After leaving the bombers and returning to enemy territory we found the airfield of Gablingen and we started our passes. On the first pass I didn't fire my guns. On the second run on the target, I wasn't in a very good position and only got in a short burst which wasn't enough to set the plane on fire. The third pass I was all lined-up on a couple of planes. The first plane I took a long burst on and it started to burn and I was just looking ahead to the next plane when the first one blew up with a terrific explosion. I was unable to manoeuvre out of the blast and flew through the flames and flying particles. The flames and smoke burnt my plane black and the flying debris damaged it.

"The left wing was torn up on the leading edge and the left wing tank must have had a large hole because I had all the gas out of it. The prop was bent out of line and caused the engine to vibrate and it felt like it was going to fall out. There was an oil leak and a stream of oil over the left wing next to the fuselage. Something flew through the canopy leaving a large hole and splattering glass all over the cockpit.

"I jettisoned my canopy, getting ready to either set it down or jump when I could get some altitude. My windscreen was covered with black soot and I couldn't see out of it. I thought my best decision was to get out of the area as fast as I could.

"I took up a heading of approximately 310 degrees and tried to climb as high as I could. After about 30–35 minutes I had managed to get up to 5,000 feet. I thought I would be able to bale from there OK. Another five minutes and the oil pressure dropped to zero and almost immediately began to stream white smoke from the exhaust. I rolled the plane over on it's back and attempted to bale out. I got about halfway out and was thrown back against the armour-plating and couldn't get out any further. I managed to fight my way back into the cockpit and straightened it back up again.

"After fighting desperately to get myself out, something happened that caused me to be jerked out of the burning plane just as it hit. I found myself lying face down six feet away from the plane which had gone straight in and was burning fiercely. I got out of my parachute and crawled to a ditch along a road a few feet away. I began to check for any injury but found I was only shaken up a little. "By this time people from a little village about a quarter of a mile down the road were beginning to crowd about me. I could not speak German so I couldn't understand much of what they were all jabbering. I found the mayor of the village and tried to talk to him without much success. I did understand that some American troops were in a nearby town of Otterberg, about seven kilometers away. The people were very friendly and the mayor took me to his home and offered me something to eat and drink. A German girl came in that could speak some English and told me that American soldiers came in to patrol the town at night and would be around soon. Two boys in a jeep picked me up and took me to their command post in the town of Otterberg. I got a Major in charge of an Aid Station to check me over and I stayed there that night.

"The next morning early, I was taken by an LI Observation plane to Y.76 at Darmstadt. That afternoon I was flown by C.47 to Nancy, France. There I received travel orders and left by train for Paris, France. I arrived in Paris Wednesday morning, receiving orders there to leave by C.47 for London on Thursday. I arrived base 19 April, 1945."

Most of the Mustangs had landed at B58 (Brussels) or A93 on the Continent in order to refuel. Red-Dog Norley had landed at Brussels, along with half-a-dozen others. Lieutenant Mike Kennedy was among them, but he drew the short straw. As he later reported:

"I landed at B.58 with Major Norley and five other pilots. Major Norley had a coolant leak so we flipped to see who had to stay with his airplane. I lost – naturally! The next morning I changed the radiator and the next day we ran up the ship and blew the gasket. I sweated out the ship Major Norley said he would send over but it did not come, so I scrounged a ride on a B.17 and a C.47 to England. I returned to base from Huntingdon in a C.64."

The operation by 334 Squadron had been a huge success. Some 44 German aircraft had been claimed as destroyed with 22 more damaged.

All for the loss of one Mustang. With the rest of the Group attacking airfields in the Prague area (Czechoslovakia), claiming 61 destroyed, it was a memorable day.

Not long afterwards on 25 April, 1945, the 4th Fighter Group had its last combat loss during a Fighter Sweep led by Colonel Stewart, to the Linz-Prague-Dresden areas. The red-nosed P.51s arrived over Linz at 8.30 am. The only loss was Lieutenant William B Hoelscher of the 334th but he returned to Debden on 9 May with the following story:

"I destroyed an Me262 over Prague aerodrome but in the process I myself picked up a 40 mm shell in my wing root and my left elevator was torn off. I pulled up and headed west, getting as far as Rakovnik, Czechoslovakia, about 50 miles due west of Prague. "I baled out from 300 feet and when I hit the ground I found I was in the middle of a bunch of Czech partisans who took care of me. They later told the SS men that another airplane had landed and picked me up, so the Jerries quit looking for me. I changed hiding places for three nights then walked to Rakovnik where I hid until the Partisans took over the town.

"I traded all my Jerry souvenirs off and got a ride to Pilsen on a motorcycle where I met a 14th Armoured Division scouting force about 30 kms from Pilsen. Then I hitched airplane rides which subsequently ended at the 4th Fighter Group, Debden, England, on 10 May, 1945."

Unfortunately his claim for the Me262 jet was not confirmed and he had to settle for a probable. The 4th had now achieved 1,003 victories, their rivals, the 56th Group, having a score of 1008 $^1/_2$. These totals were later revised. The 4th were credited with 583 $^1/_2$ air and 469 ground kills, to make 1052 $^1/_2$. The 56th scored 674 $^1/_2$ air and 311 ground kills – 985 $^1/_2$. However, the 4th had lost 241 planes to the 56th's 128, though the 56th hadn't got into combat until April 1943.

After V.E. Day, things gradually ran down. The group left Debden and moved to Steeple Morden. That was a sad day for everyone. Debden had been home for so long, first to the Eagles, then to the 4th.

Bill Spencer says: "The worst part was having to move to a regular GI base, with so many things we had not been used to, steel-mat runways, Nissen huts for quarters. Those were quite a come-down after the brick-built Officers' quarters at Debden. There were no batmen to build the fires and shine your shoes, no waitresses in the Mess and no silver napkin rings!

"Some of the Squadron Commanders had the corrugated iron inside walls of their barracks lined with wood from the crates that had held wing tanks, courtesy of the ground crews, and you'd be surprised how good they looked.

"Red Norley and Pierce McKennon even had theirs fitted up with a bar. That was nice, but with no war on, everyone got itchy to have some excitement. One night after everyone was asleep, we heard a lot of pistol shots. We got our .45s and went outside to see if we had been invaded. It turned out to be Red and Mac lying in bed shooting the empty bottles off their bar! All hell broke loose and they took off to London for a week. I don't know what the C.O. did about it, but I expect not much."

So the war was over, Debden was left behind. The 4th, I'm glad to say, went on, and does to this day. They were among the units in the Gulf War, Operation 'Desert Storm', in 1991.

The 4th had a number of claims to fame. Not only had it been born of the RAF Eagle Squadrons, and was the oldest Group in the 8th Air Force, it had been the first to engage the enemy over Berlin and over Paris. It had been the first to penetrate German air space, on 28 July 1943, and it had been awarded a Distinguished Unit Citation for destroying 189 enemy aircraft in the air and another 134 on the ground during the period 5th March to 24 April, 1944.

The 56th had some good claims to fame, too. It had received not one but two Unit Citations, had more air kills, had more aces, had been the first to fly the P-47 although, unlike the 4th, the 56th retained "Jugs and never flew the P–51.

But the one thing no other Group could take from the 4th was its history. We have tried to give some of that history here.

* * *

Epilogue

There are damn few of us left. The words that most often come to mind are those of the famous poem by Thomas Moore:

> "I feel like one
> Who treads alone
> Some banquet-hall deserted,
> Whose lights are fled,
> Whose garlands dead,
> And all but he departed."

Most of them died young, which is sad, but at least our memories of them are of handsome, fun-loving, carefree boys.

The way they were when they came to England and were "Over-paid, over-sexed and over here."

Appendix 1

71 Squadron Victories 1941–42

Date	Name	a/c	Dest	Prob	Dam	Locality	Time	Op.
1941								
15 May	PO J K Alexander	Z2756		Me109F		mid Channel	2100	Scr
2 Jul	PO W R Dunn	Z3781		Me109F		W of Lille	1235	Esc
2 Jul	SL H deC Woodhouse	Z3345	Me109E			Lille-Grave	1220	Esc
2 Jul	PO R L Mannix	Z3335		Me109E		W of Lille	1235	C29
2 Jul	PO V R Bono	Z3457			Me109E	W of Lille	1230	C29
2 Jul	PO G A Daymond	Z3185	Me109E			W of Lille	1240	Esc
4 Jul	PO K S Taylor	Z3781			Me109E	Bethune	1525	C
6 Jul	PO W R Dunn	Z3267			Me109F	Merville	1430	C35
6 Jul	FL C G Peterson	Z3170	Me109F				1430	C35
6 Jul	PO G A Daymond	Z3829	Me109E			W of Lille	1428	C35
19 Jul	PO V R Bono	Z3266		Me109		W of Lille	1410	C51
21 Jul	PO W R Dunn	Z3781	Me109F			W of Lille	1235	Est
3 Aug	PO G A Daymond		Do17z			E Orfordness	1318	Cv/P
9 Aug	PO W R Dunn	Z3267	Me109E			W Mardyck	1130	C
19 Aug	PO H S Fenlaw	Z3458			Me109	W Bourbourg	1840	C82
19 Aug	PO W R Fessler	Z3829		Me109		Hazebrouck	1840	C82
27 Aug	PO W R Dunn	P7308	Me109F			Ambleteuse	0815	C86
27 Aug	PO W R Dunn	P7308	Me109F			Ambleteuse	0820	C86
4 Sep	PO T C Wallace	AB783	Me109E			SE Mardyck	1620	C93

Date	Name	a/c	Dest	Prob	Dam	Locality	Time	Op.
4 Sep	PO R L Mannix	AD123		Me109E		Hardelot	1650	C93
4 Sep	P/ G A Daymond	AB811	Me109F			Mazingarbe	1625	C93
7 Sep	FL C G Peterson	W3627	Me109					
7 Sep	PO W R Fessler	AB811		Me109		Hazebrouck	1840	C82
18 Sep	FL C G Peterson	W3627	Me109					
19 Sep	PO J Flynn	AB807	Me109F			Channel	1650	Rhub
19 Sep	FO G A Daymond	AB812	Me109F		Me109F	Channel	1650	Rhub
21 Sep	PO C W McColpin	AB908	Me109E			Lille/coast	1630	C102
21 Sep	PO C W Tribken	AD123		Me109F		Lille/coast	1630	C102
27 Sep	PO O H Coen	AB827			Me109F	Mazingarbe	1440	C103B
27 Sep	PO S A Mauriello	AB783	Me109F			Mazingarbe	1435	C103B
27 Sep	FL C G Peterson	AB810		Me109F		Mazingarbe	1435	C103B
27 Sep	PO R O Scarborough	AB896	Me109F			Mazingarbe	1435	C103B
27 Sep	PO J J Crowley	AD123		Me109F		Mazingarbe	1435	C103B
2 Oct	SL S T Meares	W3819	Me109F			Abbeville	1345	Sweep
2 Oct	PO C W McColpin	AB908	Me109E			Abbeville	1345	Sweep
2 Oct	PO C W McColpin	AB908	Me109E			Abbeville	1345	Sweep
2 Oct	PO N Anderson	AB896				Abbeville	1345	Sweep
2 Oct	PO R O Scarborough	W3627	Me109F					
2 Oct	PO A F Roscoe	W3708	Me109E			Abbeville	1345	Sweep
16 Oct	PO C W McColpin	AB827	Hs126			Etaples	1115	Rhub
20 Oct	PO M W Fessler	AB811	Me109F	on the ground		St Inglevert	0715	Rhub
20 Oct	PO M W Fessler	AB811	Me109F	on the ground				
27 Oct	PO C W McColpin	AA857	Me109			SE Dunkirk	0725	Rhub

Date	Name	a/c	Dest	Prob	Dam	Locality	Time	Op.
7 Nov	PO T C Wallace	W3708	Me109E			Lille	1330	Rhub
8 Dec	FL G A Daymond	AB897	Me109		on the ground	Nr Lambus	1210	R.15
8 Dec	PO S A Mauriello	AB783	Me109F		on the ground	Nr Lambus	1210	R.15
1942								
9 Jan	PO R Sprague	BL376	FW190			NW Le Touquet	1440	Rhub
17 Feb	PO O H Coen	W3957			Do217	E Felixstowe	1606	Cv/F
16 Apr	PO M G McPharlin	W3759			FW190	Guines	1850	Rodeo
16 Apr	PO O H Coen	AB802			FW190	Guines	1850	Rodeo
16 Apr	PO N Anderson	W3919			FW190	Guines	1850	Rodeo
17 Apr	PO J J Lynch	W3740	1/2 Ju88			E Orfordness	0715	Cv/P
25 Apr	SL C G Peterson	BL449			FW190			
27 Apr	PO O H Coen	AD654	FW190			St Omer/sea	1215	C142
27 Apr			FW190				to	
27 Apr	PO M G McPharlin	W3709	FW190		FW190	St Omer/sea	1225	C142
27 Apr	SL C G Peterson	BL449	FW190					
27 Apr	SL C G Peterson	BL449	FW190					
30 Apr	SL S C Peterson	BL449			FW190			
9 May	PO A F Roscoe	AB941		Me109F		France	1315	Esc
19 May	SL C G Peterson	BL449			Me109		2015	Sweep
1 Jun	FL G A Daymond	BL583	FW190			Off Ostend	1345	C178
1 Jun	SL C G Peterson	BL449	FW190				1345	C178
1 Jun	PO R S Sprague	W3368			FW190	Nr Bruges	1340	C178

Date	Name	a/c	Dest	Prob	Dam	Locality	Time	Op.
19 Jul	PO J F Helgason		FW190			Dunkirk	1340	Rhub
19 Jul	PO J J Lynch							
1 Aug	PO J A Gray	AD288	FW190			Off Flushing	1505	ASR
1 Aug	PO R S Sprague	AD111			FW190	Off Flushing	1505	ASR
19 Aug	PO H Strickland	BL449			FW190	Dieppe	0530	Raid
19 Aug	SL C G Peterson	BM361	Ju88		Ju88	Dieppe		Raid
19 Aug	PO S M Anderson	BL376			Ju88	Dieppe	1350	Raid
19 Aug	PO O H Coen	BM293		Ju88		Dieppe	1400	Raid
19 Aug	PO M G McPharlin	W3767				Dieppe	1400	Raid
27 Aug	FL G A Daymond		FW190		FW190	St Omer	1315	C
27 Aug	PO A J Seaman	BM305				Gravelines	1220	
29 Aug	WC R Duke Woolley	EP179		FW190		Gris Nez	1045	C211
334th Fighter Squadron (whilst under RAF control)								
2 Oct	Lt S M Anderson	BL376	FW190				1435	C221
2 Oct	WC M Duke Woolley	BM582	FW190			SW Dunkirk	1430	C221
2 Oct	Lt J A Clark							
2 Oct	Capt O H Coen	BL582	FW190			SW Dunkirk	1435	C221
2 Oct	Lt W B Morgan	BL550			FW190	S Nieuport	1435	C221
15 Dec	Lt S M Anderson			Ju52		SW Flushing	0900	Rhub
15 Dec	Lt R A Boock							
1943								
14 Jan	Lt S M Anderson		FW190			W Ostend	1155	Rhub
14 Jan	Lt R A Boock		FW190			W Ostend	1155	Rhub

Date	Name	a/c	Dest	Prob	Dam	Locality	Time	Op.
22 Jan	Lt R A Boock		FW190			W Ostend	1730	R204
15 Apr	Col C G Peterson		FW190			Belg Coast	1750	R204
15 Apr	Lt R A Boock		FW190		FW190	Belg Coast	1750	R204
15Apr	Lt J A Clark					N Sea	1400	Rodeo
21May	Lt W M Morgan		Me109			Ghent	1359	Rodeo
21May	Lt S N Pissanos				FW190			

Appendix II
121 Squadron Victories 1941–42

Date	Name	a/c	Dest	Prob	Dam	Locality	Time	Op.
1941								
8 Aug	PO S R Edner	Z3427		Ju88		NE Hull	1450	Scr
8 Aug	Sgt J J Mooney	Z5058						
18 Aug	SL P R Powell	Z3493		Me109F		Fr Coast	1600	Sweep
16 Nov	PO H S Marting	P8133			Ju88	Flam' Head	1215	Scr
1942								
8 Mar	PO W J Daley	AD139			Me109	S Dunkirk	1620	C
23 Mar	Sgt J J Mooney	AA904	FW190			Calais	1605	Sweep
24 Mar	Sgt R Tilley	AD463		FW190		Comines/ coast	1545	C116
12 Apr	FL T W Allen	BL896			FW190	North Hazebrouck	1335	C122
12 Apr	SL H C Kennard	BL234			FW190	Aire	1330	C122
12 Apr	PO L A Skinner	AD501	FW190			Aire/Hazeb'	1330	C122
12 Apr	P O B Mahon	W3711			FW190	Aire	1330	C122
15 Apr	FL T W Allen	BL986			FW190	St Omer	1910	C125
15 Apr	PO L A Skinner	W3804	FW190		FW190	Calais	1915	C125
15 Apr	FO S R Edner	AA903	FW190			St Omer	1915	C125
24 Apr	PO W J Daley	P8794	Ju34			W Knocke	1450	C132
24 Apr	PO L A Skinner	W3804						

Date	Name	a/c	Dest	Prob	Dam	Locality	Time	Op.
28 Apr	FO S R Edner	AA903		FW190		Dunkirk	1140	C144
17 May	PO W J Daley	R6890	FW190			St Omer	1545	Sweep
17 May	PO S R Edner	AA903	FW190			St Omer	1545	Sweep
17 May	PO B Mahon	AD289			FW190	St Omer	1545	Sweep
17 May	Sgt J J Mooney	AA904			FW190	St Omer	1545	Sweep
27 May	PO W J Daley	BL986	Me109F			WWalcheron	1645	S/Rec
27 May	PO B Mahon	AD289			Me109F	WWalcheron	1645	S/Rec
27 May	Sgt F Vance	W3711			Me109F	WWalcheron	1645	S/Red
8 Jun	PO B Mahon	AD289	FW190			St Omer	1330	Rodeo
8 Jun	PO B Mahon	AD289	FW190			St Omer	1330	Rodeo
8 Jun	Sgt J J Mooney	AD423	FW190			St Omer	1330	Rodeo
8 Jun	Sgt J J Mooney	AD423	FW190			St Omer	1330	Rodeo
8 Jul	PO G O Halsey	BM597			Ju88	Gris Nez	0704	Scr
8 Jul	Sgt A C Stanhope	BM401						
19 Jul	FL S R Edner	EN918			FW190	Nieuport	1315?	OP
30 Jul	PO W J Daley	AA841			FW190	St Omer	pm	C
31 Jul	PO F R Boyles	AA841		Me109F		Berck	1500	C
31 Jul	FL S R Edner	EN918	Me109F			Berck	1500	C
31 Jul	FL S R Edner	EN918	Me109F			Berck	1500	C
31 Jul	PO B Mahon	AD289	FW190			Berck	1500	C
31 Jul	PO B Mahon	AD289	FW190			Berck	1500	C
31 Jul	SL H C Kennard	BL234	Me109F			Somme Est	1520	C
31 Jul	Sgt W P Kelly	BL490	Me109F			LeCrotoy	1455	C

Date	Name	a/c	Dest	Prob	Dam	Locality	Time	Op.
19 Aug	FL S R Edner	EN918	FW190			Dieppe	0930	Raid
19 Aug	PO G O Halsey	BM590		FW190		Dieppe	0930	Raid
19 Aug	PO F D Smith	AR423			FW190	Dieppe	0930	Raid
19 Aug	Sgt L M Blanding	EN822		FW190		Dieppe	0930	Raid
5 Sep	PO G B Fetrow	AD324						
5 Sep	Sgt F M Fink	BM590	Ju88			E of Naze	1450	Scr
5 Sep	PO D A Young	AD199						

335th Fighter Squadron (whilst under RAF control)

Date	Name	a/c	Dest	Prob	Dam	Locality	Time	Op.
2 Oct	Maj W J Daley				FW190	E Calais	1435	Sweep
2 Oct	Lt S B Fetrow		FW190			SW Dunkirk	1435	Sweep
19 Nov	t F J Smolensky		FW190			SW Flushing	1500	Rhub
21 Nov	Lt R W Evans		Fi156			SE Furnes	1135	Rhub
6 Dec	LT G B Fetrow				FW190	ne Gris Nez	1247	C241

1943

Date	Name	a/c	Dest	Prob	Dam	Locality	Time	Op.
22 Jan	Lt S M Anderson		FW190			W Dunkirk	1510	C253
22 Jan	Lt G B Fetrow				FW190	NW Dunkirk	1510	C253
16 May	Lt E D Beatie			FW190		Walcheron	1325	C253
29 May	Capt R W Evans				FW190	Divan	1530	C

133 Squadron Victories 1942

Date 1942	Name	a/c	Dest	Prob	Dam	Locality	Time	Op.
5 Feb	FL HAS Johnston	P8195	1/2Do217			E Spurn Hd	1525	Cv/P
5 Feb	FL C W McColpin	X4353			Do217	E Spurn Hd	1455	Cv/P
26 Apr	FL C W McColpin	BM300	FW190			N Boulogne	1800	Sweep
27 Apr	PO R L Pewitt	BL988		FW190		W Ostend	1500	
27 Apr	PO W H Baker	BL492		FW190		W Ostend	1500	
29 Apr	PO E Doorly	BL955			Do217	Over York		night
17 May	FL C W McColpin	MB300	Me109F	Me109F		NW LeTreport	1030	
17 May	PO M S Morris	BL996		Me109F		NW LeTreport	1030	
19 May	PO M S Morris	BL996	Me109F		Me109F	NW Fecamp	1515	
19 May	PO G Sperry	BL994			1/2Me109F	Fr Coast	1520	
19 May	F/Sgt C W Harp	BL982	FW190			NW Fecamp	1520	
19 May	F/Sgt C W Harp	BL982	FW190			NW Fecamp	1520	
24 May	PO M E Jackson				Me109F	Channel	1700	OP
29 May	SL E H Thomas	BM263			FW190	S Dunkirk	0820	
31 May	PO E D Taylor				FW190	St Valery	1950	
5 Jun	PO K K Kimbro	BM353			FW190	Cayeux	1545	
5 Jun	PO K K Kimbro	BM353			FW190	Cayeux	1545	
5 Jun	SL E H Thomas	BM263		Me109F		S Abbeville	1545	

Date	Name	a/c	Dest	Prob	Dam	Locality	Time	Op.
27 Jun	FL D Blakeslee	BM591	FW190		Ju88	Fr Coast	0715	Raid
31 Jul	PO E D Taylor	EN924	FW190		Me109F	Le Crotoy	1455	Raid
31 Jul	PO W H Baker	EN951	FW190			Le Crotoy	1455	Raid
18 Aug	FL D Blakeslee	EN951	FW190			Sangette	1345	Raid
Rodeo								
19 Aug	FL D Blakeslee	EN951		FW190		Dieppe	0800	Raid
19 Aug	F D Blakeslee	EN951			Do217	Dieppe	1050	Raid
19 Aug	FL D Blakeslee	EN951			FW190	Dieppe	1050	Raid
19 Aug	FL D Blakeslee	EN951			FW190	Dieppe	1310	Raid
19 Aug	FL R L Alexander	BL773		FW190		Dieppe	0800	Raid
19 Aug	FL R L Alexander	AB910	Do217			Dieppe	1315	Raid
19 Aug	PO W H Baker	EB834	FW190			Dieppe	0810	Raid
19 Aug	PO W H Baker	EB834			FW190	Dieppe	1100	Raid
19 Aug	PO R N Beaty	BL983			FW190	Dieppe	1050	Raid
19 Aug	PO R N Beaty	BL983			Do217	Dieppe	1050	Raid
19 Aug	FL E G Brettell	AD237	FW190			Dieppe	1050	Raid
19 Aug	FO E Doorly	AB910			Do217	Dieppe	1100	Raid
19 Aug	PO D Gentile	BM530	FW190			Dieppe	1050	Raid
19 Aug	PO D D Gudmundsen	MX-K			Do217	Dieppe	1100	Raid
19 Aug	FO J C Nelson	BM530			Do217	Dieppe	1310	Raid
19 Aug	PO G G Wright	BL773			FW190	Dieppe	1050	Raid
7 Sep	PO W H Baker	BS137		FW190		WRotterdam	1030	Raid
16 Sep	PO C H Hiley				FW190	E Deal	0640	Raid

336th Fighter Squadron (whilst under RAF control)

1943

Date	Name	a/c	Dest	Prob	Dam	Locality	Time	Op.
22 Jan	Maj O H Coen		FW190			W Dunkirk	1505	C253
22 Jan	Lt J G Matthews		Me109F			Channel	1510	C253
12 Mar	Lt D Gentile				FW190	Audruieq	pm	R183
15 Apr	Capt D Blakeslee		FW190			Ostend	1705	R204
14 May	Capt L Glover		FW190		FW190	St Nicholas	1315	Esc
14 May	Capt L Glover				FW190	St Nicholas	1315	Esc
14 May	Lt R D Hobart				FW190	E Knocke	1330	Esc
14 May	Lt Col C G Peterson		FW190		FW190	St Nicholas	1310	Esc
14 May	Capt H L Stepp Jr		FW190		FW190	W Antwerp	1310	Esc
18 May	Lt D Beeson		Me109F			Belg coast		

Rodeo

Appendix 4

71 Squadron Losses 1941–42

Date	Name			Aircraft
1941				
5 Jan	PO P H Leckrone	KIFA	Scunthorpe	
9 Feb	PO E E Orbison	KIFA	K-Lindsey	
15 Feb	PO V C Keough	KIFA	N. Sea	
26 Apr	PO J L McGinnis	KIFA	Martlesham	
17 May	PO M Kolendorski	KIA	Sweep	
2 Jul	PO W T Hall	POW	Circus 29	Z3094
9 Aug	PO K S Taylor	KIFA	N. Weald	
19 Aug	PO V W Olsen	Missing	(escaped)	Z3494
27 Aug	PO W R Dunn	WIA	Circus 86	P7308
28 Aug	PO J Weir & LAC H G Dicker	KIFA	N. Weald	Magister
7 Sep	PO H Fenlaw	KIA	Sweep	AB900
7 Sep	PO W Nicholls	POW	Sweep	AB909
7 Sep	FO E Q Tobin	KIA	Sweep	W3801
17 Sep	PO W D Geiger	POW	Circus	W3763
17 Sep	PO T P McGerty	KIA	Circus	W3509
13 Oct	PO G C Daniel	POW	Circus	AD112
15 Oct	PO R H Atkinson	KIFA	N. Weald	
20 Oct	PO O H Coen	(Evaded)	Rhubarb	AB827

Date	Name			Aircraft
22 Oct	PO L A Chatterton	KIFA	N. Weald	
27 Oct	PO M W Fessler	POW	Rhubarb	AA855
15 Nov	SL S T Meares DFC	KIFA	N. Weald	
15 Nov	PO R O Scarborough	KIFA	N. Weald	
1942				
9 Jan	PO W B Inabinet	KIFA	Martlesham	
12 Apr	PO B F Mays	KIA	Circus	AB810
27 Apr	PO J F Flynn	KIA	Circus	BM206
1 Jun	PO E G Techeira	KIA	Sweep	BM386
2 Jun	PO T G Zavakos	KIA	A5R	BM249
6 Aug	PO J F Helgason	KIFA		
19 Aug	SL C G Peterson	Baled out	Dieppe	BM361
19 Aug	PO M G McPharlin	Baled out	Dieppe	W3767
27 Aug	Sgt J E Evans	KIA	Circus	AD196
31 Aug	PO W D Taylor	KIA	Rhubarb	BM305

121 Squadron

Date	Name			Aircraft
1941				
21 Jun	PO L L Laughlin	KIFA	K-Lindsey	
15 Sep	PO E W Mason	KIFA	K-Lindsey	
3 Nov	PO F M Cox	injured	flying accident	
7 Dec	PO R F Patterson	KIA	Rhubard	W3711
12 Dec	PO K LeR Holder	KIA	Patrol	AD871

Date	Name			Aircraft
1942				
8 Jan	PO J D Gilliland	KIFA	Ipswich	
8 Mar	PO Jones	Missing	Sweep	AD463
17 Apr	FS F C Austin	KIA	Sweep	BL239
25 Apr	PO Downs	Baled out		
28 Apr	PO C O Bodding	KIA	Sweep	AD289
28 Apr	PO L A Skinner	POW	Sweep	W3804
3 May	PO F A Gamble	KIFA	N. Weald	
4 May	PO R W Freiberg	KIA	Sweep	P8794
4 May	P O R V Brossmer	KIA	Sweep	AD460
31 May	FL T W Allen	KIA	Shipping reco	W3804
16 Jun	FL J J Mooney	KIA	Rhubarb	BM578
31 Jul	SL H Kennard	WIA	Sweep	BL234
31 Jul	PO N D Young	KIA	Sweep	AA732
19 Aug	PO G B Fetrow	Baled out	Dieppe	BM401
19 Aug	FO J B Mahon	POW	Dieppe	BM405
19 Aug	PO J T Taylor	KIA	Dieppe	AD569
19 Aug	PO J M Osborne	Baled out	Dieppe	P8589
21 Sep	PO J T Slater	KIA	N. Sea	

133 Squadron

1941				
27 Sep	PO W G Soares	KIFA	Duxford	

Date	Name	Status	Location	Aircraft
27 Sep	PO C S Barrell	KIFA	Duxford	Z3781
8 Oct	FL A Mamedoff	KOAS	Flight to NI	Z3253
8 Oct	PO R N Stout	KOAS	Flight to NI	Z3677
8 Oct	PO H H McCall	KOAS	Flight to Ni	Z3457
8 Oct	PO W J White	KOAS	Flight to NI	
23 Oct	PO G R Bruce	KIFA	Eglington	
27 Oct	PO J G Coxetter	KIFA	Eglington	
1942				
16 Mar	PO H C Brown	KIA		X4353
3 Apr	PO S F Whedon	KIFA	K-Lindsey	
27 Apr	FS W C Wicker	KIA	Sweep	BM264
19 May	PO R L Pewitt	KIA	Sweep	BL988
19 May	PO D R Florence	KIA	Sweep	BM492
31 May	PO M S Morris	KIA	Sweep	BL996
31 May	PO W K Ford	KIA	Sweep	BL961
5 Jun	PO F Hancock	KIA	Sweep	BM530
20 Jun	PO W A Arends	KIA	Sweep	EP168
19 Jul	PO S M Schatzberg	KIFA	Biggin Hill	
26 Jul	PO G I Omens	KIFA	Biggin Hill	Magister
28 Jul	PO B P DeHaven	KIFA	Biggin Hill	
31 Jul	FL C C King	KIA	Circus	BM938
31 JUl	PO C W Harp	KIA	Circus	BL982
31 Jul	FS G E Eichar	KIA	Circus	BM646
4 Sep	PO R N Beaty	Baled out		BS148

Date	Name			Aircraft
6 Sep	FO E Doorly	Evaded		BS276
6 Sep	PO R D Gudmundsen	KIA		BS292
26 Sep	FL E G Brettell	POW	Escort	BS313
26 Sep	FL M E Jackson	POW	Escort	BS279
26 Sep	PO L T Ryerson	KIA	Escort	BS275
26 Sep	PO R E Smith	Evaded	Escort	BS447
26 Sep	PO W H Baker	KIA	Escort	BS446
26 Sep	PO C A Cook	POW	Escort	BS640
26 Sep	PO G B Sperry	POW	Escort	BS638
26 Sep	PO G N Middleton	POW	Escort	BS301
26 Sep	PO G G Wright	POW	Escort	BS138
26 Sep	PO G P Neville	KIA	Escort	BS140
26 Sep	PO R N Beaty	inj	Escort	BS148

Appendix 5(i)

Combat Successes of some of the top Eagle Pilots with the 8th Air Force.

John Godfrey:

1 December 1943	Messerschmitt 109	
22 December	Messerschmitt 109	
22 December	Messerschmitt 109	(half share)
6 March 1944	Messerschmitt 109	
8 March	Messerschmitt 109	(half share)
8 March	Messerschmitt 109	
8 March	Messerschmitt 109	
16 March	Messerschmitt 110	
23 March	Messerschmitt 109	
29 March	Focke Wulf 190	
29 March	Focke Wulf 190	
29 March	Heinkel III	(third share)
5 April	Junkers 88	(ground)
5 April	Messerschmitt 110	(ground)
5 April	Junkers 88	(ground – half share)
9 April	Messerschmitt 410	
9 April	Junkers 88	(fifth share)
9 April	Junkers 88	(fifth share)
22 April	Messerschmitt 109	
22 April	Messerschmitt 109	
22 April	Messerschmitt 109	
24 April	Focke Wulf 190	
29 April	Dornier 217	(ground)
29 April	Junkers 52	(ground)
29 April	Junkers 52	(ground)
30 April	Seaplane	(ground–quarter share)
1 May	Messerschmitt 109	
5 August	Junkers 52	(ground)
5 August	Junkers 52	(ground)
5 August	Junkers 52	(ground)
6 August	Messerschmitt 410	
24 August	Junkers 52	(ground)

Appendix V(ii)

24 August	Junkers 52	(ground)
24 August	Junkers 52	(ground)
24 August	Junkers 52	(ground)

Don Gentile:

19 August 1942	Focke Wulf 190	
19 August	Junkers 88	
16 December 1943	Junkers 88	(third share)
5 January 1944	Focke Wulf 190	
14 January	Focke Wulf 190	
14 January	Focke Wulf 190	
25 February	Focke Wulf 190	
3 March	Focke Wulf 190	
3 March	Focke Wulf 190	
8 March	Messerschmitt 109	(half share)
8 March	Messerschmitt 109	
8 March	Messerschmitt 109	
8 March	Messerschmitt 109	
18 March	Focke Wulf 190	
23 March	Messerschmitt 109	
23 March	Messerschmitt 109	
27 March	Messerschmitt 110	(ground)
27 March	Messerschmitt 110	(ground)
29 March	Focke Wulf 190	
29 March	Focke Wulf 190	
29 March	Messerschmitt 109	
1 April	Messerschmitt 109	
5 April	Junkers 88	(ground)
5 April	Junkers 88	(ground)
5 April	Junkers 88	(ground)
5 April	Junkers 88	(ground – half share)
5 April	Junkers 88	(ground – half share)
8 April	Focke Wulf 190	
8 April	Focke Wulf 190	
8 April	Focke Wulf 190	

Appendix V(iii)

Ralph Hofer:

8 October	Messerschmitt 109	
6 February 1944	Messerschmitt 109	
16 March	Messerschmitt 110	
18 March	Messerschmitt 109	
18 March	Messerschmitt 109	
21 March	Messerschmitt 109	
21 March	Heinkel 177	(ground)
23 March	Focke Wulf 190	
1 April	Messerschmitt 109	
8 April	Messerschmitt 109	
11 April	Messerschmitt 110	
18 April	Heinkel 177	(ground)
18 April	Heinkel 177	(ground)
1 May	Messerschmitt 109	
12 May	Messerschmitt 109	(half share)
21 May	Buchner 131	(half share)
22 May	Messerschmitt 109	
24 May	Focke Wulf 190	
24 May	Focke Wulf 190	
29 May	Heinkel 177	(ground)
29 May	Heinkel 177	(ground)
29 May	Heinkel 177	(ground)
29 May	Heinkel 177	(ground– half share)
29 May	Heinkel 177	(ground–half share)
30 May	Focke Wulf 190	(ground)
30 May	Focke Wulf 190	(ground)
30 May	Focke Wulf 190	(ground–half share)
31 May	Buchner 181	(ground)
31 May	Buchner 181	(ground)
31 May	Buchner 181	(ground)

Duane Beeson:

18 May 1943	Messerschmitt 109
26 June	Messerschmitt 109
28 July	Messerschmitt 109

Appendix V(iv)

2 October	Focke Wulf 190	
8 October	Messerschmitt 109	
8 October	Messerschmitt 109	
14 January 1944	Focke Wulf 190	
29 January	Messerschmitt 109	
29 January	Focke Wulf 190	
31 January	Messerschmitt 109	
20 February	Focke Wulf 190	
25 February	Focke Wulf 190	
28 February	Junkers 88	(ground–quarter share)
5 March	Messerschmitt 109	
18 March	Messerschmitt 109	
23 March	Messerschmitt 109	
23 March	Messerschmitt 109	
27 March	Junkers 88	(ground)
27 March	Henschel 126	(ground)
27 March	Junkers 88	(ground–half share)
1 April	Messerschmitt 109	
5 April	Junkers 88	(third share)
5 April	Junkers 88	(ground)

Don Blakeslee:

22 November 1941	Messerschmitt 109	
18 August 1942	Focke Wulf 190	
19 August	Focke Wulf 190	
15 April 1943	Focke Wulf 190	
14 May	Focke Wulf 190	
7 January 1944	Focke Wulf 190	
18 March	Focke Wulf 190	
18 April	Heinkel 177	(ground)
22 April	Messerschmitt 109	
22 April	Messerschmitt 109	
24 April	Focke Wulf 190	
24 April	Focke Wulf 190	(half share)
30 April	Seaplane	(ground–quarter share)
29 May	Messerschmitt 410	

Appendix V(v)

2 July   Messerschmitt 109

Jim Goodson:

22 June 1943   Focke Wulf 190
16 August   Focke Wulf 190
16 August   Focke Wulf 190
16 August   Focke Wulf 190
7 January 1944   Focke Wulf 190
7 January   Focke Wulf 190
16 March   Messerschmitt 110
16 March   Messerschmitt 110
18 March   Heinkel 111   (ground)
18 March   Heinkel 111   (ground)
21 March   Messerschmitt 410   (ground)
23 March   Messerschmitt 109
23 March   Messerschmitt 109
5 April   Junkers 52   (ground)
5 April   Focke Wulf 190   (ground)
5 April   Junkers 88   (ground)
5 April   Junkers 88   (ground-half share)
5 April   Junkers 88   (ground-half share)
10 April   U/I trainer   (ground)
10 April   U/I trainer   (ground)
10 April   U/I trainer   (ground)
10 April   U/I trainer   (ground)
10 April   Henschel 126   (ground)
10 April   U/I trainer   (ground-half share)
24 April   Messerschmitt 109
24 April   Messerschmitt 109
12 May   Messerschmitt 109
25 May   Focke Wulf 190
20 June   Messerschmitt 109

Jim Clark:

2 October   Focke Wulf 190   (half share)

Appendix V(vi)

16 August	Focke Wulf 190	
16 August	Focke Wulf 190	
8 October	Messerschmitt 109	
8 March 1944	Messerschmit 109	
21 March	Focke Wulf 190	
21 March	Focke Wulf 190	(ground)
23 March	Junkers 88	(ground)
27 March	Junkers 88	(ground)
27 March	Junkers 88	(ground–half share)
29 March	Focke Wulf 190	
20 June	Messerschmitt 410	

Willard Millikan:

27 September 1943	Focke Wulf 190	
20 December	Messerschmitt 109	
10 February 1944	Focke Wulf 190	
27 March	Heinkel 177	(ground)
8 April	Messerschmitt 109	
8 April	Messerschmitt 109	
8 April	Messerschmitt 109	
15 April	Heinkel 177	(ground)
19 April	Messerschmitt 109	
22 April	Messerschmitt 109	
22 April	Messerschmitt 109	
22 April	Messerschmitt 109	
22 April	Messerschmitt 109	
22 May	Messerschmitt 109	
24 May	Focke Wulf 190	

Kendell "Swede" Carlson:

31 January 1944	Messerschmitt 109	
3 March	Messerschmitt 110	
16 March	Messerschmitt 110	
5 April	Junkers 88	(ground)

Appendix V(vii)

5 April	Junkers 52	(ground)
5 April	Junkers 52	(ground)
22 April	Messerschmitt 109	
22 April	Messerschmitt 109	(half share)
16 January 1945	Focke Wulf 190	(ground)
16 January	Junkers 88	(ground)
20 February	Focke Wulf 190	(half share)
25 February	U/I 4-eng	(ground)

Winslow "Mike" Sobanski:

31 January 1944	Messerschmitt 109	
29 March	Junkers 52	(ground)
13 April	Focke Wulf 190	
19 April	Messerschmitt 109	
30 April	Messerschmitt 110	(third share)
28 May	Messerschmitt 109	

Steve Pisanos:

12 August 1943	Messerschmitt 109
29 January 1944	Messerschmitt 109
29 January 1944	Messerschmitt 109
5 March	Messerschmitt 109
5 March	Messerschmitt 109

Vermont Garrison:

16 December 1943	Junkers 88	(third share)
14 January 1944	Focke Wulf 190	
14 January 1944	Focke Wulf 190	(half share)
31 January 1944	Messerschmitt 109	
6 February	Focke Wulf 190	
10 February	Messerschmitt 109	
25 February	Focke Wulf 190	
28 February	Junkers 88	(shared/ground)

Appendix V(viii)

3 March	Messerschmitt 110	
3 March	Focke Wulf 190	

Red-Dog Norley:

16 December 1943	Junkers 88	(third share)
14 January 1944	Focke Wulf 190	(half share)
10 February	Messerschmitt 109	
27 March	Junkers 88	(ground)
8 April	Focke Wulf 190	
8 April	Focke Wulf 190	
8 April	Focke Wulf 190	
13 April	Focke Wulf 190	
22 April	Messerschmitt 109	
22 April	Messerschmitt 109	
22 April	Messerschmitt 109	
17 September	Focke Wulf 190	
2 November	Messerschmitt 163	
19 March 1945	Messerschmitt 109	
7 April	Focke Wulf 190	
16 April	Focke Wulf 190	(ground)
16 April	Focke Wulf 190	(ground)
16 April	Junkers 52	(ground)
16 April	U/I EA	(ground)

Deacon Hively:

16 August 1943	Focke Wulf 190	
5 March 1944	Messerschmitt 109	
5 March 1944	Messerschmitt 109	
21 March	Junkers 88	(shared/ground)
27 March	Junkers 88	(ground)
12 May	Messerschmitt 109	
19 May	Messerschmitt 109	
19 May	Messerschmitt 109	
19 May	Messerschmitt 109	
24 May	Messerschmitt 109	

Appendix V(ix)

2 July	Messerschmitt 109	
2 July	Messerschmitt 109	
18 November	Messerschmitt 262	(ground)
5 December	Focke Wulf 190	

Vic France:

11 December 1943	Messerschmitt 109	
29 January 1944	Focke Wulf 190	
10 February	Focke Wulf 190	
8 March	Messerschmitt 109	
21 March	Focke Wulf 190	(ground)
21 March	Focke Wulf 190	(ground)
27 March	Junkers 52	(ground)
27 March	Junkers 88	(ground)
5 April	Heinkel 111	(shared/ground)
18 April	Messerschmitt 109	(third share)

Pierce McKennon:

30 July 1943	Focke Wulf 190	
20 February 1944	Focke Wulf 190	
22 February	Messerschmitt 109	
25 February	Focke Wulf 190	
6 March	Messerschmitt 109	
21 March	Focke Wulf 190	
29 March	Focke Wulf 190	
8 April	Focke Wulf 190	
9 April	Junkers 88	(shared/ground)
9 April	Junkers 88	(shared/ground)
13 April	Focke Wulf 190	
18 April	Focke Wulf 190D	
19 April	Messerschmitt 109	
25 December	Focke Wulf 190	(half share)
9 April 1945	Junkers 52	(ground)
9 April	Junkers 52	(ground)
9 April	Messerschmitt 410	(ground)

Appendix V(x)

16 April	Dornier 217	(ground)
16 April	Dornier 217	(ground)
16 April	U/I TE	(ground)

Index